HSBC Bank Canada Papers on Asia

Editor
A.E. Safarian
University of Toronto

Managing Editor
Wendy Dobson
University of Toronto

Institute for International Business
University of Toronto

HSBC Bank Canada
加拿大滙豐銀行

Other titles in this series

East Asia in transition: Economic and security challenges

A.E. Safarian and Wendy Dobson, Editors

UNIVERSITY OF TORONTO PRESS
Toronto Buffalo London

© University of Toronto Press Incorporated 2002
Toronto Buffalo London

ISBN 0-8020-3713-5 (cloth)
ISBN 0-8020-8515-6 (paper)

National Library of Canada Cataloguing in Publication Data

Main entry under title:

East Asia in transition : economic and security challenges

(HSBC Bank Canada papers on Asia ; v. 6)
ISBN 0-8020-3713-5 (bound)   ISBN 0-8020-8515-6 (pbk.)

1. East Asia – Economic policy.   2. Financial institutions – East Asia.
3. National security – East Asia.   I. Safarian, A.E., 1924– .   II. Dobson, Wendy
III. Series: Hongkong Bank of Canada papers on Asia ; v. 6.

HC460.5.E2734 2002   338.95   C2001-903940-9

University of Toronto Press acknowledges the financial assistance to its publishing
program of the Canada Council for the Arts and the Ontario Arts Council.

University of Toronto Press acknowledges the financial support for its publishing
activities of the Government of Canada through the Book Publishing Industry
Development Program (BPIDP).

Contents

Preface

This volume takes a long view of the East Asian economies. We begin by asking, What factors will influence sustainable long-term growth in the years ahead? As the region's economies developed and modernized, the answer to this question was a combination of political stability, prudent policy frameworks for the private sector, openness for exports, and access to international technologies and capital, as well as close cooperation between government and business. These factors are all still relevant, but the 1997–98 economic crises, followed by the U.S. economic slowdown in 2000–01 and the recessionary fallout from the September 11 hijacking attacks all suggest a broader agenda for East Asia. Some of these items – China's growth prospects, population aging, structural weaknesses revealed by the economic crisis, and the prospects for security in the region – are the subjects of chapters in this volume. The common denominator to them all is the role of institutions in economic growth. We know that technological change and innovation are the sources of long-term growth, but innovations don't spring fully formed from inventors and innovators. They require enabling institutions and structures to have significant economic impacts.

When this series began in 1995, its dual purpose was to examine Canada's relationships with the East Asian economies and to reduce the information barriers resulting from distance and unfamiliarity with these markets. The first volume began with a benchmarking exercise to establish the extent of the Canadian business presence in East Asia and to examine the major barriers to information. Not surprisingly, it was

established that the Canadian business presence was relatively insignificant. With some major exceptions, Canadian firms avoided East Asian
markets. Canada's de facto business policy was NAFTA, implemented
in 1994. Canadians were looking south, to the United States and Latin
America.

Subsequent volumes have aimed at increasing the information about
key attributes of the burgeoning East Asian markets. In 1996 the topic
was East Asian capitalism. This was followed in 1997 by a focus on the
"people links" through immigration and cultural ties; and in 1998 by
fiscal and financial studies in the wake of the East Asian economic crises. In 1999, eight case studies of North American companies' specific
experiences in the East Asian markets for products and services were
completed.

Six years on, much has changed. Most evidently, the Asian economies suffered a significant crisis, a rapid rebound, only to slow again as
the world economy slowed in 2000–01 and then reeled from the hor-
rific hijackings and attacks on New York City and Washington, DC.
Since the 1997–98 crisis, East Asian governments have initiated
regional arrangements in trade and finance in reaction to NAFTA, the
advent of the Euro, and paralysis at the World Trade Organization
(WTO). The information technology revolution is also firmly under
way among governments, businesses, and consumers. In this time,
Canada's international business policy has, if anything, become more
strongly focused on the north-south relationships in the Western
Hemisphere after Canada hosted a summit of leaders to consider moving towards a Free Trade Area of the Americas in early 2001.

These changes take place in a world economy whose global institutions are facing challenges from groups criticizing the costs and failures
of globalization and from the initial reaction to tighten border security
after the September attacks. East Asians were the early and natural glo-
balizers in that market forces encouraged cross-border networks
through which goods, services, capital, information, and people have
flowed. They have benefited enormously from a combination of
domestic policies that, while they were directive of domestic industrial
policy, also promoted more open access to the world's major markets.

Despite the 1997–98 crisis, governments throughout the region remain committed to integration into world markets.

As we look to the future in this final volume, the current turmoil over the benefits and costs of globalization provide context and backdrop, but the focus is primarily on significant issues facing the region that corporations and governments should understand. Key conclusions include:

- Institutions that promoted fast growth in the past became obstacles when they failed to adapt to the changed circumstances of more open economies.
- Institutional change that is needed does not reflect a failure to "westernize" but a failure to modernize.
- The regional economic cooperation initiatives are desirable in themselves but should not be seen as substitutes for domestic institutional change.
- Institutional change will take years in the crisis economies unless there are levers to speed it up; thus growth prospects differ across the region, with China at the front of the queue. China's emergence as a significant competitor to several other economies could provide a lever to speed reforms. Overdependence on the U.S. market and anemic U.S. growth in 2001–02 could be another lever.
- Still, China's growth prospects will depend on a key change in its financial system. Recapitalization and privatization of existing state-owned banks and the entry of foreign financial institutions, as China becomes a WTO member, will not suffice. A new system of privately owned, locally based financial institutions to provide efficient financial intermediation to small and medium enterprises is required.
- Japan and China need to make major changes in their pension programs to handle the needs of their aging populations in sustainable ways. China's challenge, while further off than Japan's, is more complex because of its underdeveloped financial system and its large rural population. Reforms should include both pay-as-you-go schemes (to provide immediate benefits) and fully funded pension programs that must be phased in over time.

- Canada's business performance in East Asia is better than expected when benchmarked against 10 other countries. Significantly for policy, Canadian strengths are demonstrated in the three largest economies: China, Indonesia, and Japan. In future, Canadian governments and private-sector players should build on these strengths.

This series has featured the work of more than 30 authors from Canada, the United States, and Hong Kong. These contributions reflect the existence of an expert cadre with many accumulated years of knowledge of and experience in all the economies of East Asia, as well as of the region itself. The HSBC Bank Canada has provided generous support throughout this project. Special thanks also go to David Bond (University of British Columbia) whose advice and assistance were invaluable throughout the project. A distinguished international editorial advisory board has provided peer review and editorial advice. The editors are also grateful for the peer review provided to the authors of this volume by participants in a seminar, held at the University of Toronto, on May 28, 2001. While they bear no responsibility for the final product, Varouj Aivazian, Dwayne Benjamin, Richard Bird, David Dewitt, Bernie Frolic, Peter Pauly, and Lorna Wright from the academic community, and William Avis, Diane Bean, Gordon Fear, Oscar Freudenthal, Tom Phelps, Frederick Spoke, Neil Tait, and Kai Xing from the private sector all made valuable contributions.

The University of Toronto Press cooperates in this project. Support is also provided by Heather Munroe-Blum, Vice President, Research and International Relations, and by Roger Martin, Dean of the Joseph L. Rotman School of Management at the University of Toronto. This volume was prepared with the assistance of staff at the Institute for International Business. Liza Tham prepared the manuscript and Vivien Choy provided immeasurably invaluable leadership with all logistical matters.

Wendy Dobson
October 2001

Do institutions matter for growth?

A.E. SAFARIAN AND WENDY DOBSON

The rise and fall of regional growth

During the past three decades, East Asia has become a major growth pole in the world economy. Living standards in Japan, followed by Hong Kong, Singapore, South Korea, and Taiwan, are converging on western living standards after years of rapid economic growth. Indeed, for the past decade questions have been raised about the sustainability of these high growth rates as economies industrialized, populations urbanized and aged, and environmental costs began to mount. These questions intensified following the financial and economic crises of 1997–98. This volume, prepared once the smoke had cleared, examines key future challenges facing the region and their implications for business and public policy outside the region.

East Asians are, above all, successful traders. Their export-led growth model of economic development is now being imitated in other parts of the world. To raise living standards, East Asian governments opened their economies to the winds of external competition;[1] made local capital cheaply available and incentives relatively uniform across the board;[2] used capital controls in pragmatic ways; and developed close ties between governments and businesses. Governments liberalized

---

1 Albeit while adopting "export-oriented protectionism" that favoured local exporters.
2 See Krueger (1997).

trade policies, often unilaterally. They encouraged direct foreign investment to assist in the exploitation of natural resources, to develop labour-intensive low-cost production in multinational manufacturing value chains – particularly in the textiles and apparel, electronics, and automobile industries – and to develop modern services. East Asian exporters also benefited enormously from relatively unfettered access to western – particularly U.S. – markets as tariffs were reduced in successive multilateral trade rounds.

The financial and economic crises of 1997–98, however, revealed that all was not well with the supposed "miracle." While economies had benefited from trade openness, similar openness to international capital flows created serious vulnerabilities. Reliance on short-term debt and "soft peg" exchange rate regimes were key sources of weakness.

As important as these questionable policies were key structural and institutional problems bared by events in 1997–98 that still need to be addressed. Some economic structures and institutions were more appropriate to closed economies. Going forward, the way the East Asian economies adapt their institutions to withstand external shocks will have a significant impact on future growth prospects. East Asian businesses and other institutions differ – both within the region itself and from those in North America and Western Europe – as previous volumes in this series have revealed. The purpose of this volume is to anticipate key issues affecting the region's future prosperity, and as will be apparent in the chapters that follow, each issue has a significant institutional dimension.

What this book is about

This overview chapter draws together the findings in this volume and examines their implications. One of the main themes in these chapters is that institutions matter for the future – of both economic growth and security. That is why this first chapter focuses on institutions.

Regional economic issues

In the second chapter, Wendy Dobson (University of Toronto) examines lessons from the financial and economic crisis. Some progress has been made in addressing the structural problems revealed by the crisis but it is uneven and much remains to be done. What does get done could well determine which economies will be future winners and losers in the global economic race. Domestic economic structures are changing only slowly for reasons examined in this first chapter. Yet in marked contrast, governments have pursued deeper integration relatively rapidly through regional institutional initiatives in trade and finance. Success in these efforts to promote greater regional cooperation could affect the world economic system, depending on how they work. But their primary purpose is to develop mutual protection against future financial crises and against possible continued paralysis at the World Trade Organization (WTO). It is doubtful, however, they will be satisfactory substitutes for the basic institutional and structural changes required at national levels to reduce the vulnerabilities that come with deeper integration into the global economy.

China

No assessment of the region's future prospects would be complete without an examination of issues in the Chinese economy. In the third chapter, Professors Loren Brandt and Xiaodong Zhu (University of Toronto) argue that China's existing financial system, while it is undergoing rapid change, lacks a key institution that could support economic growth. In their view, a major factor explaining slow Chinese growth in recent years is the financial sector's inability to intermediate funds efficiently to China's rapidly growing non-state sector. The non-state sector is now the main source of China's economic dynamism, yet its growth is being undermined by lack of funds. Brandt and Zhu propose a pragmatic solution that involves the creation of new financial institutions: privately-owned, locally-based financial intermediaries for the small and medium-sized firms in the non-state sector.

Ageing populations and pension programs

Another key issue in East Asia's future is the responses of governments to aging populations, since both the Japanese and Chinese populations will age rapidly (Japan's long before China's) in the next few decades. In the fourth chapter, Professors Walid Hejazi (University of Toronto) and Pauline Shum (York University) focus on the issues and options for pension reform.[3] While Singapore, Malaysia, and Hong Kong have adopted programs that are likely to be sustainable, both Japan and China face the need for major reforms to meet the needs of aging populations. Hejazi and Shum identify key criteria for judging pension design and draw lessons from the three more advanced economies in the region, as well as from North America and Chile (the latter has developed a private pension system in addition to a public system) that might apply in China.

Security

One of the factors in East Asia's economic success has been a relatively stable security environment. In the fifth chapter Professor Brian Job (University of British Columbia) examines the future of security arrangements. The current benign post–cold war environment contains a paradox. The great powers' main concern is with the long-standing hot spots in India, Pakistan, North Korea, and the Taiwan Straits, which could boil up unexpectedly. Domestic and regional concerns are quite different, however. Democracy has advanced in the region, but economic adversity has contributed to crises of governance and to weak states. As economies have developed over the past 30 years, domestic concerns have shifted to social dislocation, civil conflicts, and leadership crises. Regional cooperation to address such issues has stalled in the face of sovereignty concerns. Thus, the security dynamic in the region is likely to be one with little movement away from the status quo unless a hot spot boils over for some unpredictable reason.

---

3 Detailed descriptions of existing pension systems in China, Hong Kong, Japan, and Singapore, as well as Canada and Chile (for comparative purposes), are provided in an appendix.

The Canadian business presence in the region

Finally, in the sixth chapter we return to one of the motivations for this series: to contribute timely analyses of the East Asian economies to assist those conducting policies towards or doing business in the region. How well are Canadian businesses doing in East Asia? Has there been improvement or deterioration over the past decade? Professors Keith Head and John Ries (University of British Columbia) pursued this theme in the first volume in 1995. In 2001, they find that, on the surface, Canadian business presence in East Asia has remained relatively small. But they also change the way they measure this presence, benchmarking against ten other western countries to gauge Canada's relative performance. They find that, taking into account country size, distance to Asia, real exchange rates, and comparative advantage, Canada's recent export performance is on a par with or better than most of the comparison group. Of significance for the future is the fact that Canada has been particularly successful in exporting to the three large, or potentially large, markets of Japan, China, and Indonesia.

Can rapid economic growth be restored?

As the backdrop to our discussion of the links between institutions and growth, we first look at East Asia's growth prospects. Can the rapid economic growth rates for which East Asia became justly famous in the past be restored in future? Or does the crisis signal the beginning of slower growth that characterizes maturing industrialized economies? There are many reasons to predict that fast growth will resume, but some significant arguments that suggest it will not, at least in some economies. High savings and investment, and investment in education and market-friendly institutions have been major contributors to East Asia's economic success (World Bank, 1993). The crisis strengthened governments' commitment to integration into the world economy. Not a single government, with the partial exception of Malaysia, erected barriers to international trade or capital. Indeed, the crisis was a catalyst for new cooperative initiatives to accelerate and manage

Table 1: East Asia in the world economy

Indicator	1999 share of world total (percent)
Gross domestic product	23
Population	33
Trade	24
Inward FDI stock	16
Foreign reserves	50
Savings	32

Source: Dobson chapter, Table 1.

closer regional economic ties, as we see in the next chapter. Democracy survived the crisis, even in Indonesia where political uncertainty deepened the economic contraction and significantly slowed recovery. The underlying economic fundamentals are impressive, with the region accounting for a quarter of world output and trade, possessing 15 percent of inward investment stocks, a third of the world's savings, and half its foreign reserves (Table 1).

In the long term, an economy's growth rate is determined by capital invested, population growth – both increases in labour force participation and in its quality – and technological change. A famous debate was touched off in the mid-1990s by economist Paul Krugman,[4] who predicted East Asian growth rates would be unsustainable because they were based mainly on investment. Past some point, the addition of more investment, without some increase in the efficiency with which this capital is employed, produces smaller and smaller increments in output because diminishing returns set in. This dismal result can be avoided by the application of new technology and information. But how new technology is introduced matters, as Lipsey et al. (1998) point out. Technologies will sit on the shelf unless there are people to apply them, as well as policy and other "enabling structures" to encourage identification of better ways to combine labour and capital and improve the efficiency with which inputs are used.

4 See Krugman (1994).

Table 2: Sources of growth in East Asia and other regions, 1960–94
(annual percentage rate)

Country/region	Output per worker	Contribution of		
		Physical capital	Education	Factor productivity
Indonesia	3.4	2.1	0.5	0.8
Korea	5.7	3.3	0.8	1.5
Malaysia	3.8	2.3	0.5	0.9
Philippines	1.2	1.2	0.5	−0.4
Singapore	5.4	3.4	0.4	1.5
Thailand	5.0	2.7	0.4	1.8
Taiwan	5.8	3.1	0.6	2.0
East Asia	4.2	2.5	0.6	1.1
South Asia	2.3	1.1	0.3	0.8
Africa	0.3	0.8	0.2	−0.6
Middle East	1.6	1.5	0.5	−0.3
Latin America	1.5	0.9	0.4	0.2
United States	1.1	0.4	0.4	0.4
Other industrial countries	2.9	1.5	0.4	1.1

Source: Collins and Bosworth (1996).

The goal is to increase the output produced per unit of input. It is commonly acknowledged that the advanced industrialized nations have been able to increase living standards over long periods of time because technological change has increased total factor productivity – GDP per unit of input. By available evidence over the past few decades, total factor productivity growth in the East Asian economies was not impressive[5] and more recent estimates for the 1980–95 period were not reassuring either (World Bank, 2000: 144).

A broader and longer measure of total factor productivity, however, shows a more favourable picture (Table 2).[6] It is true that in the 1960–94 period capital deepening accounted for relatively more of the growth in output per worker in East Asia than was the case for the United States and other industrial countries. Conversely, total factor

5 See Young (1994).
6 Collins and Bosworth (1996) as cited in Rodrik (1998a).

productivity counted for relatively less. However, if one compares the annual percentage growth of total factor productivity across regions, East Asian growth is on a par with South Asia and non-U.S. industrial countries, and far in excess of the United States, Latin America, Africa, and the Middle East.

More important, Rodrik (1998a) has drawn attention to a fundamental problem with the measurement of total factor productivity. The measurement techniques used do not allow one to rule out a high degree of labour-saving technological change in East Asia, contrary to the conclusions of Krugman and others.[7]

Whatever one's conclusions on this debate, a major issue here is the quality of the institutions that underpin an economy's wealth and growth, including those that enable technological change, capital accumulation, and educational advance. We will argue in this chapter that the quality of institutions matters a good deal in these respects, as well as for encouraging political freedoms and social gains. It will also become clear that institutional change can be considered in relatively short-run as well as long-run terms in relation to its effects on wealth.

A resumption of persistent growth requires early attention to a number of institutional issues covered at greater length in this volume and earlier ones. These include changes in exchange rate regimes, as Dobson notes in the next chapter; strengthening the oversight of financial institutions, greater transparency, and prudent regulation of financial institutions; removal of policy distortions that encourage borrowing abroad but discourage or discriminate against long-term forms of capital such as FDI (Dobson; Aivazian and Hejazi in volume 4); educational reform to encourage innovation and creativity (volume 3); reducing export-oriented protectionism; further withdrawal by governments from allocative decisions through directed lending, loan

---

7 As Rodrik (1998a: 79–85) notes, there are two possible reasons why the capital share in East Asia has remained high while capital deepening has proceeded. The conventional explanation is a high elasticity of substitution between capital and labour (close to the Cobb-Douglas case). The other possibility is rapid labour-saving technological change.

guarantees, tax credits, and trade restrictions (World Bank, 2000); revitalization of business through more transparent corporate governance (volume 2); and a change in the social contract so that aging and urban populations have stronger safety nets than simply the traditional reliance on the extended family (Bird and Chen in volume 4).

The role of institutions

How do institutions influence economic growth and what can be done to strengthen their positive effects? To consider these questions, it is helpful to classify institutions by the speed of change involved (Table 3).[8] The slowest to change (Level 1) are the customs, traditions, and beliefs that are embedded in a society, religion being a prominent example. The next slowest (Level 2) are the formal rules that make up the institutional environment, such as constitutions and property rights. These are capable of being dislodged given sufficient pressure from, for example, severe financial crises or military coups. The ongoing governance of (implicit and explicit) contractual relations changes more quickly (Level 3). This is where transaction cost economics comes into play; that is, the study of the costs of arranging a contract *ex ante* and of monitoring and enforcing it *ex post*. The incentives or disincentives involved are critical to efficient functioning of an economy whatever the institution, whether markets, firms, alliances, regulation, government bureaus, or non-profit organizations. The fourth level changes continuously and involves the ongoing processes of resource allocation and employment within the other sets of institutions.

Most of the structural issues raised in this volume fall within the second and, especially, third categories. Thus, some reforms are feasible within a decade and others within a few decades. At the same time, one should keep in mind Arrow's (1998) conclusion that institutional change must proceed slowly if institutions are to remain credible. Drawing on a variety of authors, he argues that institutions must cre-

---

8 This paragraph draws on Williamson (2000).

Table 3: Economics of institutions

Level	Frequency (years)	Purpose
L1 — Embeddedness: informal institutions, customs, traditions, norms, religion	10^2 to 10^3	Often non-calculative; spontaneous (caveat: see discussion in text)
L2 — Institutional environment: formal rules of the game – esp. property (polity, judiciary, bureaucracy)	10 to 10^2	Get the institutional environment right; 1st-order economizing
L3 — Governance: play of the game – esp. contract (aligning governance structures with transactions)	1 to 10	Get the governance structure right; 2nd-order economizing
L4 — Resource allocation and employment (prices and quantities, incentive alignment)	continuous	Get the marginal conditions right; 3rd-order economizing

L1: social theory
L2: economics of property rights / positive political theory
L3: transaction cost economics
L4: neoclassical economics / agency theory

Source: Williamson (2000), 597.

ate reasonably stable expectations if they are to operate effectively. One difficulty that then arises is that institutions suitable to one set of conditions may persist even when, under changed circumstances, their influence is less than optimal. Explanations of Japan's prolonged malaise increasingly point in this direction (for example, Bergsten et al., 2001; Smith, 1997; Katz, 1998).

Existing studies suggest strongly that institutions matter to growth, and they matter significantly. The issue was put dramatically by Temple and Johnson (1998), who noted that the long-run growth forecasts made in the early 1960s were off by huge margins. Asia was thought to be likely to do worse than Africa in general, and the wrong Asian countries were targeted for rapid growth. One reason for the forecast errors can be seen by considering the exception, a study by Adelman and Taft Morris (1967), that developed a socio-economic framework in the 1960s. Their socio-economic index was a far better *ex ante* predictor than others, when combined with initial income, essentially because social arrangements affect the structure of incentives.[9]

A more recent and quite striking example is given by Hall and Jones (1999). They argue that "social infrastructure" is the basic force driving the quality of inputs to production and productivity growth. A statistical comparison for 1988 for the five economically richest and five poorest countries in their study shows that the richest averaged investment rates 2.9 times higher, educational attainment of 8.1 years greater, and output per worker 32 times higher than the level achieved by the poorest.

At the broadest level, Sala-í-Martin (1997) noted that 22 variables show up as highly significant in various statistical tests of the determinants of growth. Fully half reflect a variety of social, political, and religious variables. North (1989) has argued that the long-run growth of productivity in western countries had as much to do with institutions

---

9 The social indicators that showed a positive relation to growth were the dominance of the immediate family over the extended family or tribe, modernization of outlook, extent of mass communication, extent of indigenous middle class, and extent of social mobility.

which reduce transaction costs, and thus increase the gains from exchange, as it had to do with the increased control over nature. Hall and Jones (1999) have shown that differences in levels of income between countries are related to whether institutions and policies exist to encourage production (for example, protection for property, openness) or whether they encourage diversion (for example, theft, corruption, expropriation). A considerable number of other studies have made a similar point in terms of institutions and policies that encourage production, as against those directed to rent seeking, that is, the use of resources to appropriate a surplus (Olson, 1982, 1996; Baumol, 1990).

With regard to East Asia, the World Bank (2000) uses a country policy and institutional index to estimate that a 20 percent improvement in macroeconomics, trade, and financial and public institutions can add between 1.2 percentage points (in the least-developed members of ASEAN) and as much as 2.0 percentage points (in South Korea and Malaysia) to a country's GDP (World Bank, 2000: 14).

Many other studies link growth to institutional quality measured in a variety of ways. Qualifications arise especially when more specific aspects of growth, institutions, and policy are examined. Many studies show, for example, that openness to trade is positively associated with growth, other things equal. Edwards (1998) uses nine measures to establish this point. When openness on capital account is considered, however, some researchers take a more qualified stand (Bhagwati, 1998; Rodrik, 1998b). For example, it may be necessary to adopt some reforms in domestic and international financial institutions before developing markets are subjected to the full force of volatile short-term capital flows, and these researchers believe that the option of a temporary reinstatement of some controls may need to be preserved.[10]

More fundamentally, one needs to consider the business organizations that are central to economic decisions for each economy, in conjunction with the government economic policies and the global economic trends within which they operate. It can be agreed that these

---

10 See Dobson and Hufbauer, 2001, ch. 1, for a fuller analysis of these and related points.

organizations may change slowly in some respects: the institutions which underlie them are mainly in levels 2 and 3 of Table 3. Yet they are obviously capable of change in response to major shocks. The large industrial investments of German banks reflect in part the funds owed on loans made to finance German recovery after the Second World War (*Economist*, 2000: 62). Japanese vertical *keiretsu* had prewar roots, but company unions (and guaranteed employment) replaced industrial unions as a result of a labour settlement ending bitter industrial conflict after the Second World War (Westney, 1995). And the Korean *chaebol* exist in part because successive Korean governments decided this organizational form would lead to a competitive advantage and offered the financial and other inducements required to sustain them (*Economist*, 1996).

The pace of change is one issue. The other is the magnitude of change required of basic business organizations. The answer to that question depends in part on the extent to which the crisis of recent years was due to, or exacerbated by, the nature of business organization.[11] The issue was put squarely by Toporowski (1998), who noted the problems that arise when institutions are defined too broadly. Hence he criticizes both those such as Hollingsworth and Boyer (1997) who tend to associate the economic success of Asian economies with their corporatist economic institutions, and also the tendency of the IMF to attribute the crisis in Asia to the same institutions. Bhagwati (2000: xviii) has made a similar point, noting that "crony capitalism" is said both to have produced the economic miracle in East Asia and also to have ended it.

One can note, first, that there is often over-generalization in the descriptions used for business organization. Volume 2 in this series detailed the diversity of East Asian capitalism: there are significant differences between the Korean *chaebol*, Japanese *keiretsu*, and overseas Chinese networks of Taiwan or Singapore, to note only some of the organizational forms involved.

---

11 It will depend also on how far such organizations are responsive to longer-term changes brought by globalization, as noted further below.

Granting this, it can also be suggested that both of the statements made by Toporowski and others can be correct. There is no one form of business organization that is superior to others in all circumstances and periods of history (just as it has been established that no one exchange rate regime holds for all time and in all countries). Chandler (1962) demonstrated some time ago that the organization of U.S. business evolved significantly over time as economic circumstances changed. A plausible explanation of what happened in Asia is that (a) the various forms of business contributed to the economic miracles of the late 20th century, but (b) the failure of these forms of business (and the related and supporting public policies) to adapt to globalization exacerbated the crisis of the mid-1990s and will continue to hamper recovery if not corrected. Lack of reform could even reduce the potential long-term growth rate if studies of institutions such as those noted earlier are correct.

Most western economies face some similar pressures in the face of both globalization and domestic developments. U.S. automobile firms went through wrenching changes in organization in order to regain market share lost to imports. The organization of business which developed so successfully in Silicon Valley is in marked contrast to the older and much less successful organizational forms for the information technology industry of the Boston area (Saxenian, 1994). In Germany and some other EU countries, stakeholder capitalism is having to cope with the virtual absence of the discipline of hostile takeovers from abroad. However, the United States and Europe have had time to develop the capital markets, secure property rights, and effective judicial systems that support major economic changes while accommodating a diversity of business sizes and organizations. In the crisis economies in East Asia, by contrast, capital markets are not yet fully developed, property rights are not adequately enforced, and there continues to be excessive reliance on family-run or highly centralized concentrations of wealth fed by public finance even in the face of disastrous economic results. It is not a case of failure to "westernize" to use Huntington's terminology. There is no need to converge in this sense. Rather it is a failure to modernize. This failure to adapt to changed economic circumstances, both in business organization and related public policy, could stand in the way of a resumption of long-term growth.

Let us put the challenge more concretely. There is much that East Asia has done well. Many of the countries show up favourably in terms of standard growth determinants such as the rate of saving and investment, educational attainment, and increasing openness to trade. Moreover, there is certainly change at the organizational level as well, which is the focus of this chapter. Such changes, unfortunately, do not go to the heart of the structural problems in much of Asia. Much more needs to be done to improve standards and transparency, publish better accounts, appoint outside directors (other than family friends) and make them accountable to shareholders and investors, and protect minority shareholder rights (volume 4 in this series; *Economist*, 2001). While China attracts a growing share of foreign direct investment and has managed to avoid the instability of smaller countries, it nevertheless has far to go in developing a judicial system, bureaucracy, company laws that are more compatible with modern business systems, a modern financial system, and the international rules of the road. In much of East Asia the move to a more rules-based system from a relations-based one is proving to be slow and uneven at national levels.

More may be at risk here than the possibility of a larger short-run adjustment in the face of another exchange crisis or the reduction of potential growth. There is a much greater risk if one believes that the effective setting and governance for business – levels 2 and 3 of Table 3 – are related to political as well as economic instability. Some countries in the region, such as Indonesia, the Philippines, and Thailand, continue to reflect considerable instability in both senses. Rodrik (1999) has argued that the effects of shocks on growth are larger the greater is the latent social conflict and the weaker are the institutions for conflict management. Latent social conflict is measured by income inequality, ethnic and linguistic diversity, and the degree of social trust, while conflict management is proxied by civil and political rights, the quality of government institutions, and provision for social insurance. Between 1960–75 and 1975–79 the sharpest drops in GNP in his model were in those societies with high measures of latent social conflict and weak conflict management institutions. Rodrik concludes that there is a need to develop more conflict-mediating institutions (such as more democracy and social insurance) as developing countries integrate more fully into the global economy. In this volume, Professor Brian Job's chapter on security and the Hejazi-Shum chapter on pension reform are both highly relevant in this respect.

Conclusions and implications for policy

One of the major questions for policy is how to bring about cumulative institutional change within feasible time periods. History indicates that, for some changes, levers are required such as massive discontent, perceived threat, or financial crises. In this sense the crisis provided a golden opportunity to modernize a number of institutions so as to foster productivity growth. Ironically, as some East Asians have pointed out, most of East Asia recovered too quickly from crisis to sustain the political will needed for deep institutional changes. Ironically as well, the world slowdown in 2000–01 may serve as a timely reminder of the need to further domestic reforms and regional cooperation so as to reduce the region's vulnerability to external shocks.

One implication for international business is the diversity of the region, not only in the traditional sense of culture and politics, but also in the strength of structural reforms. By many accounts, China has moved to the top rank in the determination and credibility of its reforms, while Japan and Indonesia have (hopefully only temporarily) sunk near the bottom. This diversity in the speed and strength of structural reform will produce differential growth prospects across the region's economies.

East Asia will continue to be a challenging place to do business in the future. There will be problems. One obvious source of problems going forward relates to security, as Job notes. But as the case studies of particular firms' experiences in volume 5 showed, while political instability and policy risks were important influences on business success, adequate planning for these was feasible, if difficult.

There will also be added opportunities. Some (not enough) organizational change is occurring, so more opportunities to network with existing organizations are opening up for foreign investors that should reduce their transaction costs of doing business. As the larger economies cope with the challenges of aging populations (e.g., via pension reform) potentially significant opportunities for Canadian financial institutions may emerge. Canadians should also assist with organizational change in areas of Canadian comparative advantage, such as finance (e.g., through the Toronto Leadership Centre, which provides training to financial supervisors). Both Canadian business and governments should pay more attention to institutional reform in East Asia.

These comments suggest implications for Canadian policies. We began this series with a chapter by Head and Ries that pointed out a paradox. Using conventional measures, Canadian penetration of Asian markets was declining, while economic growth in the region was consistently rapid. Lorna Wright, in the same volume, documented Asian perceptions of the Canadian business presence, at least in Southeast Asia, as relatively weak and tenuous. What has become painfully clear in the 2000–01 global economic downturn is that diversification of our economic relationship to include East Asia will not help protect us from U.S. business cycles because East Asia has become so closely integrated with the U.S. economy and vulnerable to its business cycle.

In the last chapter of this final volume, Head and Ries, returning to the issue of Canada's performance after seven years, use a different, benchmarking, approach that draws more positive conclusions about Canadian business. They emphasize the reasons to be optimistic about future business in East Asia. Canada is reasonably successful at exporting to the largest market – in Japan – and to potentially large markets in China and Indonesia. Once established, these business links should persist for many years, especially if China continues to reform and grow. If Indonesia, as seems possible in late 2001, is entering a period of greater political stability that allows economic reform and a resumption of growth, this market will also have considerable potential. Canadian policy should focus on developing the potential of these three markets in the years ahead.

REFERENCES

Adelman, Irma, and Cynthia Taft Morris. 1967. *Society, Politics and Economic Development.* Baltimore, Md.: Johns Hopkins University Press.

Aivazian, Varouj A., Walid Hejazi, and J.D. Han. 1998. "How much does finance matter in East Asia?" In Wendy Dobson, ed., Volume 4 in this series.

Arrow, Kenneth J. 1998. "The Place of Institutions in the Economy: A Theoretical Perspective." In Hayami and Aoki, *The Institutional Foundations of East Asian Economic Development.*

Baumol, W.J. 1990. "Entrepreneurship: Productive, Unproductive, and Destructive." *Journal of Political Economy,* 48: 893–921.

Bergsten, C. Fred, Takatoshi Ito, and Marcus Noland. 2001. *No More Bashing: Building a New Japan–United States Economic Relationship.* Washington: Institute for International Economics.

Bhagwati, Jagdish. 2000. *The Wind of the Hundred Days: How Washington Mismanaged Globalization.* Cambridge, Mass.: MIT Press.

– 1998. "The Capital Myths: The Difference between Trade in Widgets and Dollars." *Foreign Affairs,* 77/3: 7–12.

Bird, Richard M., and Duanjie Chen. 1998. "The fiscal framework for business in Asia." In Wendy Dobson, ed., Volume 4 in this series.

Chandler, A.O. 1962. *Strategy and Structure.* Cambridge, Mass.: MIT Press.

Collins, Susan, and Barry Bosworth. 1996. "Economic Growth in East Asia: Accumulation versus Assimilation." *Brookings Papers on Economic Activity,* II: 135–91.

Dobson, Wendy. 1998. "Fiscal frameworks, financial systems and the Asian crisis." In Wendy Dobson, ed., Volume 4 in this series.

Dobson, Wendy, and Gary C. Hufbauer. 2001. *World Capital Markets: Challenge to the G-10.* Washington: Institute for International Economics.

Economist, The. 2001. "In Praise of Rules: A Survey of Asian Business." April 7: 1–18.

– 2000. "Germany Unlocked." January 8: 62–63.

– 1996. "Cultural Explanations." November 9: 23–26.

Edwards, S. 1998. "Openness Productivity and Growth: What Do We Really Know?" *Economic Journal,* 108 (March): 383–98.

Hall, Robert, and Charles Jones. 1999. "Why Do Some Countries Produce So Much More Output per Worker than Others?" *Quarterly Journal of Economics,* February: 83–116.

Hayami, Y., and M. Aoki, eds. 1998. *The Institutional Foundations of East Asian Economic Development.* London: Macmillan Press Ltd.

Hollingsworth, J.R., and R. Boyer, eds. 1997. *Contemporary Capitalism: The*

Embeddedness of Institutions. Cambridge and New York: Cambridge University Press.

Katz, Richard. 1998. *Japan, the System That Soured: The Rise and Fall of the Japanese Economic Miracle.* Armonk, NY, and London: M.E. Sharpe.

Krueger, Anne O. 1997. "Trade Policy and Economic Development: How We Learn." *American Economic Review,* 87/1: 1–22.

Krugman, Paul. 1994. "The Myth of Asia's Miracle." *Foreign Affairs,* November/December: 63–78.

Lipsey, Richard, Clifford Bekar, and Kenneth Carlaw. 1998. "The Consequences of Changes in GPTs (General Purpose Technologies)." In Elhanan Helpman, ed., *General Purpose Technologies and Economic Growth.* Cambridge, Mass.: MIT Press.

North, Douglass. 1989. "Institutions and Economic Growth: An Historical Introduction." *World Development,* 17: 1319–32.

Olson, M. 1996. "Big Bills Left on the Sidewalk: Why Some Nations Are Rich and Others Poor." *Journal of Economic Perspectives,* 10/2: 3–24.

– 1982. *The Rise and Decline of Nations.* New Haven: Yale University Press.

Rodrik, Dani. 1999. "Where Did All the Growth Go? External Shocks, Social Conflict and Growth Collapses." *Journal of Economic Growth,* 4/4: 385–412.

– 1998a. "TFPG Controversies, Institutions and Economic Performance in East Asia." In Hayami and Aoki, *The Institutional Foundations of East Asian Economic Development.*

– 1998b. "Who Needs Capital Account Convertibility?" In Stanley Fischer et al., eds., *Should the IMF Pursue Capital Account Convertibility?* Princeton: Princeton University, International Finance Section.

Sala-í-Martin, Xavier. 1997. "I Just Ran Two Million Regressions." *American Economic Association Papers and Proceedings,* 87/2: 178–83.

Saxenian, Annalee. 1994. *Regional Advantage: Culture and Competition in Silicon Valley and Route 128.* Cambridge, Mass.: Harvard University Press.

Smith, Patrick. 1997. *Japan: A Reinterpretation.* New York: Pantheon Books.

Temple, Jonathan, and Paul A. Johnson. 1998. "Social Capability and Economic Growth." *Quarterly Journal of Economics,* 113/3: 965–90.

Toporowski, Ian. 1998. Review of J.R. Hollingsworth and R. Boyer, eds., *Contemporary Capitalism: The Embeddedness of Institutions. Economic Journal* (November): 1890–92.

Westney, Eleanor. 1995. "Can the Keiretsu Be Internationalized?" *Perspectives,* Centre for International Business, University of Toronto, 3/3: 4.

Williamson, Oliver. 2000. "The New Institutional Economics: Taking Stock, Looking Ahead." *Journal of Economic Literature,* 38 (September): 595–613.

World Bank. 2000. *East Asia: Recovery and Beyond.* Washington: The World Bank.

– 1993. *The East Asian Miracle: Economic Growth and Public Policy.* New York: Oxford University Press.

Young, Alwyn. 1994. "The Tyranny of Numbers: Confronting the Statistical Realities of the East Asian Growth Experience." *NBER Working Paper* no. 4680, March.

East Asia: A new regional player in the world economy?

WENDY DOBSON[1]

East Asia's changing significance

East Asia has emerged as a significant growth pole in the world economy in the past 30 years. Even after the 1997–98 financial and economic crises, when growth rates slowed from their heady levels of the previous decade, East Asia including Japan still accounts for more than 20 percent of the world economy and 24 percent of world trade (Table 1). Intra-regional trade, that is, trade among the East Asian economies, accounts for 44.5 percent of its total trade (Dobson 2001: 29). The region provides a third of the world's savings; it is host to a sixth of all inward FDI and its economies possess nearly 1 trillion dollars in foreign reserves – nearly half the world total (Table 1). Going forward, developments in the East Asian region will be significant for the world economy.

Assessing East Asia's future significance requires an understanding of the lasting effects of the Asian crisis on the region's economies. Recovery was initially dramatic and "V-shaped" in the growth of output. But the crisis forced a re-examination of key elements in the macroeconomic policy framework, particularly exchange rate regimes and capital accounts, and was the catalyst for a sea change in attitudes

---

1 Research assistance by George Georgopoulos is gratefully acknowledged.

Table 1: East Asian economies in the world economy, 1999

	I. 1999 Share of world						II. Population below the poverty line[5] (millions)	III. Foreign reserves less gold[4] 1999 (billions $US)
	GDP[1]	Population[1]	Trade[2]	Inward FDI stock[3]	Foreign reserves less gold[4]	Savings[1]		
Japan	14.54	2.13	7.12	0.81	15.73	20.130	–	286.92
China	3.28	20.92	3.41	6.41	8.64	6.356	75 (1996)	157.73
S. Korea	1.34	0.79	2.52	0.58	4.06	2.112	–	73.99
Hong Kong	0.52	0.12	3.13	2.77	5.27	0.726	–	96.24
Taiwan	0.98	0.37	2.16	–	5.82	–	–	106.20
Thailand	0.41	1.04	1.02	0.56	1.87	0.605	11.6 (1980)	34.06
Indonesia	0.47	3.46	0.76	1.37	1.45	0.517	23 (1996)	26.45
Philippines	0.25	1.29	0.62	0.23	0.73	0.184	30 (1994)	13.23
Singapore	0.28	0.05	1.93	1.66	4.21	0.674	–	76.84
Malaysia	0.25	0.38	1.46	1.02	1.68	0.513	3.56 (1989)	30.59
Vietnam	0.09	1.31	–	0.31	0.10	0.092	39.7 (1993)	1.87
Laos	0.005	0.08	0.01	0.01	0.01	0.005	2.3 (1993)	0.10
Cambodia	0.01	0.20	–	0.01	0.02	0.002	4.6 (1994)	0.39
Myanmar	0.88	0.75	0.02	0.05	0.01	–	–	0.26
Total	23.31	32.89	24.16	15.81	49.60	31.917	189.76	904.87

1 Source: World Development Report 2000/2001; exceptions are Taiwan and Myanmar: Key Indicators 2000, Asian Development Bank.
2 Trade is defined as exports plus imports. Source: IMF/IFS.
3 Inward FDI stock is the value of the share of capital and reserves (including retained profits) attributable to the parent enterprise, plus the net indebtedness of affiliates to the parent enterprise. The values are presented at book value or historical cost, reflecting prices at the time when the investment was made. Source: World Investment Report 2000.
4 Total reserves less gold is defined to include the monetary authorities' holdings of SDRs, reserve position in the IMF, and foreign exchange. Source: IMF/IFS.
5 National estimates of population below the poverty line are determined by national authorities, where the estimates are based on population-weighted subgroup estimates from household surveys. Source: World Development Report 2000/2001.
– Not available

towards "the neighbourhood" and possibilities for closer regional economic cooperation. Previously unthinkable strides have been made since 1999 toward regional institutions for monetary cooperation and trade. At the same time, though, key structural weaknesses bared by the crisis, particularly in corporate structures and financial systems, have been addressed at differing rates across the region. These weaknesses are sources of vulnerability to future external shocks – such as the global economic slowdown in 2000–01 – and contain the seeds of future difficulties. It is progress in these areas that could differentiate the region's economies into long-term winners and losers.

In this chapter, we evaluate change (and in some cases the lack of change) in policies and institutions since the crisis, and explore their future implications. We begin with exchange rate regimes and structural issues. We then examine the trends toward East Asian regionalism and their implications for the world economy and for international monetary and financial institutions. We conclude with the implications of these developments for international business in the region's economies.

Exchange rates post-crisis

More than four years after the onset of Thailand's dramatic devaluation in July 1997, it is clear that exchange-rate arrangements in the crisis economies were crucial contributors to the severity of the crisis. The monetary authorities in Indonesia, Malaysia, Thailand, and the Philippines had adopted fixed-but-adjustable exchange rate pegs that were maintained long after they should have been revised to reflect changing economic fundamentals. In the Thai case, a growing current-account deficit in the economic boom leading up to the crisis signalled to financial markets the need for policy adjustment. During the boom Thailand had attracted large inflows of foreign capital, much of it short-term bank debt, that was channelled into long-term projects such as real estate. When the inevitable exchange rate adjustment was forced by the markets, the currency crisis turned into a banking and economic crisis, in part because borrowers and foreign investors alike had assumed that there was neither exchange rate nor interest rate risk.

The Bank of Thailand's unsuccessful defence of the peg required high interest rates that pushed highly leveraged business borrowers into insolvency, taking jobs, incomes, and output with them.

The crisis illustrated a basic principle of international economics. A country cannot sustain indefinitely a combination of fixed exchange rates, monetary policy directed at domestic goals, and free movement of capital. Sooner or later, one of these policies has to give.[2] One of the interesting questions is why the fixed-but-adjustable ("soft") exchange rate pegs endured for so long, before ultimately becoming unsustainable (Thailand, for example, initiated its policy in 1983). One reason is that as economies opened their capital accounts in the 1980s and 1990s, and as private capital flows increased in volume to emerging market economies, the vulnerability of those economies to external shocks, from changes in interest rates or investor sentiment, increased. The second reason is that policy-makers moved to defend a parity (through higher interest rates or exchange market intervention) too slowly to react to shocks such as declining export demand. Speculators, anticipating devaluation, often attacked currencies successfully, causing crisis and increased financial volatility.

If the soft peg[3] is unsustainable, economic policy-makers have two choices: to adopt a "hard" peg (with a currency board, dollarization, or a currency union) or to allow the exchange rate to float. By the end of 1999, the crisis economies had moved away from soft pegs to a variety of new arrangements (Table 2). Only Hong Kong had a hard peg.[4] Indonesia, the Philippines, and Thailand claimed to have moved to free floating while others practised managed floating (Table 2). In fact, almost no East Asian economy now allows the exchange rate to float freely. Instead monetary authorities are intervening with changes in

---

2 See Edwards, 1999; Mussa et al., 2000; Williamson, 2000.

3 In the economic debate that ensued, this option was subsumed into the "intermediate" option (one that included soft pegs as well as managed floating); see Frankel, 1999 and Table 2.

4 China backed its dollar peg with capital controls; Malaysia also used selective capital controls with its currency peg.

Table 2: Exchange rate arrangements in East Asia, 1997 and 1999

Economy	1997	1999	Notes
China	Intermediate	Intermediate	Soft peg plus capital controls
Hong Kong SAR	Hard peg	Hard peg	Currency board
Indonesia	Intermediate	Float	Soft peg
Malaysia	Intermediate	Intermediate	Capital controls since 1997
Philippines	Intermediate	Float	
Singapore	Intermediate	Intermediate	Managed float
South Korea	Intermediate	Intermediate	Managed float
Thailand	Intermediate	Float	Soft peg 1970–97
Taiwan	Intermediate	Intermediate	Managed float

Source: Fischer (2001); IMF, various years.

monetary policy and intervention practices to influence exchange rate performance. The build-up of foreign-exchange reserves in all regional economies (Table 1, column III) results from central bank intervention to preserve competitiveness and to pad war chests to cover import bills and short-term international indebtedness.

While many economists ruled out soft pegs as a policy option in the wake of the crisis, some have argued that intermediate regimes are still a viable choice (Frankel, 1999; Ito et al., 1999; Williamson, 2000; Japan, Ministry of Finance, 2000). Frankel argues that many countries are, in fact, following intermediate arrangements for practical reasons. The authorities desire both some capital mobility as well as some exchange rate stability along with monetary policy independence. He observes that they do not have to give up these intermediate choices, but they must stay very much on the their toes – prepared to intervene in exchange markets and, ultimately, to change monetary policy for exchange rate reasons. Ito et al. propose an East Asian Currency Unit. Williamson (2000) criticizes managed floating on the grounds that the authorities' failure to provide transparent information on the range they prefer reduces their credibility in exchange markets. He recommends an intermediate regime known as BBC (basket, band, crawl) in which monetary authorities peg to a "Basket" of the currencies of their major trading partners and announce the exchange rate range (Band) beyond which they will intervene. He also recommends they allow the parity to (Crawl) in order to neutralize differential inflation among the major trading partners.

Frankel notes that authorities will do what makes most sense for them while running the risk that they will invite speculation if they fail to move with sufficient alacrity. Williamson's alternatives are complex to administer and are difficult for markets to understand. Nevertheless, the intermediate regime worked in the European Union. Over the long term, it is not outside the realm of possibility for East Asia.

Of course, the underlying issue is the sustainability of exchange rates and monetary policy and the close interrelationship between the two. This point is usefully emphasized by Kuttner and Posen (2001), who argue that the focus on exchange rate regimes tends to crowd out attention to relationships among the exchange rates regime, central bank autonomy, and domestic monetary policy. In Latin America, some central banks have made different choices than those in East Asia. Brazil, for example, seeks a sustainable exchange rate regime and credible monetary policy by adopting inflation targeting and a floating exchange rate. A legacy of low inflation and inflation expectations in East Asia, along with pressures from exporters for close attention to the nominal exchange rate, contributes to the policy emphasis on the exchange rate regime in the region.

In summary, most East Asian governments post-crisis are reluctant to allow exchange rates to float freely, reflecting their fears of the negative impact on exports of real and nominal exchange rate volatility. As Fischer (2001) observes: "Changes in the nominal exchange rate are likely to affect the inflation rate. Changes in the real exchange rate may have a powerful effect on the wealth of domestic citizens, and on the allocation of resources, which may have not only economic but also political effects – especially in the case of currency and appreciations, in countries where exports matter."

Managed floating has been successful over time in both Singapore and Taiwan, but for good reason. These economies have large stocks of reserves, disciplined macroeconomic policies, and well-developed, sophisticated, and liquid financial systems. In the crisis economies, as we shall see below, the situation is quite different. Weak financial systems, structural problems, and debt overhangs in Indonesia, Thailand, and the Philippines, make managed floating very risky. This practice easily turns into the soft peg, with the associated liability that, in inviting speculation in times of adversity, this option actually magnifies the risks of crisis.

At the same time, there is a change in the "angle of vision" in East Asia. The long-term goal is now one of attaining stability through permanently fixed exchange rates in a regional currency union.[5] There is increased willingness to move along a road leading to closer economic cooperation – a basic building block for eventual currency union. But as the European Union experience has demonstrated, the groundwork essential to a shared currency includes convergence in economic performance and industrial structures. Otherwise, economies with different structures adjust differently to external shocks. With exchange rate flexibility lacking as a buffer, most of the strain of adjustment falls on labour markets and employment.

Studies of the feasibility of region-wide monetary integration suggest that the conditions necessary for smooth adjustment to external shocks do not yet exist. Bayoumi and Eichengreen (1994) found that the Japanese, South Korean, and Taiwanese economies had sufficient similarities to be one possible regional currency grouping. Hong Kong SAR, Indonesia, Malaysia, Singapore, and possibly Thailand were seen to be another. Note that China was not seen to be part of any grouping. Kwan (1998) studied the feasibility of regional monetary union using the yen as the common currency. Kohsaka (2000) found that East Asian economies adjusted to simulations of aggregate supply and aggregate demand shocks in a manner similar to the European economies. The implication of this latest work is that the risks for the Asian economies, heterogeneous as they still may be, do not differ much from those that Europeans currently face.

---

5 A Vision Group organized by the leaders of the ASEAN economies, Japan, South Korea, and China, has also recommended an East Asia currency union in the long term (see the discussion below).

Structural factors post-crisis[6]

Structural or microeconomic weaknesses in the East Asian economies were another key source of vulnerability to external shocks. The unbalanced structure of domestic financial systems was one weakness. These systems tend to be dominated by banks supplying debt finance; hence, there is little diversity in the supply of long-term financial instruments. Such systems were slow to adapt to the added external risks from mobile international capital flows.

East Asian financial sectors have improved, but they still trail best international practice (see Table 3.3 in Dobson and Jacquet, 1998 and Claessens and Glaessner, 1998). As economies develop and become more complex, diverse financial systems are required to permit savers and investors to interact with confidence with borrowers and issuers not known to them. Stronger banks, diversified institutional frameworks that supply financial instruments of longer duration, and flows of transparent information, as well as payments and settlement arrangements, make possible deep and liquid financial markets that can withstand external shocks. Strong supervisory oversight and enforcement of prudential standards, adequate infrastructure, and modern accounting and legal frameworks that promote transparency are all required to strengthen financial systems. At the same time, several constraints must be addressed: the lack of trained manpower, lack of independent supervisors, and the vested interests in existing systems.

Highly leveraged corporations were another source of weakness. Many corporations became highly leveraged during the high growth years, in part because of the lack of alternatives to bank debt, but also because of corporate governance practices such as close relationships between banks and the firms in business groups and family conglomerates. Some firms borrowed heavily abroad in unhedged foreign currencies. Some governments also biased policies and incentives to favour

---

6 This section draws on Dobson and Jacquet (1998), Claessens et al. (2001), and Claessens et al. (1999).

foreign over domestic capital (for example, Thailand taxed foreign capital more lightly than the other forms and South Korea restricted FDI inflows but encouraged foreign debt).

One of the initial consequences of unanticipated external shocks from exchange rate and interest rate changes was a rise in corporate defaults and increased non-performing loans in financial institutions. The capital flow reversals and related regional economic slowdown depressed asset prices and contributed to complex coordination problems among corporations, investors, financial institutions, and governments. One of the primary issues in responding to these developments was to facilitate corporate debt workouts to reduce the debt overhang.

The magnitude and nature of corporate distress in the wake of the East Asian crisis indicated that better bankruptcy procedures were required to restore corporate financial health. Beyond that, stronger and more transparent corporate governance seems to be indicated, particularly for firms engaging in international business, with better representation of the interests of minority shareholders. A recent World Bank study (Kaufman et al., 1999) compared indicators of national and corporate governance in more than 155 countries in the 1997–98 period. The authors compiled indicators of the process by which those who govern countries are selected and replaced (voice), capacity to implement sound policy (regulatory framework), and respect for rules (rule of law). Rankings (which range from –2.5 at the low end to +2.5 at the high end) for the East Asian economies (Table 3) indicate lower scores for the crisis economies (negative scores to less than 1), particularly with respect to regulatory framework and rule of law, than those for the international financial centres in Hong Kong and Singapore.

Addressing the debt overhangs left by the crisis requires consistent frameworks of incentives to bring both banks and corporations to the negotiating table. The heat of crisis is perhaps the best time to make such changes, yet the records of the crisis economies in creating such frameworks are mixed. For example, both Indonesia and Thailand have created bankruptcy codes since the crisis, but use of them has been minimal. South Korea created favourable tax treatment for corporations that successfully restructured debts with their creditors, yet

Table 3: Governance indicators, 1997–98

Economy	Voice	Regulatory framework	Rule of law
China	−1.296	−0.07	−0.040
Hong Kong SAR	−0.074	1.207	1.333
Indonesia	−1.165	0.121	−0.918
Malaysia	−0.144	0.477	0.834
Philippines	0.614	0.565	−0.078
Singapore	0.040	1.245	1.939
South Korea	1.002	0.219	0.943
Taiwan	0.706	0.829	0.928
Thailand	0.215	0.192	0.413
Median (9 economies)			
Japan	1.163	0.389	1.422
United States	1.505	1.135	1.254
Canada	1.362	0.869	1.549

Source: Kaufman et al. (1999).

the available evidence suggests these tax rules have been used mainly for cosmetic purposes rather than for real change. Thailand, Korea, and Malaysia have each developed procedures whereby majority accords among creditors can be used to force all creditors into debt restructurings; Indonesia has moved more slowly in this direction.

Another measure employed by governments in each of the crisis economies is the Asset Management Corporation (AMC), to which non-performing assets were moved from the books of corporations in preparation of closing them or fixing them and selling them. The centralized AMC used by Indonesia does not seem to have achieved its goals of expediting bank and corporate restructuring. Malaysia's was more successful, helped by a strong bankruptcy regime. Thailand used a more decentralized framework that has not been regarded as very successful, in part because of a weak institutional framework (accounting and legal rules, capital positions of banks and ownership links). The evidence from South Korea is mixed. Claessens et al. (2001) conclude that the centralized AMC structure has not achieved its goals. The OECD's 2001 country report on South Korea applauds its progress, but concludes there is still a long way to go before the government stops propping up banks and *chaebol* and switches resources into a social safety net for individuals (*Financial Times*, 2001). Overholt (2001), by contrast, lauds the authorities for a complete reorganization of the banking system, for putting 14 out of 30 of the largest *chaebol* out of business, and for fundamentally altering how the five largest will function in future.

Since the crisis, public ownership of banks and corporations in the crisis countries has increased. Nationalization has also complicated the resolution of the crisis by creating counter-productive incentives through perceptions of public-sector bailouts. But public ownership can also provide an opportunity to change ownership structures – for example, by reducing the concentration of family ownership, by reallocating ownership to the general public or to employees, and by selling assets to foreign entities. The latter course, in the case of banks, can lead to their recapitalization and to a more competitive and efficient financial system (Dobson and Jacquet, 1998). Allowing greater foreign entry by banks is a course used in Thailand, but with limited success because of political opposition to foreigners acquiring such assets at "fire sale" prices.

One of the great sources of uncertainty in the region, unrelated to the crisis, relates to China's structural reforms. China's progress is discussed in more detail by Brandt and Zhu elsewhere in this volume. Many observers are quite optimistic that China will successfully tread the fine line between reform imperatives and their social and political consequences. Overholt (2001), for example, cites China as "the global hero of reform, laying off perhaps 45m workers, cutting its government in half, and getting the military out of business." If China successfully restructures, its resulting increased competitiveness will be an added external prod to its neighbours.[7] Reports of a marked slowing of the privatization drive in late 2001 imply that, for the time being, the limits of political tolerance of economic change have been reached (Kynge and McGregor, 2001).

---

7 Holland (2001)

In summary, some progress has been made in addressing the structural problems revealed by the 1997–98 crisis, but much more is required. Slow progress in addressing these microeconomic issues provides a marked contrast with governments' speedy commitment to develop regional institutions in trade and finance.

The emergence of East Asian regionalism

In drawing their own lessons from the crisis, East Asians recognize the need to remove structural obstacles to the free play of market forces, but they argue these changes cannot realistically be made overnight. At the same time, many recognize that East Asians require additional financial arrangements that will enable them to build their own infrastructure for more efficient intermediation of their own substantial savings. Given the fact of their growing economic clout in the world economy, these strengths can be turned to advantage in reducing vulnerability to external shocks.

The crisis was a catalyst for regional financial initiatives, both for "plumbing" and architecture. The plumbing refers to initiatives to improve intermediation among the financial centres in the region. With respect to architecture, major initiatives are being taken to promote closer monetary cooperation. The rationale is developmental. Macroeconomic performance, as well as structural weaknesses in national financial systems, can spill over from one economy to its neighbours' through interest rates, capital flows, exchange rates, and trade flows, as well as through migratory flows. It helps to have a hand on the policy levers of one's neighbours through surveillance discussions and through technical assistance for institution building. Investments in the closer relationships can pay off in terms of early warnings of future crises and in cooperative management of crises.

East Asia's export-led growth has been highly dependent on market access to the major OECD economies. If OECD growth momentum declines or market access becomes less certain, other sources of growth must be found. One is growth in domestic demand. Another is region-wide liberalization through sub-regional FTAs. The only WTO members who are not also members of some regional trade arrangement are Japan and South Korea. For historical reasons, Japan has been exclusively committed to the multilateral trade liberalization process. In 1998, however, Japanese policy began an unprecedented shift towards bilateral negotiations. By early 2001, a number of studies of and commitments to negotiate FTAs had proliferated in the region. The emergence of NAFTA and the advent of the euro, along with lack of U.S. participation and leadership at the global level is seen to make the second route imperative, both as a contingency plan and as strategic pressure on the U.S. Congress and the U.S. president.

These choices will have an impact on the international economy. Regional financial arrangements to provide emergency financing to central banks could create distortions in international capital markets and add to moral hazard[8] unless they are carefully crafted. Intermediate exchange rate arrangements could attract speculative activity and volatility, although significant voices disagree (Frankel, 1999; Williamson, 2000). There is also considerable scepticism that capital controls can be administered in ways that avoid serious distortions (Edwards, 1999).

More concern is voiced about regional trading arrangements because it is not clear that these will be non-discriminatory. Bhagwati and Panagariya (1996) make a closely argued theoretical case that they are a mistake. Krueger (1999) surveys the debate over whether preferential trading arrangements (PTAs) are building blocks or stumbling blocks to global trade liberalization. The empirical evidence on PTAs indicates they are trade-creating. Some governments use them as a device to lock in domestic reforms; others use them as strategic threats to encourage laggards back to the multilateral bargaining table. PTAs are also channels by which governments can move faster and in innovative ways that are not possible in the increasingly cumbersome mul-

---

8 Moral hazard refers to the impact on incentives of the prospect of regional funding on possibly easier terms than that available from the International Monetary Fund. Governments, central banks, and financial-sector regulators might be more relaxed about risk taking by national financial institutions if there is an expectation that they will be bailed out.

tilateral rounds. Producers use PTAs to accelerate tariff reductions on intermediate goods.

Stumbling-block proponents emphasize the dangers of trade diversion. They prefer unilateral liberalization to preferential arrangements, but would prefer that trade ministers focus their scarce resources on multilateral liberalization. Krueger points out that the few sophisticated models of the costs and benefits of PTAs show that PTAs create trade. There are few other empirical studies on which to base conclusions. She concludes that PTAs are here to stay. The challenge is to make them compatible with multilateral liberalization. Of course, as is well known, unilateral liberalization has been a common practice in East Asia. APEC members, in committing in 1994 to free trade in the region by 2010 for developed economies and by 2020 for less-developed economies, have had to rely almost exclusively on unilateral liberalization (known as "concerted unilateralism") up to now.

The initiatives for regional institutions are being driven by ASEAN+3 (the Association of Southeast Asian Nations plus Japan, China, and South Korea). ASEAN is East Asia's longest-standing regional grouping.[9] It has a history of difficulties in achieving closer economic cooperation because of its traditional principle of non-interference and consensus decision-making. In the early 1990s it negotiated the ASEAN free trade area (AFTA). Implementation has slowed to crawl since the Asian crisis, in large part because of Indonesia's political and economic turmoil and because of Malaysian resistance to tariff reductions in the auto sector.

In contrast, plans for ASEAN+3 have developed rapidly since late 1999 following a summit of leaders in Manila. These plans include a Vision Group, led by a former South Korean foreign minister, which completed work in mid-2001 on a report to leaders. The draft vision includes an East Asian community, free-trade area, investment area, common regional currency, and other far-reaching cooperative arrange-

---

9 Its 10 members include Brunei, Indonesia, Malaysia, Philippines, Singapore, and Thailand with the recent additions of Cambodia, Laos, Myanmar, and Vietnam.

ments to promote development of the less developed members. The moving forces behind this grouping are the Northeast Asians. Although decisions are largely taken by consensus, a "2 + 2" mechanism has been developed for technical cooperation projects. If two ASEAN members agree to request a development project and two of Japan, South Korea, and China agree to fund it, this agreement provides the basis to proceed. The financial clout and resolve of the "plus three" will be major factors in future development of the regional grouping.

Regional trade initiatives

A number of trade-liberalizing initiatives are in various states of play (Table 4), ranging from the well-established AFTA to study of a possible regional FTA. The implications of these potential arrangements may not always be fully understood by their proposers, so considerable study is probably required before formal negotiations begin. Free-trade arrangements, for example, make little economic sense between two economies with complementary industrial structures. The gains from liberalization are to be realized from reducing tariffs and the many technical barriers that prevent specialization and intra-industry trade. This is especially true in services. In addition, such agreements will not be WTO-compliant unless they aim to free up trade in essentially all sectors on a non-discriminatory basis.

    As Table 4 indicates, the list of proposals is a long one, but only a few have been implemented. Two countries, Singapore and Japan, are major movers. One of Singapore's objectives in pursuing FTAs with neighbours such as New Zealand and Japan and non-neighbours such as Canada and the United States is to create an incentive for its foot-dragging AFTA partners to become more serious about faster implementation of AFTA. Another objective is strategic: to head off concerns about a discriminatory block by stimulating cross-regional ties. Japan seeks a new form of *gaiatsu* (foreign pressure) to stimulate needed domestic reforms. Japan is also concerned to break its sense of isolation created by the severity of its own domestic crisis and by its inability to project effective leadership in the regional crisis. Negotia-

Table 4: Subregional trading arrangements, APEC
region, 2001

Under study
Singapore – Chile
Singapore – Mexico
Singapore – Canada
Singapore – United States

Korea – Chile
Korea – Mexico
Korea – New Zealand

Japan – Mexico
Japan – Canada
Japan – Chile

New Zealand – Chile

Chile – United States

ASEAN – China
ASEAN – Japan
East Asian Free Trade Area

"P-5" (US, New Zealand, Australia, Singapore, Chile)

AFTA – CER closer links study

Being negotiated
Japan – Singapore

Negotiated/implemented
Canada – Chile
Singapore – New Zealand

Sources: Author; Scollay (2001).

tions with Singapore moved quickly in part because agriculture is an insignificant item in bilateral trade. While the Singapore–New Zealand agreement is between two very small economies,[10] that between Singapore and Japan is potentially significant, judging by the report of an official binational study group that laid the groundwork for negotiations.[11] This report recommends the elements of a free-

---

10 Even so, the agreement itself is a textbook example.
11 See Japan, Government of, and ... Singapore, 2000.

trade agreement (reduction of tariff and non-tariff barriers; creation of dispute-resolution mechanisms; and inclusion of goods, services, investment, intellectual property, government procurement, and competition policy). It also contains proposals to break new ground through bilateral cooperation on a wide range of "new" issues in electronic commerce, multi-media, science and technology, and trade and investment promotion. An agreement was reached in October 2001 that will be signed by the end of 2001.

Because of the new ground it proposed to cover, the Japan–Singapore negotiation was potentially significant. It could have provided a flexible structure for future Japanese bilateral negotiations as well as have a useful WTO-consistent model that others could adapt. But what was actually produced demonstrated that Japan is hampered in these initiatives by its agriculture, fish, and forestry lobbies. Excluding these sectors from the negotiations, as turned out to be the case, sets a dangerous precedent that probably dooms any other Japanese free-trade initiatives.[12] Instead, these will be more modest moves toward liberalizing services and investment flows between the two countries.

Regional financial arrangements and monetary integration

The road to monetary integration is a very long one, but governments have decided to begin the trip. Sub-regional financial arrangements began informally in the ASEAN economies when several central banks agreed to currency swaps in 1996–97. These agreements had relatively little effect during the crisis, but cooperative arrangements took a major leap forward when the idea was expanded and formalized among ASEAN+3 central banks in May 2000. In what has become known as the Chiengmai Initiative (after the location at which the scheme was agreed) the ASEAN+3 central-bank governors and finance

---

12 Japan is also talking to countries such as Australia, which has a substantial agriculture sector, with the aim of liberalizing economic relations in areas other than agriculture. Such talks are seen to be part of new economic partnerships, but not FTAs.

ministers agreed to work out currency swap arrangements among central banks in Northeast and Southeast Asia. These arrangements are part of the Network of Bilateral Swap Arrangements (NBSA), which will supplement the reserves of such countries as Singapore with Japanese, South Korean, and Chinese foreign exchange reserves. Details of the scheme are being worked out for quick activation and disbursement of swaps. In 2001 Japan finalized agreements with South Korea, Malaysia, and Thailand in which borrowers will be permitted to draw 10 percent of their allowance without conditions; beyond that amount, IMF conditionality applies. Japanese officials informally indicated their expectation that within two years as many as 22 agreements would be finalized. The amounts, however, are small, totalling roughly $7 billion announced in 2001. It is also anticipated that monitoring and surveillance of member economies' performance will take place in the ASEAN+3 meetings of central bankers and finance minister (see, for example, Japan, MOF, 2000). This network will take some time to become operational, and the magnitude of its resources will be relatively modest.

Work is also under way on arrangements to increase the region's ability to intermediate its substantial savings. Some Executive Meeting of East Asia and Pacific (EMEAP) member central banks are working on bilateral payments and clearance mechanisms for specific financial instruments that could eventually grow into regional networks.

As indicated earlier, the economic feasibility of region-wide monetary integration is under study. Existing studies say little about institutional and political feasibility. To realize the benefits of monetary union, countries must have similar macroeconomic policy objectives. Their central banks should have some institutional similarities and be independent of political pressure. They should have similar economic structures; trade and capital markets should be closely integrated and labour must be mobile. While trade and investment flows increasingly link the Asian economies, financial intermediation is still underdeveloped; labour movements are restricted; central banks are not independent; and governments still guard national sovereignty closely.

In summary, while region-wide monetary integration is not in the cards in the short term, some significant steps towards closer monetary cooperation have been taken by policy-makers that will strengthen regional financial infrastructure and build the shared understanding necessary for collective efforts to prevent and manage crises.

Regional crisis prevention and management

In the short term, the test of the monetary arrangements being negotiated is whether they will play any role in preventing a future crisis, or transfer the means into regional hands to manage one if it occurs. Clearly the magnitudes referred to above fall far short of the financial clout necessary to bridge a country's short-term financial requirements. Similarly, the arrangements for closer monitoring and surveillance of a country's economic performance in ASEAN+3 forums have not been seriously tested.[13] But a start has been made. Furthermore, Malaysia's experience with selective and temporary capital controls has provided support for short-term intervention by small, open export-oriented economies with floating exchange rates that are overwhelmed by volatile international capital flows. Many economies are practising managed floating, allowing them to build up reserve positions that speculators have to respect. The Miyazawa Plan, which replaced the Asian Monetary Fund proposal, assisted a number of crisis countries and guarantees foreign borrowing by some of them.

Will the new regionalism persist?

East Asian integration had a defining impact on the world economy in the past decade as the region became an economic growth pole in the world economy. Will deeper integration in East Asia have a further defining impact on the international economic system and its institu-

---

13 As Fischer (2001) points out, neither new exchange rate arrangements nor closer surveillance will have much impact on crisis prevention if governments choose not to listen to outside advice or early warnings when they are proffered.

tions? The earlier discussion of these regional initiatives suggests four issues that should be monitored.

1. Are the bilateral and sub-regional trade initiatives filling a vacuum created by paralysis at the WTO that will be abandoned if WTO momentum is restored?

The resumption of WTO talks will likely have a major impact on regional developments. The reason is that two (Japan and South Korea) of the three countries most keen to negotiate FTAs have underestimated the strength of the opposition from their farm lobbies. Japanese policy to promise its farmers that agriculture will only be tackled at the WTO, where the widest possible range of trade-offs can be found, may be insufficient to induce these groups even to discuss common bilateral interests in agriculture, forestry, and fishing. Excepting agriculture entirely from bilateral discussions will doom the FTAs, where some, but not blanket, exceptions are possible. Another obstacle to these bilateral agreements could come from businesses, if they find that each bilateral agreement has its own rules of origin and dispute settlement procedures. Business may press for reduction of barriers among larger areas to simplify these arrangements or for a return to the WTO.

2. Will regional economic surveillance mechanisms "add value" in preventing international crises?

Experience has shown that effective surveillance relies on peer pressure during good times and requires "interference," in the form of constructive criticism of each other's economic performance and policies – as well as conditions in return for financial assistance – with those that get into trouble. Peers must be willing to supply constructive criticism and those in potential or actual difficulty must be willing to accept objective analysis. Unless governments are willing to enter into this kind of give and take, the regional mechanism will simply become another overlay of officialdom.

3. Will East Asians do things differently (such as restricting certain international private-sector financial players, making liberal use of capital controls, and imposing weaker conditions on troubled economies) than the rest of the world?

Substantially different approaches to financial development or to crisis management will invite arbitrage, introduce moral hazard, and create distortions in capital markets. Weak conditionality will simply delay the necessary strengthening of domestic financial systems. East Asian economies did not turn their backs on world capital markets in the recent crises; but international experience demonstrates that strong financial and corporate governance systems are essential to withstand external financial shocks.

4. Is the ASEAN+3 political and institutional framework sufficiently durable to carry out effective crisis prevention and management?

The ASEAN+3 initiatives will have to be integrated by skilful leaders and brought to life by some sort of administrative mechanism. European experience strongly suggests the importance of a political framework for economic integration. Asia's history and diversity is such that there is no grand vision comparable to the Franco-German vision of integration to end European wars. The Asian custom of consensus and incrementalism suggests the need for strong leadership from a country such as Indonesia or Thailand, or from a coalition of leaders with legitimacy, support, and longevity. Gyohten (2000) proposes an intermediate step to address these difficulties. He suggests launching a core group of economically homogeneous (market-oriented) countries such as Japan, South Korea, Singapore, Australia, New Zealand, Hong Kong, and Taiwan (the latter two if China agrees) to demonstrate how regional cooperation might work, before attempting closer cooperation among a more heterogeneous group.

The administrative issues are not insignificant either. How will monetary cooperation and other forms of economic cooperation be integrated into a coherent whole? Can this be done incrementally and in a pragmatic way? East Asian aversion to international bureaucracy is evident in the minimalist arrangements for APEC. Yet implementing a grand design for integration such as Europe's, while based on political consensus, required a "centre" with permanent expertise.

China will be a major factor in the answers to these questions in three respects. First, stable relationships among China, Japan, and the United States will be necessary for a regional initiative to be successful. If this trilateral relationship destabilizes, regional efforts will be submerged by geopolitical issues. Since the 1997–98 crises, support from the Northeast Asians – South Korea, Japan, and China – has been the driving force behind ASEAN+3 initiatives. Despite old antagonisms, leaders of the three economies have demonstrated their commitment to cooperate on regional issues. Second, China's internal balance will affect its neighbours. China faces huge challenges to transform its state-owned enterprises (SOEs) into profitable enterprises. The continued problems of the SOEs will influence its objectives of modernizing its financial institutions and building a safe and sound private banking system. Exacerbation of its internal problems could spill over into the region through two channels. One channel is trade: slower growth of internal demand and higher unemployment would reduce demand for imports from its neighbours and could also intensify its export drive, which could have negative impacts on the competitiveness of its neighbours in third-country markets. The second channel is through the financial system, particularly if China were to allow a significant effective exchange rate devaluation. Third, once it accedes to the WTO, China will have to decide where it will focus. It is possible that WTO obligations will crowd out regional matters and regional relationships could suffer.

Conclusions and implications for international business

There are two major implications of these developments. One is East Asia's impact on the world economic system. The other is the impact of developments in the world economy on East Asia.

East Asia's new openness to regional trade and financial institutions marks a sea change in attitudes towards cooperation. While it would be a mistake to underestimate the catalytic effects of the financial crisis and perceived external threats posed by NAFTA, the successful launch of the euro and continued paralysis of the WTO, these institutional initiatives are likely to develop slowly for several reasons.

First, strong leadership is lacking, so the way forward will be uneven and uncertain. It is unlikely that any one or two Asian leaders will have the legitimacy to provide a blueprint or the overall leadership that were critical factors in Europe's deeper integration. An incremental process based on consensus decisions is more likely.

Second, deeper integration in East Asia does not occur in a vacuum. Europe and the United States have managed the world economy for the past 50 years. It will be important that East Asians view their process in this broader strategic context. Implementation in 2001 of the Chiengmai Initiative for swap arrangements indicates such an awareness: the initial modest bilateral arrangements spearheaded by Japan require IMF linkage once drawings reach 10 percent of the total allowable; and growing emphasis on the need for a regional surveillance mechanism indicates an awareness of the moral hazard dangers that accompany such an arrangement. Singapore's emphasis on cross-regional FTAs, evident in Table 4, also indicates a broader strategic intent.

Third, while the list of proposed FTAs is a lengthy one, there are significant obstacles to their realization. Agriculture has proved to be a major stumbling block, particularly for Japan and South Korea. WTO-consistent arrangements require liberalization of essentially all trade. This means that agriculture must be included, at least as a negotiating issue.[14] FTAs are probably doomed in the absence of renewed WTO negotiations, where the broadest-possible trade-offs can be made. Paradoxically, however, launching the new WTO round, which might provide a way to reassure these groups, will also probably reduce

---

14 Exceptions and lengthy periods of adjustment for sensitive sectors can be negotiated, but the entire sector cannot be exempted.

the overall interest in and resources for bilateral talks. Even so, liberalization of services and FDI, as well as cooperation in developing "new economy" links through cooperation on information technology (IT) – while not amounting to FTAs – could contribute new liberalizing momentum in sectors that are key to future prosperity.

A more immediate and pressing issue is the potential impact on East Asian economies of the world slowdown in 2001–02. In 1998, U.S. demand for East Asian exports provided a powerful engine pulling the economies back to health. The weakening of this market, along with the risk profiles of heavily indebted Argentina and Turkey, have raised concerns about a new crisis in the region. Early warning indicators of potential financial crisis, such as the sustainability of an economy's trade and finance in the face of external shocks (Table 5), suggest renewed worries about some – but not all – economies in the region. Indonesia's profile is the most worrisome: ratios of foreign debt, fiscal imbalance, and continued short-term indebtedness are all unsustainable. Malaysia and Taiwan have large fiscal imbalances. Hong Kong, Malaysia, and Singapore continue to depend heavily on the U.S. export market. And Hong Kong, China, and Malaysia still fix their exchange rates. If Argentina abandons its currency-board arrangements and devalues, currencies in both Hong Kong and Malaysia will come under pressure. China is likely to escape, as it did in 1998, because of its relatively closed capital account, current account surplus, and small debt.

Offsetting these concerns, however, are the facts that all have large foreign exchange reserves and large current account surpluses. With the exception of Indonesia, most economies are less leveraged than in 1997 (South Korea, for example, has reduced its reliance on short-term borrowing dramatically; the ratio of short-term debt to reserves has fallen from 300 percent in 1997 to 38 percent in 2001 [*Economist*, 2001]). Real exchange rates are substantially devalued since 1997 in the crisis economies (although the real exchange rate has appreciated in China).

The persistent challenge for most crisis economies lies in their institutions. Slow growth bares the rocks of structural weaknesses. Financial

Table 5: Economic indicators, East Asian economies, 2001

Economy	Foreign debt (% of exports)	Budget balance (% GDP)	Short-term debt (a), (% of reserves)	Current account balance (% GDP)	Exports to US (% GDP)	Real exchange rate (b), change since January 1997 (%)
China	47	−2.8	11	0.9	4.7	+13
Hong Kong	19	−0.3	11	3.6	*28.7*	0
Indonesia	*186*	*−4.6*	*108*	2.7	6.0	−43
Malaysia	39	*−7.0*	20	6.3	*23.9*	−19
Philippines	108	−3.8	55	9.3	16.1	−32
Singapore	5	1.7	3	21.4	*26.2*	−8
South Korea	60	−0.4	38	2.8	8.2	−16
Taiwan	24	*−6.3*	22	3.5	11.2	−14
Thailand	86	−3.0	53	4.7	13.1	−20

Notes: (a) Disbursed external debt having original maturity up to one year. (b) J.P. Morgan trade-weighted index. Bold, italicized entries indicate unsustainable ratios.

Source: *The Economist* (2001).

systems are still fragile in Thailand, Indonesia, and the Philippines and more improvement in corporate governance is required outside of the international financial centres of Hong Kong and Singapore. The prolonged economic slumps in Thailand and Japan illustrate how inadequate structural reforms can trap resources in moribund institutions and depress the entire economy. If these slumps persist and conditions get much worse, internal pressures may increase to turn inward as an alternative to the dependence on export-led growth of the past three decades.

Yet to restore prosperity, the crisis economies should do just the opposite. As they lose competitiveness in goods production to China, the newest ASEAN members, South Asian, and even African economies, they should adjust by shifting to production of services and higher value-added goods – in line with 30 years of experience of industrial upgrading. The next stage means liberalizing previously protected service industries and investing more heavily in education and infrastructure including IT. The response to the 1997–98 crisis was to deepen regional linkages and restore international competitiveness. Overall, the economic record depicted in Table 5 is a good one. Indonesia is the exception, in part because of its political difficulties. These may start to abate if President Megawati Sukarnoputri's promising start in late 2001 is any indication. It is also difficult to underestimate the positive impact on the region that a determined and credible reform effort in Japan could have. So there is reason to be optimistic, without minimizing the difficulties and the pain of adjustment. Of all the emerging market economies, the leading East Asian economies have the best track record on which to build for the future.

REFERENCES

Asian Development Bank. 2000. *Key Economic Indicators*. Manila: Asian Development Bank.
Bayoumi, Tamim, and Barry Eichengreen. 1994. "One Money or Many?" *Princeton Studies in International Finance* no. 76. Princeton, NJ: Princeton University, International Finance Section.

Bhagwati, Jagdish, and Arvind Panagariya, eds. 1996. *The Economics of Preferential Trade Agreements.* Washington: The AEI Press.

Claessens, Stijn, Simeon Djankov, and Daniela Klingebiel. 1999. "Financial Restructuring in East Asia: Halfway There?" World Bank: available on the Internet or in mimeo form.

Claessens, Stijn, and Tom Glaessner. 1998. "Internationalization of Financial Services in Asia." World Bank: unpublished manuscript.

Claessens, Stijn, Daniela Klingebiel, and Luc Laeven. 2001 (July). "Financial Restructuring in Banking and Corporate Sector Crises: What Policies to Pursue?" *NBER Working Paper* no. 8386. Cambridge, Mass: NBER.

Dobson, Wendy. 2001. "East Asia in the World Economy." In Charles Morrison, coordinator, *East Asia in the World Economy.* Trilateral Commission Papers. New York: Trilateral Commission.

Dobson, Wendy, and Pierre Jacquet. 1998. *Financial Services Liberalization in the WTO.* Washington: Institute for International Economics.

Economist, The. 2001. "Special Report: Emerging Markets." July 21: 20–22.

Edwards, Sebastian. 1999. "How Effective Are Capital Controls?" *Journal of Economic Perspectives*, 13/4: 65–84.

Financial Times. 2001. "Korea's Conundrum." August 3.

Fischer, Stanley. 2001. "Distinguished Lecture on Economics in Government – Exchange Rate Regimes: Is the Bipolar View Correct?" *Journal of Economic Perspectives.* 15/2: 3–24.

Frankel, Jeffrey A. 1999. "No Single Currency Regime Is Right for All Countries or at All Times." *Essays in International Finance* no. 215. Princeton, NJ: Princeton University, International Finance Section.

Gyohten, Toyoo. 2000. "Revitalization of Asia." www.glocom.org.

Holland, Tom. 2001. "Asia's Red-Queen Economies." *Far Eastern Economic Review*, September 6: 54–56.

International Monetary Fund. *Annual Report.* Various years.

Ito, Takatoshi, Eiji Ogawa, and Yuri Sasaki. 1999. "A Regional Currency System in East Asia." In *Stabilization of Currencies and Financial Systems in East Asia and International Financial Cooperation.* Tokyo: Institute for International Monetary Affairs.

Japan, Government of, and Government of Singapore. 2000 (September). *Japan-Singapore Economic Agreement for a New Age Partnership.* (Joint Study Group Report.) Tokyo and Singapore.

Japan, Ministry of Finance. 2000. "Exchange Rate Regimes for Emerging Market Economies." Discussion paper jointly prepared by French and Japanese staff. www.mof.go.jp.

Kaufman, Daniel, Art Kraay, and Pablo Zoido-Lobaton. 1999. "Governance Matters." *World Bank Policy Research Department Working Paper* no. 2196.

Kohsaka, Akira. 2000. "Macroeconomic interdependence in the APEC region." In Ippei Yamazawa, ed., *APEC: Challenges and Tasks for the Twenty-first Century*. London: Routledge, 19–56.

Krueger, Anne O. 1999. "Are Preferential Trading Arrangements Trade-Liberalizing or Protectionist?" *Journal of Economic Perspectives*, 13/4: 105–24.

Kuttner, Kenneth N., and Adam S. Posen. 2001. "Beyond Bipolar: A Three-Dimensional Assessment of Monetary Frameworks." *Institute for International Economics Working Papers* WP01-7. Washington: Institute for International Economics.

Kwan, C.H. 1998. "The Theory of Optimum Currency Areas and the Possibility of Forming a Yen Bloc in Asia." *Journal of Asian Economics*, 9/4: 555–80.

Kynge, James, and Richard McGregor. 2001. "Stability to the People." *Financial Times*. October 26.

Mussa, Michael, Paul Masson, Alexander Swoboda, Esteban Jadresic, Paolo Mauo, and Andrew Berg. 2000. *Exchange Rate Regimes in an Increasingly Integrated World Economy*. IMF Occasional Paper 193. Washington: IMF.

Overholt, William H. 2001 (July). "Reform, Risk and Opportunity in Northeast Asia." *Nomura Strategy Update*. Hong Kong: Nomura International.

Scollay, Robert, and John P. Gilbert. 2001 (May). *New Regional Trading Arrangements in the Asia Pacific?* Washington: Institute for International Economics.

United Nations Committee for Trade and Development (UNCTAD). 2000. *World Investment Report*. Geneva: United Nations.

Williamson, John. 2000. *Exchange-Rate Regimes for Emerging Markets: Reviving the Intermediate Option*. Washington: Institute for International Economics.

World Bank. 2000. *World Development Report 2000/2001*. Washington: World Bank.

What ails China?
A long-run perspective on growth and
inflation (or deflation) in China

LOREN BRANDT AND XIAODONG ZHU

Overview

Since 1994, China has experienced a prolonged period of declining inflation during which growth has also fallen sharply. Over much of the last three years prices have actually declined. The simultaneous reduction in growth and inflation has led many to attribute the macroeconomic problems China is now facing to the condition of weak aggregate demand. Not unexpectedly, the Chinese government has cut interest rates several times and has vigorously pursued an expansionary Keynesian spending policy in hopes of stimulating aggregate demand. However, these measures have had only limited effects. Prices in most sectors continue to fall, and output growth remains sluggish.[1] The persistent decline in economic activity in the last several years is in stark contrast to a highly cyclical pattern of growth between 1978 and 1994, during which high inflation rather than deflation was the main concern of the government.

In this chapter, we provide an explanation for the behavior of out-

---

1 Official Chinese statistics for the period 1998–2000 run counter to the view of sluggish growth. They report GNP increasing at robust rates of 7.5–8 percent. The general view among experts in and outside of China, however, is that the official data exaggerate GNP growth for these years. Actual growth may have been only half that suggested by official figures.

put growth and price-level changes in China that can account for both the cyclical pattern between 1980 and 1994 and the secular decline in recent years. Our analysis suggests that the reason for the declining growth is not weak aggregate demand. Thus, traditional aggregate demand policies have not and will not be very helpful. Rather, we contend that the lacklustre growth is a result of financial disintermediation, which has caused slower growth of investment in the non-state sector. The financial disintermediation, moreover, is a result of the government's financial repression policy over the last two decades and its recent effort in centralizing the financial system. For the economy to grow more rapidly, the Chinese government needs to eliminate financial repression and allow the entry of new, privately owned, locally based financial institutions.

Central to our explanation are the government's commitment to the state sector and the behaviour in the financial system. Before 1994, the central government maintained a strong commitment to employment growth in the state sector. Severe fiscal constraints forced the central government to look to the financial sector as a source of revenue for supporting the state sector. While there was some financial decentralization, the central government continued to impose control on the financial system's credit allocation. During this period, more than 80 percent of the banking system's credits were directed to the state sector, and lending to the non-state sector can best be described as a process of *intermediation by diversion*. Because of higher average returns in the more productive non-state sector, whenever possible, state-owned banks (SOBs) diverted credits intended for the state sector to the non-state sector. While this increased output growth, it also forced the government to rely more heavily on money creation to finance the transfers to the state sector, which led to high inflation. The cyclical pattern of growth and inflation up through 1994 was the result of the government's inability to control the state banks' credit diversion in the face of financial decentralization and the periodic need to resort to recentralization and administrative control of credit allocation to reduce inflation.

The cyclical growth process, however, was inefficient and unsustainable. The government's use of the financial system to support the state sector resulted in soft budget constraints for both the SOBs and for state-owned enterprises (SOEs) and was the main reason for their deteriorating financial performance. As the productivity gap between the state and the non-state sector widened, there was a steady increase in the size of the transfers required to support SOEs. Mounting losses of the SOEs led to a rapid increase in non-performing loans in the SOBs, putting the whole financial system at risk. There is also a limit to how much revenue can be raised through money creation, and the rapidly rising inflation in 1993–94 indicated that the required transfers were pushing this limit.

It was largely because of these difficulties that beginning in 1994 we see an overall tightening in policy towards the SOBs and SOEs. The People's Bank of China (PBOC), China's central bank, centralized and significantly reduced its lending to the SOBs, and the government began an effort to commercialize the SOBs by putting them in the position of assuming increasing responsibility for their losses and bad loans. The government was able to do so by reducing its long-standing commitment to the state sector. It privatized some small SOEs, allowed large SOEs to lay off workers, and shifted much of the costs of these lay-offs to local governments. As an integral part of the overall tightening policy, the government also lowered the money supply's growth rate significantly, leading to the prolonged decline in inflation.

While these measures have had a desired consequence of hardening the budget constraints of the SOBs and the SOEs, they have also had an important unintended consequence: disintermediation in the financial system and a decline in lending to the non-state sector. This has occurred for several reasons. First, the SOBs have become highly risk averse because of their bad-debt problem and their increased responsibility for their losses. Second, banks are handicapped in identifying good projects due to a lack of information and human capital. Both of these factors have contributed to a voluntary tightening of credit by the SOBs. Third, the financial system has become more centralized in recent years, making the financial institutions more biased against lending to small and medium enterprises (SMEs) in the non-state sector.

Fourth, as part of its financial repression policy, the central government has clamped down on and closed many informal financial institutions such as rural credit cooperative foundations (RCFs) that were not directly under its control. This action has denied the non-state sector a valuable source of financial intermediation. Since 1994, the growth of credit to the non-state sector has declined sharply. It is this decline in credit growth to the non-state sector that is largely responsible for the economy's continued decline in output growth the last several years.

There are several policy implications regarding China's financial system that we can draw from our analysis. First, relaxing constraints on the financial institutions through new infusions of funds from the PBOC, as was often done in the past, is not the solution. Second, major policy initiatives, including the re-capitalization and commercialization of the SOBs, the much-discussed entry of foreign banks with WTO, and opening the capital markets to non-state firms, while very important for large firms, will only have limited effects on overall growth prospects. Third, it will not be efficient simply to target SMEs for increased lending by existing financial institutions or by any newly established centralized financial institutions.[2] To solve China's economic woes in both the short and long term the government should adopt a more radical strategy of reform for the financial system: allowing the entry of new, privately owned, locally based financial institutions that can provide efficient financial intermediations for the SMEs.

The rest of the paper is organized as follows. In the next section, we examine the main determinants of price-level changes and output growth in China. The analysis in this section highlights the stable relationships between the money supply and inflation, and between credit allocation, non-state sector investment, and output growth. It also shows that the declining inflation and output growth is a direct result of a tightening of monetary policy and a decline in credit expansion. The impact of the Asian financial crisis on deflation is also discussed in this section. Since the behaviour in the financial system is central to our

---

2 The monetary commission of the PBOC has recently recommended that the government establish a new state-owned bank specializing in making loans to SMEs.

analysis, we provide a brief overview of China's financial system in the third section. In the fourth section, we analyse the monetary and credit policy employed by the government up through 1994, paying particular attention to the role of credit diversion by the banks in the growth and inflation cycles. In the fifth section, we examine the major policy regime shift that dates from 1994, and its implication for money supply, financial intermediation, and growth. In the sixth section we analyse the fundamental reason for the declining growth in China, financial disintermediation. Based on our analysis, we explain in the seventh section why fiscal and monetary policy have been ineffective in recent years and why they are not going to be effective in the near future. In the final section we examine the policy implications of our analysis for China's financial reforms and the design of China's financial system.

What determines price-level changes and output growth?

Money supply and inflation

China's current deflation follows in the wake of a steady decline in the rate of inflation. After peaking late in 1994, inflation fell for three years until deflation set in beginning in 1998. Inflation is usually a monetary phenomenon, and in China this is also the case.

Over the last 20 years, there is a very strong relationship between the behaviour of M0, the narrowest measure of the money supply, and the changes in the retail price index in China.[3] In Brandt and Zhu (2000), we show that the increase in M0 as a percentage of GDP predicts inflation exceedingly well for the period up through 1994. This close relationship between the inflation rate and the increase in M0 continues to hold for the period after 1994. (See Figure 1.) The declining inflation rate is a direct result of the sharp reductions in the increase in money supply since 1994.

---

3 Because banks' decisions on reserves and loans are heavily influenced by the government's credit policy, which varies significantly over time, more broadly defined money such as M1 and M2 are not good measures of monetary policy.

Figure 1: Money creation and inflation

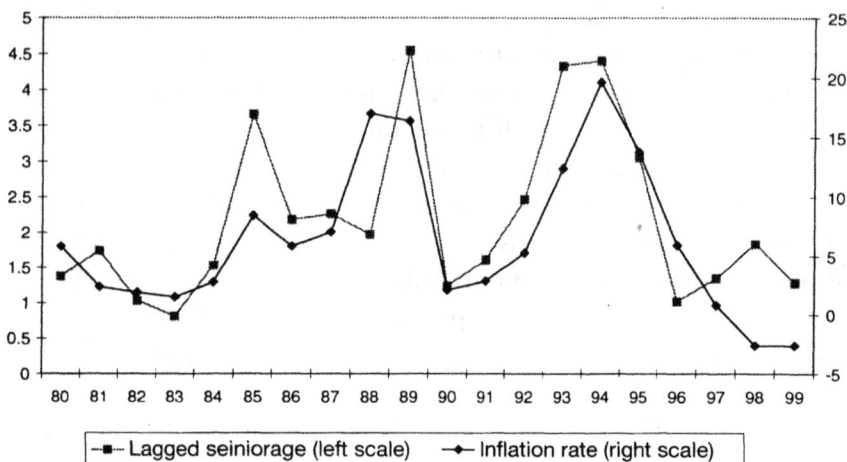

--■-- Lagged seiniorage (left scale) --◆-- Inflation rate (right scale)

Source: *Zhongguo Tongji Nianjian* (Statistical Yearbook of China), various issues.

The Asian financial crisis and deflation

While tight monetary policy can account for the generally low inflation rate experienced in the last several years, it cannot fully account for the *deflation* that started in 1998. Some have suggested that the deflation is a result of excess capacity. Lardy (1999), for example, argues that excess capacity has created a tendency for manufacturers to cut prices in an effort to sell their products. There is a problem, however, with this argument.[4] Excess capacity is not a new phenomenon in China. For the last 20 years or so, inventory investment as a percentage of GDP has averaged 6.3 percent. During the period 1995–98, inventory investment actually declined monotonically from 6.7 percent to 4.6 percent of GDP.[5] Yet, the average inflation rate was very high in

---

4 For a criticism of the excess-capacity argument in the context of Japan's deflation, see Krugman (1999).

5 Unless stated otherwise, all the numbers cited in this paper are from various issues of the Statistical Yearbook of China.

Table 1: Price indices by goods category

	Dec. 1996	Dec. 1997	Dec. 1998	Dec. 1999	Dec. 2000
RPI[1]	104.4	98.8	97.3	97.0	99.6
CPI[2]	107.0	100.4	99.0	99.0	101.5
Food	105.0	97.1	97.2	95.6	99.8
Clothing	105.9	101.9	97.9	97.5	99.8
HH articles	102.6	101.9	97.9	97.7	97.5
Health care	107.4	103.0	102.1	100.0	100.7
Housing	112.0	105.2	100.0	102.9	105.2
Services	118.3	112.5	109.6	114.5	112.8
Imports				94.9	
Exports			92.3	92.5	

1 Retail price index
2 Consumer price index

Source: All data are from the Statistical Yearbook of China except the price indices for imports and exports, which are from the World Bank.

those years. So, by itself, excess capacity does not necessarily lead to price-cutting behaviour.

A more plausible explanation for the deflation is that it is a response to the competitive pressure created by the devaluation of several other Asian currencies. Since China effectively maintains a fixed exchange rate with the U.S. dollar, the devaluation of the Asian currencies put downward pressure on the prices of tradable goods.[6] Table 1 lists price indices of several major goods and services, as well as imports and exports. The price of exports fell most, averaging slightly less than 8 percent in 1998 and 1999, followed by prices of imports. It is clear that domestic goods that are most subject to international competition, such as food and household appliances, experienced the next strongest decline in prices. On the other hand, services and housing, which are internationally non-tradable, have experienced inflation, rather than deflation.

Thus, deflation may simply be a result of market adjustment of the real exchange rate in response to external shocks under a fixed exchange-

---

6 The continuing deflation in Hong Kong appears to be the result of similar forces related to the peg of the HK dollar to the U.S. dollar.

rate regime, which may have actually helped to dampen the impact of the Asian financial crisis on China's exports and overall growth. What, then, caused the growth slowdown? We attempt to answer this question in the next section.

Credit allocation, non-state sector investment, and growth

Over the last two decades, China's non-state sector, which includes collective and private enterprises, has been the main source of output growth. In 1978, when the economic reform started, only 22 percent of industrial output was produced in the non-state sector. Since then, the non-state sector's contribution has increased steadily, and by 1998 accounted for 72 percent of industrial output. Central to growth in the non-state sector, and thus to overall growth, is the level of investment in the sector. Figure 2 shows the strong positive relationship between GNP growth and the growth rate of non-state sector investment. When we regress GNP growth on the growth rates of investment in the state and the non-state sectors, only the non-state sector's growth rate is significant.

Investment in the non-state sector, however, is constrained by the availability of credit. Figure 3 shows the important role that bank credit and, in recent years, foreign investment plays in determining the growth of investment in the non-state sector. Over the last couple of years, however, both sources of funds have declined significantly, leading to a slowdown in investment growth in the non-state sector and, therefore, slower output growth for the whole economy. Since 1994, the rate of growth of credit to the non-state sector has averaged less than 6 percent, compared to 30 percent before 1994. The rate of growth of foreign funded non-state investment also declined considerably beginning in 1994, and after averaging 66 percent for the period before 1994, has only averaged 27 percent since then.

Summary

Money supply and credit to the non-state sector have consistently been the two key factors determining price-level changes and growth

Figure 2: Non-state investment and growth

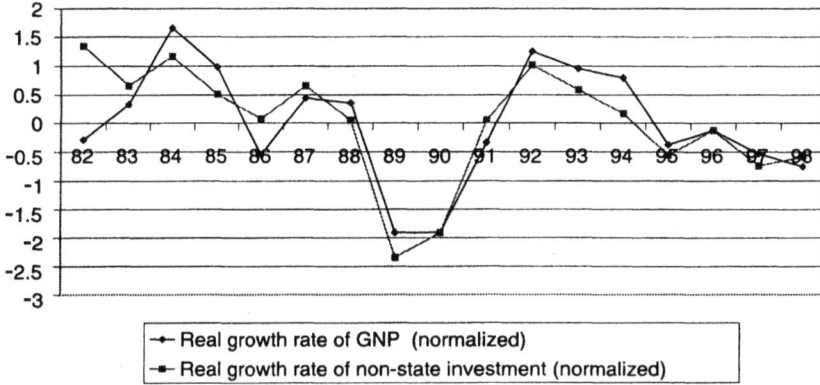

Legend:
—◆— Real growth rate of GNP (normalized)
—■— Real growth rate of non-state investment (normalized)

Figure 3: Bank credit and investment in the non-state sector

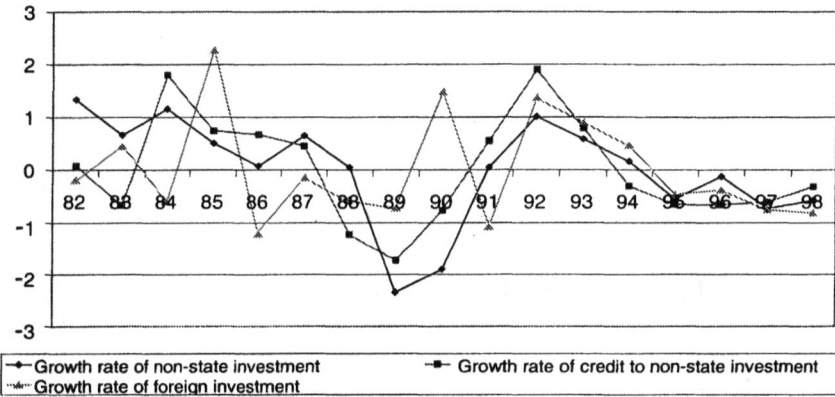

Legend:
—◆— Growth rate of non-state investment   —■— Growth rate of credit to non-state investment
····*···· Growth rate of foreign investment

Note: All series have been normalized by subtracting the mean and then dividing by the standard deviation of each series.

Source: *Zhongguo Tongji Nianjian*, various issues.

throughout the reform period. The recent decline in inflation and output growth is a direct result of a tightening of money supply and a decline in credit growth, a problem that has been confounded by the Asian financial crisis. To understand China's current macroeconomic problem, then, we need to analyse how monetary policy and credit allocation by the financial institutions are determined in China. The key to this analysis is the behaviour in the financial sector.

A brief overview of China's financial system

Before the reforms, China had a mono-bank system in which the PBOC simply served as a cashier of the government. Household savings in the form of deposits were minimal, amounting to only about 5 percent of GNP, and no real intermediation went on. There were also no capital markets. Allocation of fixed investment and working capital to firms was determined administratively by the overall economic plan, and came largely in the form of grants that were financed out of fiscal revenue.

In the early 1980s, the banking system was restructured. The PBOC became the central bank, and its commercial divisions were converted into four state-owned specialized banks. Grants were gradually converted into loans that were financed by the rapid build-up in household deposits in China's financial institutions.[7] However, the government continued a policy of financial repression. The overriding objective of the state banking system has been to provide resources for the state sector, and the development of new financial intermediaries has been constrained. Capital markets have faced similar obstacles and been largely used to mobilize resources for fiscal purposes (through the development of a government debt market), or for financing restructuring of SOEs. In Table 2, we provide incomplete data for the years between 1987 and 1999 on the financing of the non-financial sector by source: banks, non-bank financial institutions (NBFIs), and capital markets.

Even with financial repression, over much of this period we do observe some decentralization within the state-controlled financial system. SOBs were given some discretion in their lending decisions

---

7 Since the early 1980s, China's savings rate has averaged 35 percent of national income. Approximately half of the annual savings is intermediated by China's financial institutions through the increase in deposits. By 1998, total deposits in all of China's financial institutions were 9.6 trillion RMB, which represents 123 percent of GNP.

Table 2: Enterprise financing by source (%)

Year	Banks	NBFIs	Government bonds	Stock issue	Enterprise debt	State sector[1]
1987	71.6	23.3	5.1			59.8
1988	72.7	20.5	5.3		1.4	67.6
1989	82.1	10.9	5.6		1.4	80.6
1990	78.3	16.0	4.3		1.4	73.4
1991	72.4	19.6	4.4	0.1	3.5	67.1
1992	61.2	24.2	5.8	1.6	7.2	57.1
1993	66.5	24.3	3.8	5.2	0.3	63.8
1994	67.1	19.5	9.6	3.7		69.2
1995	63.0	25.2	10.4	1.4		63.2
1996	64.3	21.7	10.7	3.4	−.1	70.9
1997	73.2	11.6	7.1	8.0	.2	70.1
1998	64.1	17.5	12.2	5.9	.3	71.5
1999	47.8	17.8	25.8	8.6		63.7

1 This includes the portion of lending by the banks that went to state-sector firms, plus government bonds, and stock issue.

Source: *Zhongguo Jinrong Tongji Nianjian*, various issues.

through the use of an *indicative* credit plan. In addition to the rural credit cooperatives (RCCs), other non-bank financial institutions were also established, including the urban credit cooperatives (UCCs) and trust and investment companies (TICs). Inter-bank markets were established to facilitate the flow of funds among banks and the NBFIs. The primary motivation for these measures by the central government was to enhance the efficiency with which credit was allocated.

Since they were less bound by the credit plan, and typically had more discretion than the SOBs in making lending decisions, the NBFIs played an important role in intermediating funds to the non-state sector. However, these institutions also had serious shortcomings. On the one hand, they operated under a weakly developed and often inconsistent regulatory environment. Oversight and supervision were often minimal. On the other hand, they were often owned by the local governments or subsidiaries of the SOBs and operated under soft budget constraints. Some NBFIs even had direct financial ties to the local offices of the PBOC, the institution that was in principle supposed to monitor their behaviour.[8] This combination of a lax regulatory environment and soft budget constraints contributed to problems of moral hazard and excessive risk-taking in lending decisions.

China also has an informal financial sector that fell almost entirely outside of the purview of state control. Activity in this sector extended from lending by emerging rural credit foundations (RCFs) to intermediation by illegal private banks, to a host of fund-raising schemes by firms in the state and non-state sectors alike. This activity tended to be cyclical and was most likely to surface during periods of rapid growth when there was a combination of a high demand for credit and lax state control over the financial sector. Periodically, especially during periods of economic retrenchment, efforts were made to clamp down on these kinds of activity.

The seemingly paradoxical policy of financial repression and partial financial decentralization reflects a trade-off the government faces between its commitment to support the state sector and the need to promote the growth of the whole economy. In the next section we show how the government's choices in trading off these two factors resulted in growth and inflation cycles before 1994.

Intermediation by diversion and inflation cycles: 1978–1993[9]

Before 1994, China's monetary policy can be characterized as a stop-go policy: it tightened whenever inflation accelerated, but loosened again once inflation was under control. Correspondingly, growth and inflation were highly cyclical. (See Figure 4.) At the root of these dynamics were the government's commitment to the state sector and the behaviour of credit allocation between the state and non-state sectors.

Ever since the economic reforms started in 1978, productivity and

---

8 Based on interviews with PBOC officials and local financial institutions in Hubei in December 1994.

9 The analysis in this section is based on Brandt and Zhu (2000), where we document in detail the role of credit allocation by state-owned banks in growth and inflation cycles.

Figure 4: Growth and inflation

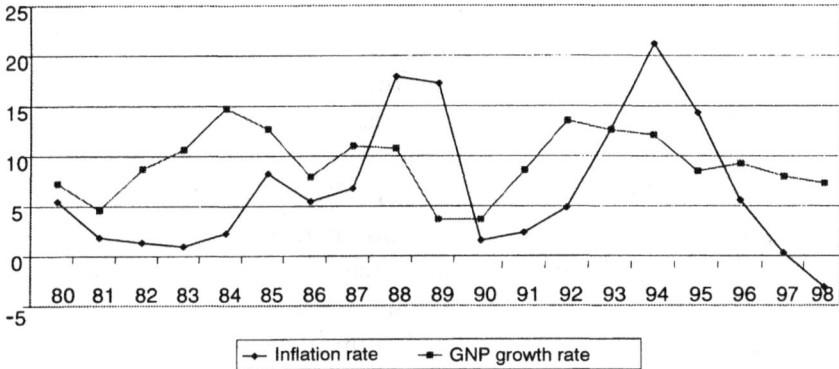

Source: *Zhongguo Tongji Nianjian*, various issues.

output growth in the state sector have been significantly lower than that in the non-state sector. Up through 1993, however, the central government maintained a strong commitment to employment in the state sector that enabled it to grow on a par with that achieved in the non-state sector. Because the state sector's share of output was declining, maintaining this commitment required a steady flow of transfers to the state sector. Facing severe fiscal constraints, the central government financed the transfers mainly with cheap credit from the state banking system and money creation. To ensure that a large portion of total bank credit was directed to the state sector, the government used the credit plan as its principal instrument to control the banking system's credit allocation.

In most years, the credit plan was used as an indicative plan under which SOBs were given some discretion in lending activity to enable them to use their superior information to allocate credit more efficiently. They used this discretion, however, to divert bank resources intended for the state sector under the plan to the non-state sector, in which returns were higher. Lending to the non-state sector was also facilitated by the development of the inter-bank market and the NBFIs.

The diversion of credit to the non-state sector contributed to an increase in investment in the more productive non-state sector. As we documented in the second section, this had a positive effect on growth in the economy. This behaviour, however, left the banks without the resources needed to fund the commitments for fixed and working capital investment outlined in the plan that were essential to supporting employment growth in the state sector. The gap in funding requirements was filled by lending from the PBOC to the SOBs, which contributed to money-supply increases and inflation.

The threat of hyperinflation ultimately required the government to reassert full control over credit allocation in the economy. This meant eliminating any discretion of the SOBs through the implementation of the *administrative* credit plan, restricting fund flows in the inter-bank market, and tightening reins on the NBFIs. These measures were successful in eliminating any leakage out of the state banking system, and thus reduced the funding demands on the PBOC. Inflation fell with the reduction in PBOC lending. The use of the administrative plan, however, came at the cost of lower economic growth as a lower percentage of resources made their way to the more productive non-state sector, and all discretion in credit allocation was eliminated. The high costs associated with these administrative measures explain the government's delay in their implementation, and thus, the cycles.

Policy regime shift in 1994: downsizing the state sector

By 1994, China had experienced three episodes of high inflation. The macroeconomic problems caused by the inefficiency of the state sector steadily worsened. Our estimates (Brandt and Zhu, 2000) for the period between 1986 and 1993 suggest that as the productivity gap between the state and non-state sectors widened, there was a steady increase in the size of the transfers required to support SOEs in industry, a majority of which were financed by loans from SOBs. Since many of these loans were not being repaid, a bad debt problem developed, which put the entire financial system at risk. Estimates differ, but by 1993 total non-performing loans were as much as 25 percent of GDP (Lau and Qian, 1994).

The deterioration of the SOBs' loan portfolio put strong pressure on the central bank to use money creation to finance the transfers. There is a limit to how much revenue can be raised through money creation. As the gap between the state and the non-state sectors widened, there were signs indicating that the required transfers were nearing this limit. Symptomatic of these growing pressures, in each of the three cycles the peak inflation rate was progressively higher, pushing nearly 50 percent on an annual basis during the last of the cycles.

The recurring inflation and deteriorating performance of the state-owned enterprises and banks made the government realize that the stop-go policy was not sustainable and that it could not maintain its support to the state sector indefinitely without running the risk of hyperinflation and a collapse of the banking system. It is against this background that the government in 1994 finally started to tackle directly the fundamental problem of the economy: inefficiency of the state-owned enterprises and banks caused by soft budget constraints.

Several steps were taken in 1994 to harden the budget constraints. First and foremost, the government reduced its long-standing commitment to support employment growth in the state sector, which was the main reason for the soft budget constraints. The government started a policy of privatizing small SOEs at the county level and downsizing SOEs at the city level (Cao et al., 1997). Second, the PBOC centralized and reduced its loans to SOBs, which had been an important source of funds for loans to the SOEs. Third, the government began an effort to commercialize the SOBs by putting them in the position of assuming increasing responsibility for their losses and bad debts.

The result of these policy changes has been impressive. After growing at roughly the same rate as the rest of the economy for the period 1979–94, employment in the state sector started to decline significantly in 1995 (see Table 3). Between 1995 and 1999, employment in the state sector was reduced by 26.9 million, while employment in the non-state sector increased by 50 million. The reduction of state-sector employment was most pronounced in industry. During this four-year period, the industrial SOEs let go 45 percent of their workers (or 19.9 million).

The PBOC was fairly successful as well in tightening its lending to

Table 3: Policy regime shifts in 1994

Year	Non-agricultural employment growth	Non-agricultural employment growth in state sector	Growth of PCB loan to SOBs	Seiniorage as percentage of GNP	SOBs' credit growth
1986	2.83	3.82	18.72	2.26	28.54
1987	2.93	3.44	2.35	1.97	18.99
1988	2.94	3.42	20.53	4.54	16.81
1989	1.83	1.24	22.92	1.24	17.61
1990	1.61	2.35	19.39	1.61	22.22
1991	1.39	3.07	14.99	2.46	18.98
1992	1.17	2.11	12.66	4.34	19.79
1993	1.25	0.28	40.07	4.41	22.42
1994	1.24	2.69	8.14	3.06	22.60
1995	1.11	0.42	9.88	1.02	21.43
1996	1.33	−0.15	9.73	1.35	20.41
1997	1.09	−1.78	−1.10	1.85	25.05
1998	0.51	−17.98	−7.92	1.31	15.38
1999	0.90	−5.37	7.25	2.75	7.68
1986–94 average	1.91	2.49	17.75	2.88	20.88
1995–99 average	0.99	−4.97	3.57	1.66	17.99

Source: *Zhongguo Tongji Nianjian* and *Zhongguo Jinrong Tongji Nianjian*, various issues.

SOBs. After averaging almost 17 percent before 1994, the growth rate of PBOC loans to SOBs never exceeded 10 percent after 1994. Between 1996 and 1999, PBOC lending to SOBs actually declined in absolute terms. This tightening of the PBOC lending is the main reason for the sharp decline in money-supply growth since 1994.

Changing the behaviour of the SOBs turned out to be the hardest task. However, there are signs that the government's effort to tighten the SOBs' budget constraint is finally taking effect. After averaging 21 percent for the period 1980–97, the SOBs' credit growth rate declined to 15.4 percent in 1998 and 7.7 percent in 1999. (See Table 3) It also appears that the SOBs have become more discriminating in their lending decisions. The percentage of SOB working-capital loans that went to the SOEs declined from 91 percent in 1996 to below 67 percent in 1997–98 and to only 7.8 percent in 1999. Since cheap working capital loans were a major component of government transfers to the SOEs, the sharp reduction in working-capital loans to SOEs represents a significant hardening of the SOEs' budget constraint.

These policy changes have made the economy more efficient by reducing resource flows into the inefficient state sector. First, they forced the downsizing and even closing down of many money-losing SOEs formerly supported by working-capital loans. Second, they reduced inefficient and often wasteful investment by SOEs. Between 1995 and 1999, the real growth rate of fixed investment by SOEs in industry averaged only 0.2 percent, compared to 11.8 percent for the period 1982–94.

Financial disintermediation

The reduction in growth of credit to the state sector does not imply that the resource flow into the non-state sector has increased. As we documented in the second section, the real growth rate of investment in the non-state sector has also declined sharply, mainly due to the reduction in growth of credit to the sector. Given the government's effort to commercialize banks, one might have expected that SOBs would lend more to the non-state sector. After all, rates of return are higher in the non-state sector, and in 1998 the central government eliminated credit quotas for the SOBs. Why has the credit to the non-state sector continued to be so tight?

There are several factors that have contributed to the current problem of financial disintermediation. First, the SOBs have become highly risk-averse because of the bad-debt problem and their increased responsibility for losses. Second, the banks are handicapped in identifying good projects due to a lack of information and human capital. Third, the financial system has become more centralized in recent years, making the financial institutions more biased against lending to the SMEs in the non-state sector. Fourth, the government has continued to clamp down on informal financial institutions and markets, severely limiting their role in financial intermediation. Reflecting the effect of these factors, we see a steady decline of the loan-deposit ratio for all financial institutions. Since 1995, the increase in loans by all financial institutions has only been 60 percent of the increase in deposits.

These developments are ultimately products of the financial repression policy pursued by the government. We elaborate on each of these factors below.

Bad debt, budget constraint hardening, and bank conservatism

The SOBs have become much more cautious in making loan decisions in recent years. Before, without having to take full responsibility for bad loans, the SOBs pursued projects with higher expected returns regardless of their risk. Since projects in the non-state sector *on average* have higher returns, SOBs had incentives to divert funds to finance investment in the non-state sector. With the recent hardening of their budget constraints, the SOBs know that bad loans are much less likely to be refinanced by new loans from the PBOC. In addition, with the increasing emphasis by the government on reducing bad loans, managers in the SOBs also know that they are more likely to be held personally responsible for making bad loans and face the possibility of dismissal. Both of these factors have made SOBs more sensitive to risk and less inclined to make loan decisions based on expected returns alone. Most enterprises in the non-state sector are small or medium-sized, and like SMEs everywhere, they inherently are more risky than large firms. As a result, the SOBs have become highly risk-averse in making loans to non-state firms.

Lack of information and human capital

Bank lending to the non-state sector is further hampered by the inability of SOB managers to distinguish between good and bad projects. Given that their main responsibility was to provide credits to the state sector, the SOBs have limited experience in lending to non-state firms. In addition, because of soft budget constraints, SOB managers had few incentives to gather information about non-state firms when they did lend (through diversion) to the non-state sector. Their lending to the non-state sector was mainly based on the high average returns in the sector. As a result, SOBs managers currently lack information and the ability to process information that is needed for them to make sound lending decisions. This problem is exacerbated by the lack of good accounting standards and reliable financial information on non-state firms.

Re-centralization of the financial system

Partly in response to the diversion problem encountered in the period prior to 1994, the government has adopted several measures the last few years that made China's financial system significantly more centralized.

First, while the central government has eliminated credit quotas for each of the four state-owned specialized banks, the lending decisions within these banks have become much more centralized. Within each of the four state-owned banks, control (decision) rights of local branches over lending behaviour, e.g., extension of new loans, renewals, etc., have been cut back and increasingly consolidated in higher-level branches. In 1997, for example, the Construction Bank "allocated" more than half of the new deposits to the head office for management. In the Industrial and Commerce Bank, 93 percent of the county-level branches had their loan-making rights seriously rescinded in 1997. Starting the same year, most of the new working-capital loans were administered by the head office of the Industrial and Commerce Bank, most of which were directed to a few key SOEs.[10] This trend has been further supported by the recent reforms of the inter-bank market, which have contributed to a vertical (as opposed to horizontal) flow of funds within the state banking system and cut off the access of local branches to discretionary funds for lending through this

---

10 The other two SOBs report taking similar measures to centralize administration and put funds usage under the control of the head office. The Bank of Communications also reported an increase in the degree of centralized administration, with more than three-quarters of loans being in branches under the direct jurisdiction of headquarters.

channel.[11] Thus, even if branch managers have information and the ability to identify good projects in their local area, they may not have the authority to lend to those projects. One of the consequences of the reforms of the inter-bank market has been a significant reduction in the size of the inter-bank market.[12]   .

Second, centralization is also reflected in the conversion of a large number of independent, quasi-private, largely district-level urban credit cooperatives (UCCs) into a centralized, municipal-level urban credit cooperative bank (UCB). (See Sehrt, 1999.) The change in ownership that accompanied this reform – notably, establishing dominant ownership by municipal governments in each UCB – has tended to centralize decision-making. In addition, this reform has required an increase in reserves held by these institutions in the PBOC, and thus reduced the discretionary funds at the local level.

Finally, in 1994 there was a clamp-down on activity by trust and investment companies (TICs), which had played an important role in intermediating funds at the local level. Numerous TICs were shut down and restrictions on the kinds of activity that they could engage in, including accessing funds through the inter-bank market, were more strictly enforced.

Severe restrictions on financial institution development

It is because formal financial institutions were largely ill-suited as intermediaries for the SMEs in the non-state sector that informal financial institutions emerged periodically to fill the gap. Examples include private banks and rural credit foundations (RCFs). A variety of innovative, but illegal fund-raising schemes were often also used. Yet as part of its financial repression policy, the government has constantly attempted to close down these institutions and restrict these practices, depriving the non-state firms of a valuable source of financial interme-

---

11 Access to the inter-bank market is limited to the head offices of the 19 major domestic banks, 35 short-term financial centres, and money brokerages run by the PBC.

12 See *Zhongguo Jinrong Nianjian* (1997), 6.

diation. In 1996, for example, the PBOC issued a directive banning all private banks.[13] In 1999, RCFs, under pressure from the rural credit cooperatives (RCCs), were officially shut down and folded into the RCCs.[14] There are also numerous reports of crackdowns on illegal fund-raising schemes.[15]

Growth in capital markets and crowding out

The sharp decline in the loan-deposit ratio and the declining rate of growth of bank credit are indicative of the reduction in the role of banks in China as financial intermediaries. Over the last five years, however, there has been increased activity both in the stock market as well as in the bond market. Table 2 provides data for the years between 1987 and 1999 on the financing of the non-financial sector by source: banks, non-bank financial institutions (NBFIs), the government bond market, the stock market, and the enterprise bond market. Are these new sources of finance simply offsetting the decline in the role played by banks, and helping to more efficiently allocate credit to the most promising of firms? Probably not.

Much of the increase in capital-market activities is directed to the state sector. Although a few larger private firms have recently been able to do IPOs, most issues are by larger SOEs. Moreover, the central government has increasingly tapped the capital market to finance Keynesian counter-cyclical expenditure. In 1999, for example, more than a quarter of all new credit went to the government. Preliminary numbers (not reported) for 2000 suggest much the same tendency. Although the role of bank lending in general and bank lending to the state sector

---

13 See reference to the directive "Guanyu qudi siren qianzhuang de tongzhi" in *Zhongguo Jinrong Nianjian* (1997), 38.

14 Several interpretations for this decision have been given, but one key factor may be the effect on the RCCs of the growing competition from the RCFs. On this point, see Park et al. (1999) and Holz (forthcoming).

15 These crackdowns are discussed frequently in China's Financial Yearbook, and other sources. Unfortunately, not much detail is provided.

has declined, it appears that much of this is being counteracted by mobilization of resources for the state sector in other ways. Even with the decline in bank lending to SOEs in 1999, more than 60 percent of all new credit was still effectively going to the state sector. Even if we allow for the possibility that the use of these funds is slightly more selective than earlier bank lending to the SOEs, the real concern is that these capital-market activities are effectively crowding out savings that would otherwise be directed to the SME sector.

The ineffectiveness of fiscal and monetary policy

What can the government do to return the economy to a higher but sustainable growth regime? Based on our analysis above we explain in this section why fiscal and monetary policy have not been effective in promoting growth in recent years and why they will not be effective in the near future.

Fiscal policy

Over the last couple of years, the central government has relied on deficit-financed public investment to stimulate growth. In 1998, for example, the government ran a deficit of 92.2 billion RMB, or 9.3 percent of total government expenditure. In 1999, the deficit almost doubled to 175.9 billion RMB, or 2.1 percent of GNP.[16] The impact, however, has been very limited. The Japanese government has pursued a similar policy for several years now, without much impact on that economy's growth either. As we argued earlier, the main reason for sluggish growth in China is not a lack of demand, but rather a lack of intermediaries that can channel savings into efficient investment projects. Fiscal policy does not help in solving this problem. Instead, it crowds out resources that can potentially be used for investment in the non-state sector.

Fiscal policy may have played a positive role in redistribution.

---

16 *Zhongguo Tongji Zhaiyao* (2000), 58.

Regional inequality has increased sharply in recent years.[17] In the past, the government relied heavily on the financial system to redistribute resources across regions. With the bad-debt problem and the government's effort to harden budget constraints, redistribution through the financial system becomes less appealing,[18] and the government relies much more on fiscal policy as an instrument for redistribution. From a social-welfare point of view, using fiscal policy to redistribute may be desirable, but its effect on the economy should not be mistaken: it redistributes income with little and possibly negative impact on growth.

Monetary policy

The central government has also tried to use monetary policy to stimulate growth. Before 1994, this was mainly done by increasing PBOC lending to the SOBs and relaxing restrictions on credit allocation by the SOBs, which allowed intermediation by diversion. As we discussed in previous sections, while this policy helped stimulate growth it was inflationary and unsustainable. A return to such policy would undermine the government's effort in hardening the budget constraints on both the SOBs and the SOEs, contribute to further increases in bad debt, generate high inflation, and put the financial system and the whole economy at grave risk.

Given that relaxing PBOC lending is not a viable option, the government tried in recent years to use the interest rate as an instrument for its operation of monetary policy. The central government has cut interest rates several times in hope of stimulating investment demand, but investment remains sluggish. There are two reasons for the ineffec-

---

17 While inter-regional inequality has increased, intra-regional inequality has increased just as rapidly, so that contribution of inter-regional inequality to overall inequality has remained fairly constant. See Benjamin et al. (2002).

18 This does not mean, however, that the government has stopped using the financial system for redistribution completely. As part of the policy of promoting development in western China, the government has encouraged banks to lend to projects that are partially financed by the central government.

tiveness of the interest rate policy. First, most SOEs are highly inefficient and have problems finding investment projects that provide
positive returns. Even if the interest rate were zero, the SOEs would
find their projects to have negative net present values. This lack of
good projects and the recent hardening of budget constraints have
reduced the SOEs' demand for investment significantly.[19] Second,
even though there are highly profitable projects in the non-state sector
that would have positive net present values at a market-clearing interest rate, they are not financed by the banks because of the latter's
inability to distinguish between good and bad projects. This problem
is due to the SOBs' lack of information and human capital, and lowering interest rates will not help much.

What kind of a financial system does China need?

Our analysis shows that the main problem China is now facing is financial disintermediation: the lack of intermediaries that can direct savings
to efficient investment in the non-state sector. How can China over-
come this problem? Will the financial reforms that are being carried out
by the government help? What kind of a financial system does China
need? Drawing on the recent literature on financial system design and
based on our analysis in previous sections, we provide here a discussion
on the specific measures that China needs to take to transform the
financial system into one that can meet China's development needs.

The institutional environment and the choice of financial system

The relationship between financial sector development and economic

---

19 Note that this is in stark contrast with their behaviour in the period before 1994,
when the SOEs' demand for investment seemed insatiable. During that period, the
SOEs operated under soft budget constraints. They expected that any losses they
incurred as a result of bad investment would be refinanced, and their bad debt would
likely be forgiven. Therefore, they were willing to undertake almost any investment
projects that were financed by bank loans.

growth has long been debated in the literature, at least since Schumpeter (1911). Recently, several authors have provided empirical evidence on the positive role of financial sector development on growth.[20] However, different economies have followed different paths of financial sector development with seemingly similar growth performance. For example, the United States and United Kingdom have developed arm's-length systems, with financial markets playing a very important role. Germany and Japan, by contrast, built relationship-based systems, with financial markets playing only a minor role. Both types of financial system have supported sustained growth in these economies. Which of these two kinds of financial system is better for China today?

A few years ago, mainly motivated by Japan's (and Germany's, for that matter) strong economic performance in the 1970s and 1980s, the advantages of the relationship-based system over the Anglo-Saxon arm's-length system were frequently discussed. Some have also suggested that China should adopt Japan's main-bank system. (See Qian, 1994.) With Japan's prolonged recession in the 1990s and the recent Asian financial crisis, however, the weaknesses of Japan's main-bank system have been exposed, and discussions have turned to the superiority of the market-based financial system in the U.S. and U.K. Why have different systems performed differently in different periods? What are the underlying conditions that determine the performance of a particular financial system? Several recent studies shed some light on these questions.

Legal system

In a market-based system, investors rely on legal contracts rather than personal or institutional relationships in dealing with firms. Therefore, it is vitally important to have a well-established legal system that can

---

20 See King and Levine (1993), Jayaratne and Strahan (1996), Rajan and Zingales (1998), Levine (2000), and Levine et al. (2000). Rajan and Zingales (1999) provide a good survey of this literature.

provide legal protection of investors' contractual rights. Thus, most countries with market-based financial systems have a common-law tradition, which offers greater protection for contractual rights. (See La Porta et al., 1997.)

The legal system is also found to be a factor in determining the average size of the firms. Kumar et al. (1999) show that countries with better protection of contractual rights, such as those with a common-law tradition, tend to have more large-size firms. As we will discuss later, large firms have a comparative advantage in financing through capital markets. Therefore, a market-based financial system is better suited for countries with a better legal system because they also tend to have larger firms.

When there is not a well-established legal system to protect contractual rights, investors have to adopt a more hands-on approach in identifying projects and monitoring firms to protect their investment. In this case, financial institutions can serve as intermediaries between investors and firms by performing information-gathering and monitoring services for the investors.

Information

Both financial markets and financial intermediaries play informational roles. Financial markets help provide information about firms through price signals. Financial intermediaries, on the other hand, generate information about firms through their relationship with the firms and their monitoring effort. Both have their advantages and disadvantages.

Financial markets can aggregate information from a wide range of sources and process information by aggregating a wide range of opinions. But there is a free-rider problem: private information gathered by an investor will be signalled to all investors through prices. Thus, individual investors have weak incentives to gather information about firms and instead rely on price signals as their source of information. So, financial markets are most effective when information is easy to obtain but difficult to process. In these situations, the free-rider problem is not very important (because the cost of acquiring information is low), and markets can process information more efficiently by aggregating opinions from a large number of investors. This is why technological firms whose projects face high uncertainties tend to be financed through the equity market or venture capital market.

When information is difficult or very costly to obtain, however, the free-rider problem is more serious. In this case, concentrating financing in a small number of investors or institutions and providing them with long-term business will help provide strong incentives for these investors or institutions to gather information. In these situations, financial intermediaries have advantages over decentralized markets.

Thus, countries that have good accounting standards and financial reporting and auditing systems will have lower information costs and, therefore, be better able to take advantage of capital markets. Countries with poor and unreliable financial information about firms, by contrast, will rely more on financial intermediaries.

Firm size

Large firms have a comparative advantage in using capital markets as their source of outside financing for at least two reasons. First, financing through capital markets involves large set-up costs. So there are increasing returns to scale that favour large firms. Second, good firms without established records will suffer information dilution costs in capital markets because market investors cannot distinguish them from bad firms, and small firms are more likely to be the ones without established records. (See Diamond, 1991 and Rajan, 1992.)

On the other hand, it is the SMEs, not large firms, that rely more on outside financing. Thus, financial intermediaries are more important than capital markets in economies that rely more on SMEs for output growth.

Stage of development

While the U.S. financial system has been viewed as the typical market-based financial system, it is worth noting that U.S. firms historically have relied heavily on relationship-based financing.[21] So, which finan-

---

21 See Calomiris and Rammirez (1996).

cial system is good for the economy also depends on the stage of the economy's development. This is not surprising, since well-functioning legal systems, good accounting standards, efficient capital markets, and firms with well-established records are all functions of economic development: they are more likely to emerge at later stages of economic development.

The financial system for China

China is at an early stage of economic development. It does not have a well-functioning legal system, financial information about firms is limited, accounting standards are weak, and non-state SMEs are the major source of economic growth. All these conditions suggest that in the short to medium term financial intermediaries should play a more important role than capital markets in China's economic development. However, China's current financial system is dominated by the SOBs. Our earlier discussion indicates that the SOBs have not been effective as financial intermediaries. Some of the problems that inhibit effective intermediation by the SOBs, such as the bad-debt problem and government intervention, may gradually be removed through re-capitalization and commercialization. Other problems, such as the lack of human capital and competition, may also be addressed through training and by allowing the entry of foreign banks. It may take a very long time before these reforms can successfully be completed, but China is moving in that direction.[22] However, even if the SOBs are fully re-capitalized and become truly commercial banks with the objective of maximizing profits, they will still not be effective financial intermediaries for the SMEs because of their centralized-hierarchical organizational structure.

Because SMEs generally are risky and lack reliable accounting information, lending to them requires an intensive effort by local branch managers to identify good firms and projects in their region. In a centralized-hierarchical organization, capital-allocation decisions are made

---

22 See Lardy (1999), however, for an agnostic view.

at the centre, and local managers face uncertainty regarding the availability of capital when they discover a good project. As a result, local managers have weak incentives to exert effort in identifying good projects.[23] Instead, they are more likely to deal with more established firms that they can easily convince the centre to lend. This bias against SMEs by centralized-hierarchical financial institutions is supported by the experience of recent bank mergers in the United States. Berger et al. (1998) found that lending to small business declined after banks were merged, even though there was evidence that projects whose funding was cut off were profitable.

This bias against SMEs cannot be resolved by decentralizing capital-allocation decisions within the hierarchically organized banks for two reasons. First, the banks' headquarters always have incentives to move capital across regions to maximize total returns and, therefore, will find it difficult to maintain a credible commitment to guaranteed capital for any particular local branch. Second, even if the headquarters can maintain a credible commitment to decentralized capital-allocation decisions, it will have difficulty credibly committing to not bail out bad projects financed by the local branches. In other words, the centralized ownership structure will give rise to soft budget constraints. (See Dewatripoint and Maskin, 1995.)

Allowing the entry of foreign banks will not solve the problem either. As we explained above, relationship banking is important in China and foreign banks have a comparative disadvantage in building up relationships with Chinese firms. It is more likely that their clients will be multinational firms and some more-established Chinese firms. The majority of the SMEs in the non-state sector will not benefit much from the foreign banks.

The only way to ensure that the financial system will meet the financing needs of the SMEs in the non-state sector, then, is to establish locally based, small, single-manager financial institutions. To ensure that managers have the right incentives to exert an effort to

---

23 Our argument here draws on a recent theoretical paper by Stein (2000).

identify good SMEs for investment, they should be given the ultimate right of control in allocating capital. To ensure hard budget constraints, these institutions should not be owned by a centralized organization. One way to establish such institutions is to allow the entry of private banks owned by the managers.

The experience of the dual financial system in Taiwan

The experience of the dual financial system in Taiwan provides a good example for China. Taiwan 30 years ago was very similar to China today. It was at an early stage of economic development, it did not have a well-functioning legal system, financial information about firms was limited, accounting standards were weak, and private SMEs were the major source of growth and dynamism in the economy.

The banking system in Taiwan was also very similar to that in China today.[24] It was heavily regulated, with interest rates being controlled by the central bank of Taiwan. It was dominated by a few large state-owned banks, with very strict restrictions on entry. The formal financial system in Taiwan also discriminated heavily in favour of state-owned firms and larger private businesses, which received a disproportionate amount of their credit from the banking sector. From 1964 to 1990, credits from banks and other formal financial institutions accounted for 88 percent of the state-owned firms' outside financing, compared to only 60 percent for the private firms (Shea, 1994).

The banks in Taiwan were very conservative as well, wary of bad debts. As a result, they preferred to lend to less risky large firms. From 1976 to 1987, the percentage of total credits that went to the SMEs in Taiwan was less than 5 percent for the state-owned comprehensive banks, and less than 29 percent for the whole banking system (Lin and Peng, 1994). In contrast, SMEs were the source of 70 percent of employment and 55 percent of output.

---

24 For a discussion on Taiwan's dual financial system, see Shea (1994), and for a more detailed comparison between the formal financial systems in Taiwan and China, see Zhu (1998).

Despite the discrimination by formal financial institutions, the SMEs were the most important sector for Taiwan's growth. This was made possible by numerous informal financial institutions and curb markets that helped intermediate savings to investment in the SMEs. They include financial instalment credit companies, leasing companies, investment companies, rotating credit societies, deposits in firms, and loans against post-dated cheques. Data for the period 1964–90 show that this sector consistently supplied one-quarter of the outside financing for all enterprises in Taiwan, and more than one-third of the outside financing for private enterprises. Smaller firms were much more reliant on the curb market. Shea (1994) presents estimates by assets of firms and finds that those with less than one million $NT obtained about 90 percent of their credits from the informal sector, 1–10 million $NT, 60 percent; 10–100, 45 percent; 100–1000, 25 percent; and 1000+, 10.3 percent.

The informal financial sector operated in a competitive environment with lax regulation. Unlike in China, the government in Taiwan did not try to clamp down or impose interest rate controls on the informal financial sector. The interest rates offered in the curb market were considerably higher, often by a factor of two or three, which diverted savings from the formal financial institutions and provided needed financing for SMEs.

It is important to note that the basically unregulated informal financial sector did not create chaos in the financial system, and that the diversion of savings from the formal financial institutions did not undermine the solvency of these banks. There were no bank runs. In fact, Taiwan did not even have a system of deposit insurance until 1985, and then participation by financial institutions was voluntary.[25]

---

25 As of March 1990, membership in the deposit insurance system included the following private institutions: all commercial banks (4), all medium-sized business banks (7), and all trust and investment companies (6), as well as 27 out of 33 foreign banks. Only 3 of the 11 government banks joined, however, as did fewer than half of all smaller institutions such as credit cooperatives, which were otherwise unregulated. Yang (1994: 315).

The experience in Taiwan suggests that a basically unregulated informal financial sector can coexist with a highly regulated formal financial sector and function well in serving the needs of the SMEs.

Proposal for a new financial system

There are about 25,000 rural townships in China. And on average there is about one rural credit cooperative (RCC) in each township. Their existence suggests that there is a large demand for rural financial institutions. However, the RCCs are tightly regulated by the central bank and have not been able to efficiently intermediate funds to the rural SMEs. We envisage the evolution of a dual financial system with a new set of private financial institutions that are locally based and largely outside state control. The rules of the game under which these institutions will operate will differ in key respects from those that govern existing institutions. Government regulations should be minimal and should not serve as a substitute for monitoring by depositors. In particular, depositors should be made fully aware of the risks they face by putting money into these institutions, and regulations should not give depositors any false sense of safety about their deposits.

- *These institutions should have some minimum capital requirement and no deposit insurance.* The former will make these banks truly accountable for their lending behaviour by putting owner's capital at risk. The absence of deposit insurance, on the other hand, will encourage information finding and monitoring by depositors. Given that it maybe difficult to verify and enforce the capital requirement for these small local banks, it is important that the depositors understand clearly that their deposits are not insured and that they are responsible for the risk they take when putting their money in these banks. This will induce depositors to choose banks carefully and monitor the banks closely. On the other hand, with no deposit insurance the banks would also have incentives to voluntarily reveal information about their assets and liabilities in order to assure potential depositors about the safety of their deposits and thus attract deposits.

In fact, the potential for bank runs itself may play a disciplinary role on bank behaviour and reduce bank failures (Diamond and Rajan, 1999). There are many examples of well-functioning banking systems that lack deposit insurance. Hong Kong has never had deposit insurance, and there have been no bank runs. Before 1967, Canada did not have deposit insurance, and there were rarely any bank failures and there were no bank runs (Carr et al., 1994).

- *These institutions must have hard budget constraints.* An implication of this requirement is that the government should commit to not bailing these banks out in the event of failure and to shutting them down when they become insolvent. Since public ownership will undermine the credibility of such a commitment, these institutions should be privately owned. The depositors should be informed clearly about the private ownership of these institutions. Some of the problems China had with RCFs were partly due to the depositors' perception that these institutions were backed by local governments. As a result, depositors presumed that their deposits were implicitly guaranteed by the governments. They did not pay much attention to which RCF they put their money in nor did they monitor the RCFs after depositing their funds.
- *Depositors' rights will be protected through bankruptcy law,* which provides them with some claim to the institution's assets in the event of failure, but they will face potential deposit risk. As noted above, they are not provided deposit insurance, and know this ex-ante. This feature will help increase the monitoring role of depositors in the governance of these institutions.
- *Interest liberalization will be allowed* that will compensate depositors for the potential risk, and will allow financial institutions to price credit risk appropriately. Depositors will be able to choose between lower return, and insured deposits in the state banking system, and higher return, but uninsured deposits in these new institutions.

The development of these new financial institutions does not mean that the existing, largely state-owned financial institutions and capital markets will not play a role. Rather, these institutions and markets will cater to larger firms and possibly new firms in the emerging high-tech sector. These new institutions will also play an important role in the long run. Over time, the best of these institutions will grow and evolve into comprehensive, regional-based (as opposed to locally-based) financial institutions. As they become more integrated into China's financial system, they will begin to serve a wider clientele. However, as long as there are small firms with unmet financial needs, the demand for some local-based intermediaries will remain. Those institutions that succeed the test of the market and expand over time will introduce much-needed competition for China's SOBs, much as China's township and village enterprises did in the 1980s. This kind of competition is likely to be much more effective than that offered by foreign banks, largely because of the differences in the kinds of firms the latter are likely to serve.

In conclusion, this paper provides a framework for thinking about China's current economic difficulties, which is equally capable of explaining pre-1994 dynamics. It puts at centre stage the functioning of the financial system and the allocation of credit and investment in the non-state sector. Contrary to much conventional wisdom, we do not believe that weak aggregate demand lies behind the sluggish growth, and thus are doubtful that expansionary fiscal policy or a loosening of monetary policy can have the desired effect. Rather, the problem is the inability of the financial system to intermediate efficiently China's enormous savings and, more specifically, to direct a larger portion of those savings to China's dynamic small and medium-sized non-state enterprises, which have been the driving force in the economy for almost two decades. Our analysis suggests a rethinking of issues related to the design of China's financial system, and a renewed attention to the development of locally-based, decentralized financial institutions outside of the purview of state control.

REFERENCES

Benjamin, Dwayne, Loren Brandt, Paul Glewwe, and Guo Li. Forthcoming. "Markets, Human Capital and Income Inequality in an Economy in Transition: The Case of Rural China." In Richard Freeman, ed., *Inequality Around the World: Where We Are and Where We Are Headed*. London: Palgrave in association with the IEA.

Berger, Allen N., Anthony Saunders, Joseph M. Scalise, and Gregory F. Udell. 1998. "The Effects of Bank Mergers and Acquisitions on Small Business Lending." *Journal of Financial Economics*, 50: 187–229.

Brandt, Loren, and Xiaodong Zhu. 2000. "Redistribution in a Decentralized Economy: Growth and Inflation in China under Reform." *Journal of Political Economy*, 108/2: 422–39.

Calomiris, Charles, and Carlos Rammirez. 1996. "The Role of Financial Relationships in the History of American Corporate Finance." *Journal of Applied Corporate Finance*, 9/2: 52–74.

Cao, Yuanzheng, Yingyi Qian, and Barrry Weingast. 1997. "From Federalism, Chinese Style, to Privatization, Chinese Style." *Economics of Transition*, March 1999, 7/1: 103–31.

Carr, J.L., G.F. Mathewson, and N.C. Quigley. 1994. *Ensuring Failure: Financial System Stability and Deposit Insurance in Canada*. Toronto: C.D. Howe Institute.

Dewatripoint, Mathias, and Eric Maskin. 1995. "Credit and Efficiency in Centralized and Decentralized Economies." *Review of Economics Studies*, 62: 541–56.

Diamond, D.W. 1991. "Reputation Acquisition in Debt Markets." *Journal of Political Economy*, 98: 828–62.

Diamond, D.W., and Raghuram G. Rajan. 1999. "Liquidity Risk, Liquidity Creation and Financial Fragility: A Theory of Banking." *NBER Working Paper* no. 7430.

Holz, Carsten. Forthcoming. "China's Monetary Reform: The Counterrevolution from the Countryside." *Journal of Contemporary China*.

Jayaratne, Jith, and Phillip E. Strahan. 1996. "The Finance-Growth Nexus: Evidence from Bank Branch Deregulation." *Quarterly Journal of Economics*, 41: 639–71.

King, R., and R. Levine. 1993. "Finance and Growth: Schumpeter Might Be Right." *Quarterly Journal of Economics*, 108: 681–737.

Krugman, Paul. 1999. "Can Deflation Be Prevented?" Mimeo, MIT.

Kumar, K., R. Rajan, and L. Zingales. 1999. "What Are the Determinants of Firm Size?" Mimeo, University of Chicago.

La Porta, R. Florencio, Lopez de Silanes, Andrei Shleifer, and Robert Vishny. 1997. "The Legal Determinants of External Finance." *Journal of Finance*, 52/3 (July): 1130–50.

Lardy, Nicholas R. 1999. "When Will China's Financial System Meet China's Needs?" Paper presented at Conference on Policy Reform in China, Stanford University.

Lau, Lawrence, and Yingyi Qian. 1994. "Financial Reorganization of Banks and Enterprise in China: A Proposal." Paper presented at "Jinglun International Conference on China's Reform: The Next Step." August 22–24.

Levine, Ross. 2000. "Bank-based or Market-based Financial Systems: Which Is Better?" University of Minnesota working paper.

– 1997. "Financial Development and Economic Growth: Views and Agenda." *Journal of Economic Literature*, 35: 688–726.

Levine, Ross, Norman Loayza, and Thorsten Beck. 2000. "Financial Intermediation and Growth: Causality and Causes." *Journal of Monetary Economics*, 46/1: 31–77.

Lin, Z., and B. Peng. 1994. "A Comparison of Financing for SMEs and Others." In *The Development of Taiwan SMEs* (Chinese). Taibei: Niajin Press.

Park, Albert, Loren Brandt, and John Giles. Forthcoming. "Competition under Credit Rationing: Theory and Evidence from Rural China." *Journal of Development Economics*.

Qian, Yingyi. 1994. "Financial System Reform in China: Lessons from Japan's Main Bank System." In Masahiko Aoki, Hugh Patrick, eds., *The Japanese Main Bank System: Its Relevance for Developing and Transforming Economies.* Oxford and New York: Oxford University Press.

Rajan, Raghuram G. 1992. "Insiders and Outsiders: The Choice between Informed and Arm's-Length Debt." *Journal of Finance*, 47/4: 1367–1400.

Rajan, Raghuram G., and Luigi Zingales. 1999. "Financial Systems, Industrial Structure, and Growth." University of Chicago working paper.

– 1998. "Financial Dependence and Growth." *American Economic Review*, 88: 559–86.

Schumpeter, J.A. 1911. *A Theory of Economic Development.* Cambridge, Mass.: Harvard University Press.

Sehrt, Kaja. 1999. "A Bank for Every Government: The Incorporation of Credit Cooperatives in the PRC." Mimeo, Dartmouth College, Hanover, NH.

Shea, Jia-Dong. 1994. "Taiwan: Development and Structural Change of the Banking System." In Hugh T. Patrick and Yung Chul Park, eds., *The Financial Development of Japan, Korea, and Taiwan.* New York: Oxford University Press.

Stein, Jeremy C. 2000. "Information Production and Capital Allocation: Decentralized vs. Hierarchical Firms." *NBER Working Paper* no. 7705.

Yang, Ya-hwei. 1994. "Taiwan: Development and Structural Change of the Banking System." In Patrick and Park, 288–324 (see Shea).

Zhongguo Jinrong Tongji Nianjian (Almanac of China's Finance and Banking). Beijing: China Finance Publishing House, various years.

Zhongguo Tongji Nianjian (Statistical Yearbook of China). Beijing: China Statistical Publishing House.

Zhongguo Tongji Zhaiyao (China Statistical Abstract). Beijing: China Statistical Publishing House, various years.

Zhu, Xiaodong. 1998. "Financial System and Macro-Stability: A Comparison between Taiwan and China." (Chinese). In Xinhai Fang and Sunfeng Song, eds., *Raising International Competitiveness: Taiwan's Experience and Its Implications for Mainland China*. Beijing: China Economic Press.

East Asia's ageing populations: Pension reform and its implications

WALID HEJAZI AND PAULINE SHUM

Improvements in public health coupled with rising living standards have contributed to longer life expectancy around the world. With birth rates declining in many countries, the elderly dependency ratio (the number of people age 65 or older divided by the working-age population, typically between the ages of 15 and 64) is projected to climb for at least the next 50 years (Kohl and O'Brien, 1998).

Much has been written about the impact of ageing on pension reform in the OECD economies. The purpose of this chapter is to focus on a sample of East Asian countries where the problem is a pressing one and where the response has varied. Singapore, for example, has had a comprehensive social security program since the 1950s. Hong Kong, by contrast, has just implemented a mandatory pension system in 2000. China, where one-fifth of the world's population resides, faces a particularly difficult task. The pension burden on state-owned enterprises – many of which are in financial distress – is reaching a crisis. China's large rural population has little formal retirement protection. The lack of a mature, well-functioning capital market further exacerbates the problem and limits China's choices. Japan's population is ageing faster than that of any other country in the world (Turner et al., 1998). Even though Japan is East Asia's richest country, it has yet to undertake significant pension reforms to address this reality.

In this chapter we examine some of the choices China and Japan face in addressing their demographic challenges. For guidance and comparative purposes, we examine pension-system design in two other Asian economies, Singapore and Hong Kong, as well as those in Canada and Chile.[1] The Canadian system is one with which most readers will be familiar, and the Chilean system, reformed in 1981, has served as a model for social security reform in many countries, both developing and developed.

The chapter is organized as follows. In the next section, we provide some technical background: the changing demographic structure in certain East Asian economies; some historical description of national pension plans and debates; and a description of existing pension arrangements in Japan, Singapore, Hong Kong, Canada, and Chile. In the third section, we apply several criteria to a comparative analysis of these pension systems. The key criteria by which to judge pension design include sustainability, institutional factors, portfolio allocation and savings, coverage and social welfare, and portability. In the fourth section, we apply these criteria in a discussion of options available to the Chinese authorities. Finally, we draw conclusions.

Background issues

Demographic structures in East Asia

Demographic structures are changing throughout the region. In this section we examine demographic developments and projections in a sample of East Asian countries. Canada, the United States, and Chile are also included for comparison purposes. The data used in the construction of the following figures are obtained from UNDP (1999).

The population data for 1975, 1997, and projections for 2015 (Figure 1) emphasize China's relative size and the fact that this pattern is not

---

1 Of course, a number of East Asian economies face similar issues; the economies chosen for comparison here are at either end of the spectrum. Singapore has one of the most established social security systems, while the public pension plan in Hong Kong is brand new.

expected to change over the next 15 years. Life expectancy (Figure 2) has risen across the board over the past two decades as infant mortality has declined and public health has improved. Japanese life expectancies are the longest, reaching 80 years in 1997, followed by Canada, Hong Kong, Singapore, the United States, and Chile. Indonesia, the Philippines, Thailand, and China have the lowest life expectancies. Indonesia, Chile, and the Philippines are among those experiencing the largest absolute increases in life expectancy, however.

Fertility rates are declining (Figure 3). Over the 1975–97 period fertility rates have declined in all countries except the United States. The largest declines occurred in Indonesia, China, the Philippines, and Malaysia, but by 1997, Japan and Hong Kong had the lowest fertility rates.

These trends together imply that population growth rates will decline and the percentage of the population over the age of 65 will increase, as Figures 4 and 5 illustrate. Malaysia had the highest growth rate over the past 25 years at 2.5 percent, but this growth rate is projected to fall to 1.5 percent over the next 15 years. Japan had the lowest population growth rate over the past 25 years at 0.6 percent, and this is expected to fall to zero over the next 15 years.

In most East Asian economies the proportion of total population over the age of 65 is projected to increase by 30 to 50 percent over the 1997–2015 period. Japan is projected to have the highest ratio of retired individuals, followed by Canada and the United States.[2] The Philippines and Malaysia will have the lowest ratios.

The number of people age 65 or older as a ratio of the working-age population – the elderly dependency ratio (Figure 6) – will also rise, with the highest dependency ratio and largest projected increase over the next 15 years occurring in Japan. The dependency ratio in 1997 was 23 percent, and is expected to increase to over 40 percent by 2015. The

---

2 In only 25 years Japan's share of population over the age of 65 doubled, whereas similar doubling took most other developed countries 50 years. In Sweden, it took 120 years (Watanabe, 1997).

Figure 1: Population

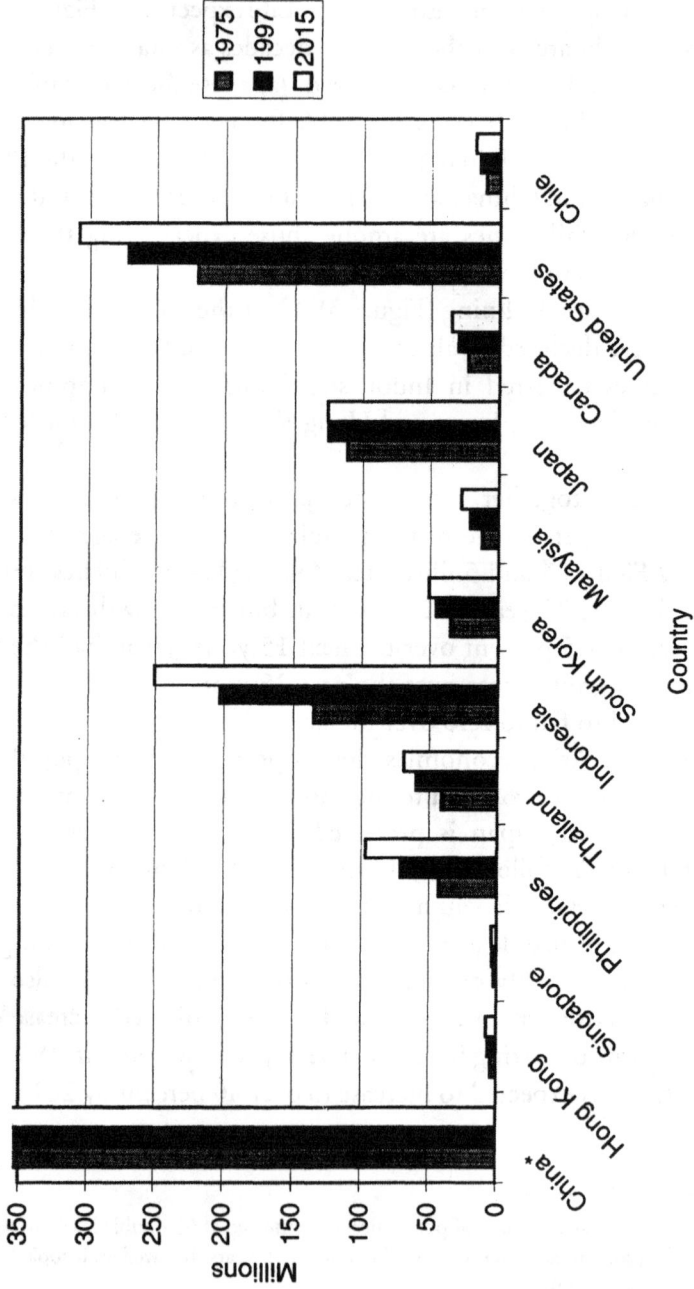

Legend: 1975, 1997, 2015

X-axis (Country): China*, Hong Kong, Singapore, Philippines, Thailand, Indonesia, South Korea, Malaysia, Japan, Canada, United States, Chile

Y-axis (Millions): 0, 50, 100, 150, 200, 250, 300, 350

*China's population was 927 million in 1975, rising to 1.2 billion and 1.4 billion in 1997 and 2015, respectively.

Source: UNDP (1999).

Figure 2: Life epectancy at birth

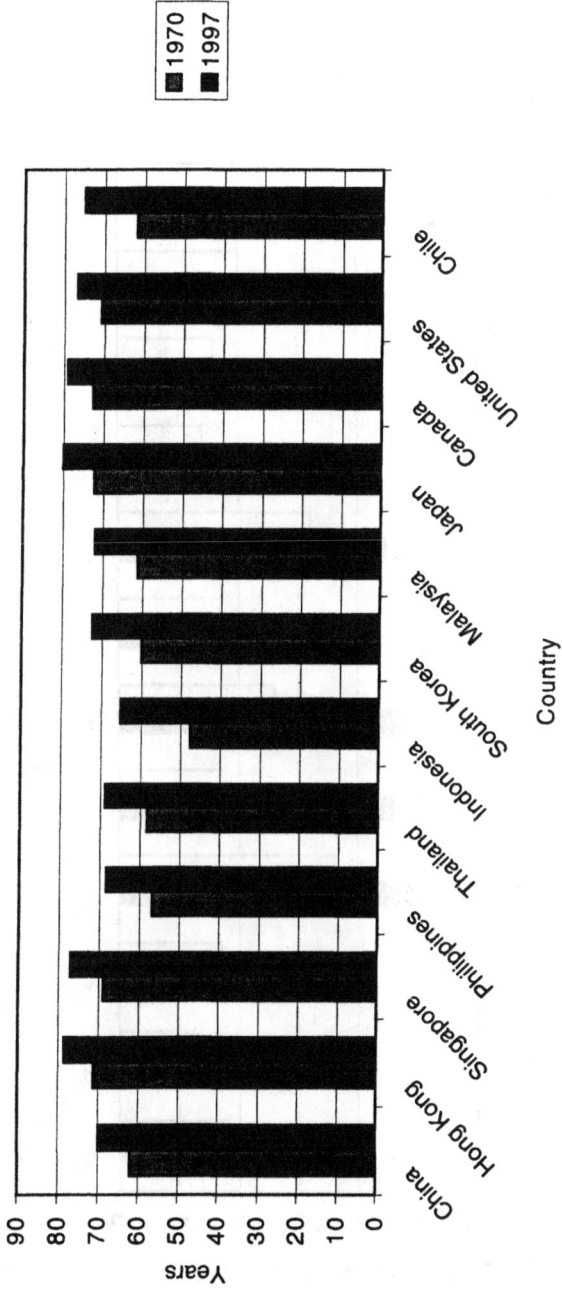

Source: UNDP (1999).

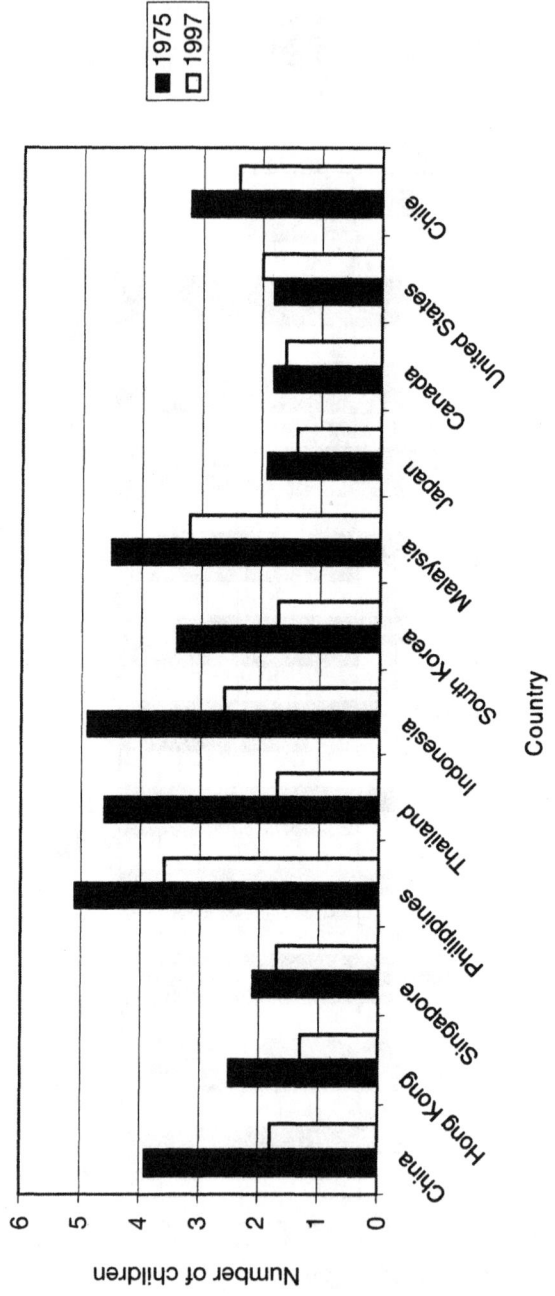

Figure 3: Fertility rates

Source: UNDP (1999).

Figure 4: Population growth rates

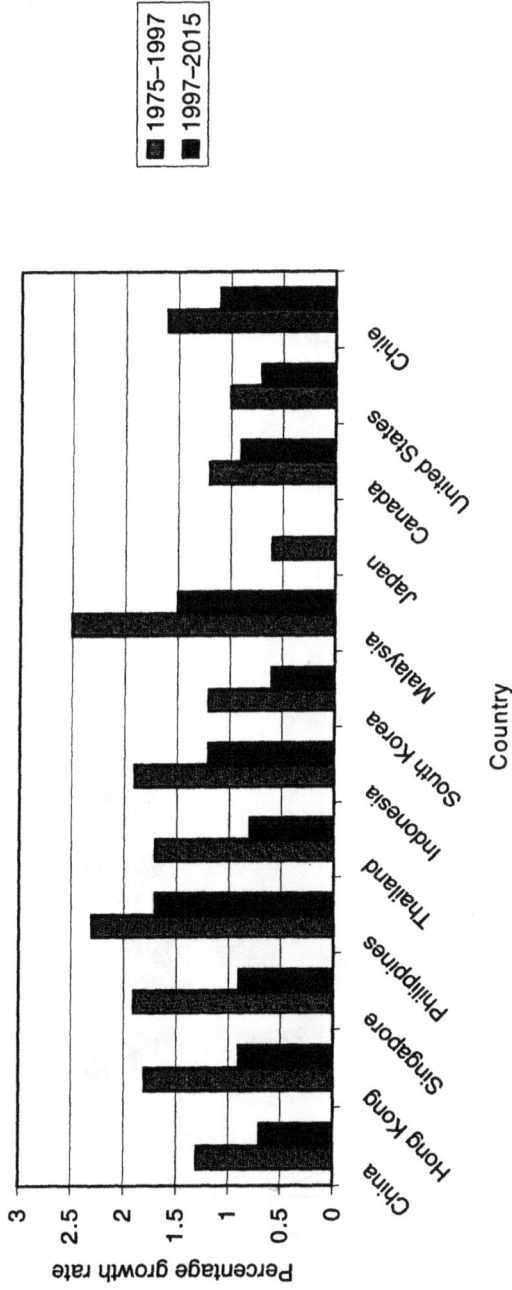

Source: UNDP (1999).

Figure 5: Percentage of total population over age 65

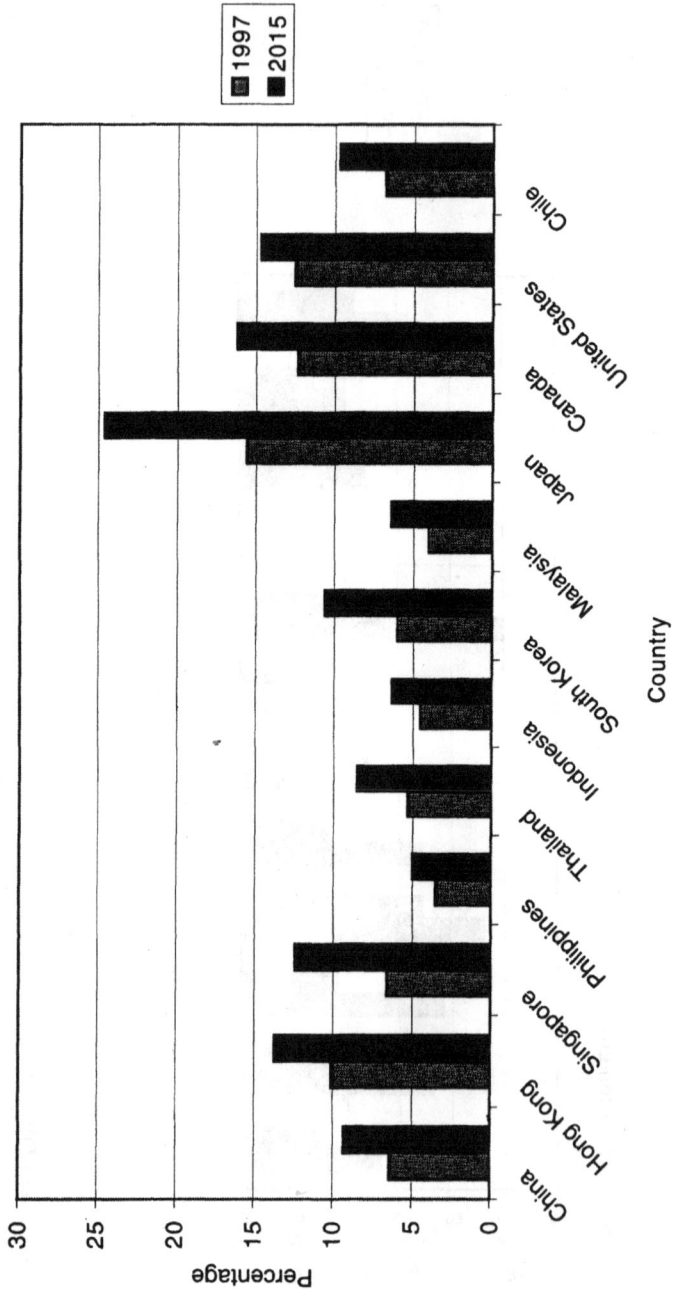

Source: UNDP (1999).

Figure 6: Elderly dependency ratio

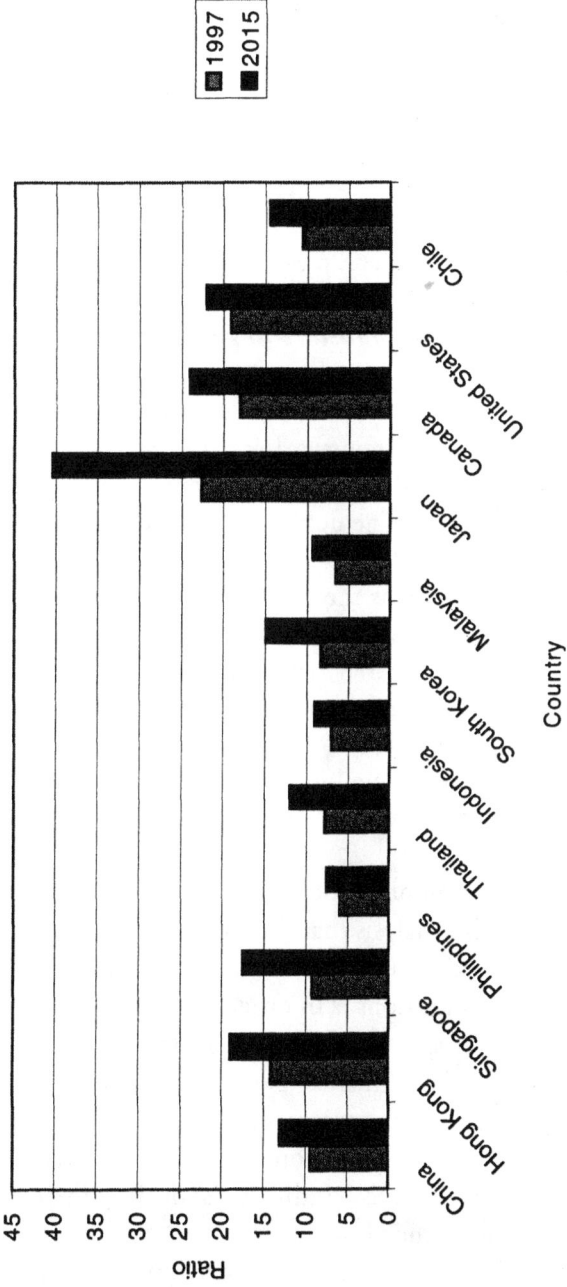

Source: UNDP (1999).

dependency ratios for the United States and Canada are also expected to increase above 20 percent over the next 15 years. The dependency ratios for the East Asian economies are also increasing, but at rates below those in Japan, Canada, and the United States.

As the elderly dependency ratio rises the burden on any social security scheme will also increase, especially if those currently employed must finance those who are retired. As the elderly dependency ratio rises over time, the burden on each working individual increases.

National pension plans: historical perspectives

The history and structure of some major pension programs discussed below help to lay out a framework for the criteria and choices that governments face in introducing new programs (as in China) or reforming old ones (as in Japan). The public debate and policy discussion is most advanced in the United States.

Historically, as long as the majority of the world's population lived and worked on farms, economic security was provided by the extended family. Since the industrial revolution and with the urbanization of most countries, these arrangements have become unsustainable. The financial crisis in the 1930s threatened the economic lives of many people and hastened the adoption in the United States of a national social insurance program. The Social Security Act (SSA) was signed into law in 1935.

The pension component of the SSA is an *unfunded* or "pay-as-you-go" system. In the analysis that follows, both the funding and pay-out parameters will be seen to be essential to pension design, so a digression to provide definitions is in order. In an *unfunded*, or "pay-as-you-go" system, retirement benefits are paid from current payroll taxes. In other words, workers finance pensioners today, and expect future workers to finance their retirement. A *funded* system is one in which pension benefits are derived from the stream of returns generated by the funds contributed by individuals during their working years. Chile's system is a funded one.

The rates of return in the two systems differ. In the funded system, the rate of return is equal to the marginal return on capital, assuming that pension contributions are invested in productive capital stock. In an unfunded system, the rate of return is equal to the growth rate in wages if the population distribution remains constant. If the elderly dependency ratio is rising, then the rate of return in an unfunded system is less than the growth rate in wages.

Hybrids of the two systems also exist, with Canada's being one such example. In 1998 reforms to the Canada Pension Plan (CPP) moved it away from pure pay-as-you-go financing towards fuller funding from two sources (see Canada, 1998). First, the reforms increase the pre-funding: the size of the public plan's reserves were increased from two years of payments to five years. Second, reforms allow for a portion of the reserves to be invested in the hopes of increasing returns on these assets. Canada also now allows 14 percent of these reserves to be invested in financial markets by an independent advisory board as a way to increase rates of return. In 2000, the entire 14 percent was invested in domestic and foreign stocks (see Canada Pension Plan Investment Board, 2001).

Defined-contribution and defined-benefit schemes are the two most common payout schemes. Under a defined-contribution scheme, the contribution rate is defined in advance – for example, 5 percent of wages – but the amount of pension benefits is uncertain and depends on asset returns. Most funded systems are defined-contribution schemes. Under a defined-benefit scheme, pension benefits are defined in advance by the sponsor – usually according to a formula that depends on a worker's years of service – regardless of the contribution rate or asset returns. Most pay-as-you-go systems and union pension plans fit this category.

Returning to the historical development of pension systems, the pay-as-you-go system provides financial security after retirement, but it also plays a redistributive role. High-wage earners receive a higher level of benefits than low-wage earners, but the benefit formula is skewed in favour of low-wage earners, who receive a higher percentage of their pre-retirement earnings. In the United States, for example, it is estimated that the Social Security system reduces poverty among the aged.[3] Current estimates put 11 percent of U.S. senior citizens living in poverty with Social Security; this number would increase to nearly 50 percent without Social Security, which replaces as much as 40 percent of the average worker's pre-retirement income.

In 1984, after the U.S. Social Security System ran into a serious financing crisis, several changes were made, including the reduction of social security benefits and a temporary suspension of indexation of these benefits to the rate of inflation. Further changes have included the introduction of taxes on social security benefits (Kohl and O'Brien, 1998; Davis, 1995).

In the 21 century, changing demographics are now driving the need for further reform. In 30 years, the number of workers paying into social security per beneficiary will drop from 3.4 to 2.1. Benefit payments will begin to exceed social security taxes in 2015, and the social security trust fund (reserves) will be exhausted in 2037 (U.S. Social Security Administration, 2000b). If no changes are made, the government will only be able to pay out 72 percent of promised benefits at that time. Options for further reforms include (1) making up the shortfall with government budget surpluses; (2) raising the retirement age further; (3) creating a Chilean-style system of individual, funded accounts;[4] and (4) allowing the government to invest social security reserves in the stock market. Proponents of this last option argue that the government is better able to manage a market downturn than are individuals (U.S. Social Security Administration, 2000a). However, critics are concerned that the government may end up owning a sizeable share of private companies (ibid.).

This summary of the U.S. debate provides a useful benchmark for a brief comparative description of pension arrangements in East Asian economies, Canada, and Chile.

---

3 See United States Social Security Administration (2000a).
4 A summary of the Chilean pension system can be found in the next section. A detailed description is provided in the appendix.

Japan

Japan is the country with the most advanced ageing problem (Peterson, 1999). With an elderly dependency ratio of 41 percent expected by 2015, Japan's current pay-as-you-go system will be unsustainable without major restructuring (Nishi, 1998; Watanabe, 1997). The existing Japanese system has two layers. The first is for employees in the private sector, and the second is a nation-wide scheme. Current OECD estimates put total pension liabilities in the first layer at approximately US$ 400 billion, and the liabilities in the second layer at 10 times that size. By 2025, workers' monthly contributions will have to increase from the current rate of 17 percent of salaries to 30 percent (Watanabe, 1997). At the same time, pension benefits will have to be cut (Watanabe, 1997; Kohl and O'Brien, 1998), as has been the case already in the United States. Currently, the vast majority of Japan's pension deposits earn returns that are well below those earned in other developed countries (Nishi, 1998). This is due in part to the conservative allocation of Japanese pension assets, and in part to poor financial returns in the domestic markets. Recent moves to allow pension funds to be invested globally and less conservatively, such as the 1995 U.S.-Japan Pension Accord, could allow foreign (mostly U.S.) firms to compete for the management of Japanese pension assets. If returns improve, part of the under-funding problem will be alleviated.

Singapore[5]

The Singapore government established an employment-related Central Provident Fund (CPF) scheme in 1955. The CPF is a private, funded system, but it is different from other pension schemes in that it does more than provide financial support for the retired population. Contributions and accrued benefits can be used for other purposes, such as housing, medical expenses, and education. Hence, the CPF is a

---

5 Much of this summary is based on the Government of Singapore's website: www.cpf.gov.sg.

multi-dimensional scheme. Its goal is to encourage Singaporeans to save and essentially take care of themselves with minimal government assistance. Contributions to the CPF were initially held mostly in deposits administered by a government agency. In November 1998, investment guidelines for CPF-approved unit trusts were liberalized to allow CPF members to diversify their investments. Portfolio allocation is still restricted by law to a 10 percent limit on gold, and a 50 percent limit on equities and corporate bonds. The CPF is a comprehensive and creative system.

Hong Kong[6]

The Hong Kong government introduced a compulsory pension system on December 1, 2000. The Mandatory Provident Fund (MPF) scheme is employment-related, and privately managed by approved trustees. Assets are invested in the financial market with relatively few restrictions. Employers select the trustees, but employees have some flexibility in the choice of investment products. The government-appointed Mandatory Provident Fund Authority is responsible for regulation and supervision. The contribution rate is 10 percent of salaries, half of it from the employee, and half of it from the employer. Both parties can elect to make additional contributions. To limit risk exposure, investment guidelines are set by the government. Scheme members can make a lump-sum withdrawal from the MPF when they reach the age of 65. Because the MPF was only introduced in 2000, it provides little benefit to workers who are currently close to retirement. The welfare implications of this limitation are discussed below.

Canada

Canada has a mixed pension system. It includes the mandatory pay-as-you-go Canada Pension Plan (CPP), as well as the voluntary Registered Retirement Savings Plan (RRSP). Official estimates, published in Gov-

---

6 This description is based on the Government of Hong Kong's website: www.mpfahk.org.

ernment of Canada (1997), suggested that if left untouched, the CPP would run out of reserves by 2015. To avoid this shortfall, several changes were made in 1998. First, the regularly-scheduled increase in CPP premiums was accelerated, thus increasing the CPP reserves from two years of benefits to five years. Second, the contribution base was expanded by freezing the annual basic exemption at C$ 3500; as time passes, inflation will expand the base of contributory earnings. Third, the way benefits are calculated has been changed. Specifically, under the old system, the formula for calculating retirement pensions was based on maximum pensionable earnings for the average of the last three years of employment. A modest reduction in benefits was effected; under the new system, the main change in the benefits formula was to extend the pensionable earnings maximum to average the last five years of employment. Finally, the rules for disability pensions were tightened (see Canada, 1998).

Independently evaluating these changes, Pesando (2001) confirms the modest impact of the benefit reductions resulting from these reforms, with their success in improving the funded status of the CPP. In addition to the accelerated increases in CPP contributions, the reserves in the fund are no longer invested solely in relatively low-return federal and provincial securities. Instead they are invested in a broader range of financial instruments, managed by an independent body. Taken together, these changes have restored the sustainability of the Canadian pension system. The Canadian government has argued that the success of the CPP reforms has made it possible to rescue the pay-as-you-go system. Sustainability is more likely, however, because the CPP benefits represent a relatively small portion of total retirement income in Canada (i.e., private funding plays a significant role, as is shown in the appendix).

Chile[7]

The Chilean pension system, introduced in 1981, has been imitated

---

7 See Ruiz-Tagle and Castro (1997) and Pinera (1997).

by several Latin American economies and is also being considered seriously by several other countries, including the United States and China. In 1981, Chile replaced its pay-as-you-go system with a system of private, individual-based Pension Savings Accounts (PSAs). Workers are required to contribute a minimum of 10 percent of their monthly salaries to their PSAs. All PSA assets must be invested in traded securities. Contributions are tax-deductible, and the returns earned in the PSA are tax-free. Taxes are paid when funds are withdrawn during retirement. Individuals receive a passbook that records the value of their retirement accounts, and they can update their PSA balances at any time. Workers can increase their contributions at any time up to an additional amount of US$ 2000 per month.

Summary

In summary, the pension systems in our sample of countries cover a spectrum ranging from completely funded systems in Singapore, Hong Kong, and Chile to completely unfunded systems in the United States and Japan, and a partially funded system in Canada. Chile provides an example of a country where, as demographic changes impacted the financial soundness of the unfunded system, reforms were implemented to ensure full funding. Significantly, however, the United States and Japan are two exceptions where such reforms have not been made. (There are no examples of movement in the opposite direction, away from funded to unfunded systems.)

As we have seen, reforming national pension systems is not straightforward. Changes must be evaluated against some key criteria – sustainability, institutional factors, portfolio allocation and savings, coverage and social welfare, and portability. Reforming existing pension schemes or making decisions on implementing new schemes requires the consideration of each of these criteria. That is the subject of the next section.

As will become clear, although fully funded systems are sustainable, they require well-developed financial institutions and financial markets. In addition, phasing in a funded system can take as long as 50 years. At the same time, although an unfunded system is not sustainable in most countries in which populations are rapidly ageing, it provides instant pensions to the elderly, and allows the government an additional tool to subsidize the retirement of the elderly poor. How countries address this trade-off is also the subject of the next section.

National pension plans: comparative analysis

What are the relative merits of pension systems in each of the countries described above? They can be assessed according to the five criteria referred to above. These criteria, which experience has shown characterize a successful pension system, are sustainability, institutional factors, portfolio allocation and savings, coverage and social welfare, and portability.

Sustainability

The traditional pay-as-you-go pension system would be sustainable if the population structure were stationary. An ageing population undermines sustainability because the contribution rate would have to be increased significantly in order to provide the same stream of pension benefits, or the benefits would have to be reduced substantially. Such changes would cause large intergenerational transfers.

Several issues must be considered in ensuring sustainability. An increase in the contribution rate is also an effective increase in the payroll tax and therefore has a macroeconomic impact. Governments can also raise general taxes to pay for shortfalls in retirement benefits, but these may not fit well with other economic objectives. Higher taxes can lead to lower compliance rates (that is, more refusals to contribute) and to negative impacts on labour supply as workers make informal employment arrangements to avoid contributing to social security. Both effects work against the notion of a self-financing pension scheme. Reducing retirement benefits effectively breaks the government's contract with retirees, and hence may reduce the government's credibility with the current working population.

In Japan, the contribution rate is currently set at 17.35 percent of pensionable income. It is expected to increase dramatically without fundamental reform. The Japanese government has introduced some reforms, mainly with respect to management and portfolio allocation – not with respect to the fundamental issue of ensuring a system of funded pensions, either public or private. Although these are positive steps, they are unlikely to be sufficient to return the Japanese pay-as-you-go system to a sustainable position.

In Chile, demographic changes together with a poor incentive structure for both contributing and participating caused the contribution rate to climb to 50 percent of income in the mid-1970s, making the system unsustainable. Significant changes implemented in 1974 included uniform rules for all pensions and an increase in the effective retirement age by five years. The introduction of a fully funded system in 1981 saw the beginning of the end for the pay-as-you-go system, which is now being phased out.[8]

In Canada, the CPP makes up a relatively small portion of total retirement income. In 1997, for example, only 28.8 percent of all pension income was derived from the public pension system. Old Age Security, which is universally available to people over the age of 65, accounts for 27.5 percent of pension incomes and 43.8 percent comes from private retirement savings plans that have a tax-deferral benefit (Canada, 1997). Hence, even in the absence of any reforms to the CPP, it was projected that the premiums would increase to 14.2 percent of pensionable income (Canada, 1999). The size of the increase is in part attributable to the approach taken in the design of Canada's retirement income program. This approach, consistent with OECD recommendations for pensions systems, has both funded and unfunded elements, and provides incentives for private savings (such as the tax incentives for RRSPs) in addition to both employer/occupational pensions and the CPP.

The Canadian government has argued that its reforms, undertaken

---

8 The pay-as-you-go system still exists in Chile. It will coexist with the fully funded system until all pensions have been fully paid to those who were entitled under the old system, expected in 2045 (Ruiz-Tagle and Castro 1997).

in 1997, have returned the unfunded CPP to a position of sustainability (Canada, 1998). This view, however, is not unanimous. For example, Pesando (2001) argues that two assumptions underlying the government's analysis are questionable, namely, those regarding the inflation rate and expected real returns. He argues that if the inflation rate is higher than the CPP assumes, or if the real returns on the invested portion of CPP reserves are lower than assumed (both of which are likely), the 9.9 percent maximum contribution rate will likely have to rise above 10 percent.

When the Hong Kong government introduced the Mandatory Provident Fund in December 2000, the government chose a Chilean-style fully-funded system. From the citation below, it appears that the reason Hong Kong shied away from the pay-as-you-go system can be explained by the preferences of the authorities in Beijing:

> There is usually more acrimony than comedy in the long-running row between Britain and China over the future of Hong Kong. Yet a smile may have flickered across the face of Chris Patten, Hong Kong's governor, even as China scuppered his plans to introduce a (pay-as-you-go) pension scheme in the colony. Zhou Nan, Communist China's main representative in Hong Kong, harrumphed that Mr. Patten, a British conservative, was trying to bring "costly Euro-socialist" ideas to Hong Kong. (*Economist*, 1995)

Institutional factors

Pension-system reform should go hand-in-hand with financial-sector reform. In a pay-as-you-go system, current contributions are used to finance current pensions, with any excess funds being transferred to the government, where they are either included in general revenues or saved in a trust fund depending on the country. In contrast, with a funded system, contributions are channelled directly into financial markets. Unless these funds are channelled into riskless assets such as government securities, the efficiency and depth of financial markets are critical to the success of a funded system. Where financial markets are well developed, governments must therefore ensure strong finan-cial-market supervision, transparency, and the timely disclosure of rel-evant information. This will ensure that pension-system managers are disciplined and monitored by financial markets, and will protect against managers who consistently undertake poor investment projects as well as against fraud. Where financial markets and institutions are still being developed, government regulation of pension-fund portfolio management and allocation will be necessary.

Another relevant institutional factor is the official retirement age. The official retirement age in most Asian countries falls below the international average of 65 years, except for Hong Kong. The typical retirement age in Asia is between age 55 and 60 (West and Kinsella, 1998). Hence, the elderly dependency ratio typically used to illus-trate the urgency of pension reform underestimates the problem in Asia. While increasing the retirement age may reduce a government's or a company's pension liability, it may also increase youth unem-ployment (because older workers tend to hang on to available jobs longer).

Although ageing is occurring most rapidly in Japan, the inadequacy of pension support can, in part, be explained by key institutional fea-tures of the Japanese economy. For example, the *keiretsu* relationship between pension-plan sponsors and investment management compa-nies has contributed to the poor performance of pension-fund man-agement. In such an economic structure, the performance of the fund manager is of secondary importance to managerial appointments that are driven by business relationships. Another important factor is the rivalry between the Ministry of Finance and the Ministry of Health and Welfare (Nishi, 1998). The former regulates trust banks, insur-ance companies, and investment advisory companies, whereas the lat-ter regulates the pension-plan sponsors. Still another feature of the Japanese economy that hinders reform is the lack of well-defined legis-lation obliging Japanese boards of directors to manage pension assets for the benefit of plan participants (ibid.). This opaqueness contrasts sharply to U.S. rules on the fiduciary responsibilities of pension-fund boards that are quite clear.

Portfolio allocation and savings

One of the arguments favouring a funded system is that returns are potentially higher when pension assets are invested in financial markets. However, the risk-reward trade-off implies that higher returns are achieved through more risk-taking. Campbell and Feldstein (1999) include eleven studies of alternative models of risk preferences to assess the market risks associated with funded systems where assets are invested in financial markets. The dilemma inherent in such investment is that, while assets invested in financial markets may generate higher returns than otherwise, more risk-taking may also be involved to obtain those returns. Campbell and Feldstein find that in a funded system, the added risk assumed by participants is moderate relative to the improved return. If this finding is generally true, then authorities can either reduce the contribution rates, or increase the retirement benefits. What is also attractive about market investment is the added flexibility to adapt to differences in individuals' risk preferences. These results are reinforced by Feldstein and Ranguelova (2000).

Governments in most countries with funded systems restrict the allocation of pension assets. Setting these restrictions requires a delicate balance between investment flexibility and risk-taking. It is important to provide flexibility in the range of investment options to cater to different risk preferences. Offsetting this advantage, however, is the need for governments to limit the risks that individuals and pension-fund managers are permitted to incur.

The impact of alternative pension systems on saving is unclear. A pay-as-you-go system does little to increase savings, since it is financed by a payroll tax. In theory, a funded system will require higher total savings, assuming that prefunding does not induce a shift in the composition of savings. Empirical evidence, however, gives mixed results. Samwick (2000) studies the impact on savings rates of the characteristics of pension systems and determinants of aggregate savings, and also tests whether less reliance on a pay-as-you-go system is associated with higher national savings. Using data for 121 countries from the 1970–94 period, he finds that the savings rate does not change when countries move from pay-as-you-go to funded systems. In contrast, Baillu and Reisen (1997), using a similar methodology on data from a sample of 11 countries from the 1982–93 period find statistically significant evidence for an interaction between funded pensions and aggregate savings. In short, theory does not provide a predictable relationship on which policy can be based.

The other attribute of portfolio allocation and savings is the rising role of offshore investment allocation. As cross-border capital flows increase and as authorities recognize the need to diversify pension assets, more foreign exposure in pension funds is being permitted. For example, the Canadian government increased the allowable foreign content in RRSPs from 20 to 30 percent in 2000.[9] Hong Kong has no limit. Singapore allows foreign assets to be held only indirectly, through unit trusts (similar to mutual funds).[10] In Japan, foreign securities can account for up to 30 percent of pension fund assets; in 2000 25 percent were allocated to equity and 5 percent to bonds (Nishi, 1998).

Coverage and social welfare

Another key criterion by which a pension system is judged is the extent to which pension arrangements cover the entire workforce and provide adequate retirement income where pension arrangements are inadequate. The availability of a well-functioning social-welfare network becomes an important issue. Canada, for example, has two income-tested programs that supplement the universally available Old Age Security benefits for those over the age of 65. The first is a Guaranteed Income Supplement that provides income support to low-income seniors; the second is a Spouse's Allowance that provides income to low-income survivors of pensioners. These benefits are paid out of

---

9 As sophisticated financial products have proliferated, investors have been able to increase their foreign content above this limit using derivative products.
10 A unit trust is a fund managed by a professional investment manager in which investors' money is invested in three asset classes: cash, bonds, and stocks.

general government revenues. Singapore has a social-welfare network to care for the elderly in addition to the CPF. In October 1998, an inter-ministry committee was also struck to "shape national policies to meet the needs of an aging population more comprehensively" (www.cpf.gov.sg).

Hong Kong, which has recently introduced its funded system, faces a significant transition problem since the benefits of the system are not available to workers who are close to retirement.[11] (Indeed, it is expected that the MPF scheme will take at least 30 years to reach maturity.) The tradition in Hong Kong, as in most East Asian economies, is for the family to look after its elderly members. The Hong Kong government has stated explicitly that it will continue to rely on this tradition. For example, public housing allocation policies have been revised further to encourage families to live with their elderly members.[12] In terms of social assistance, the Comprehensive Social Security Assistance (CSSA) scheme provides welfare to individuals at the poverty level.

Japan has mature public and private sector employment-related pension systems.[13] These sources of retirement income are supplemented extensively by private savings. Savings rates in Japan, at 30 percent, are significantly higher than the OECD average of 22 percent. Furthermore, labour-force participation rates for the elderly are quite high in Japan: 75 percent of males between the ages of 60 and 64 are active members of the labour force, as are 54 percent of males between the ages of 65 and 69. These high participation rates are one factor behind the high savings rates, as people tend to continue saving as long as they work. From the standpoint of "active ageing," the Japanese have taken comprehensive measures to encourage employment of older people (Japan, 1999).

Japan's social security system also includes a mechanism to provide

---

11 The Hong Kong Council of Social Service proposed a pay-as-you-go scheme in 1994 that would have provided immediate benefits, but the proposal was rejected.
12 See Hong Kong (1999).
13 See www.mhlw.go.jp.

minimum income levels to those who have not contributed and hence are ineligible for retirement income. Public pension benefits currently cover more than 60 percent of the income for elderly-only households. The current pension system consists of two tiers. The national pension is the first tier. The second tier consists of employee and corporate pensions, insurance for the employees of private companies, and mutual-aid pensions for public service employees.

Portability

The final criterion by which pension systems can be judged is the portability of pensions. Are pensions tied to employment or can employees move their pension assets to new jobs? The guaranteed employment and lifetime jobs that used to be the norm in many parts of East Asia are disappearing as new economies are restructured and modernized. Portable pensions are becoming more of an issue because they promote labour mobility and improve allocative efficiency in an economy.

In Hong Kong, an industry scheme within the MPF is set up for this purpose in industries such as construction and food services where labour mobility is high. This arrangement facilitates mobility, and it also allows workers within an industry to pool their resources for investment purposes. While workers in other industries lack such an arrangement, their pensions are relatively portable since the pension accounts are tied to workers, not employers. The only inconvenience is that when a worker changes jobs, he or she may have to reallocate pension assets according to the scheme used by the new employer. Similarly, the Central Provident Fund in Singapore allows workers to set up their own individual accounts, which are portable.

Mandatory public pension schemes, such as the CPP in Canada, are portable in the sense that moving from one employer to another (within the same country) has no impact on the value of the pension or the benefit stream. However, tax-sheltered, employer-sponsored pension funds are tied to the employer, and exit clauses may vary across employers. When the employee leaves the firm, there are implications for the value of the pension. The Japanese model has similar implications.

In the Chilean system of individual pension accounts, the pension is tied to the employee and not the employer. Furthermore, workers have access to the daily market value of their retirement accounts. These features have served to increase labour market flexibility and efficiency, and many believe has contributed to the success of the Chilean economy.

Summary implications

Ageing populations have rendered a purely unfunded pay-as-you-go pension system unsustainable. Maintaining such systems requires increasing payroll taxes and reducing benefits as populations age. The evidence suggests that raising contribution levels by itself is not enough. A combined strategy of reduced benefits and increased contributions is necessary to return such pension systems to sustainability. In addition, as the World Bank recommends, national pension systems should contain both funded and unfunded components. But reforming pension systems must go hand in hand with financial-market reform. Funded pension programs that allow investment in financial markets should only be allowed when financial markets are well developed so that prices provide accurate signals of risk, asset quality, and performance and supervision provides safeguards against fraud.

In a world of increased labour mobility and changing industrial structures, portability of pensions becomes increasingly important as it serves to improve labour-market efficiency. Therefore, funded pensions like those in Chile or RRSPs in Canada are very attractive as they are tied to the employee and not the employer. Changing jobs therefore has no impact on the value of these assets.

These issues are especially pertinent to pension reforms in Japan and the United States, and in the development and expansion of the Chinese pension system. Although the Japanese authorities are considering the implementation of funded pension accounts, they have not yet done so.

China's choices: comparative analysis applied

As the preceding summary implies, these comparative findings imply certain choices for China. Falling birth rates since the introduction of the one-child policy in 1979 and rising life expectancy will change China's elderly dependency ratio from ten workers per retiree in 1995 to three workers per retiree in 2050 (World Bank 1997).[14]

Before economic reform began in the early 1980s, state-owned enterprises (SOEs) dominated the Chinese economy, and provided their (essentially urban) workers with an "iron rice bowl": SOE workers were taken care of for life through a pay-as-you-go system. Retirement benefits were taken from current operational costs; the government absorbed the deficits. The move to a more market-oriented economy has had a devastating impact on SOE competitiveness. With rapidly aging workforces, SOEs – those that manage to break even – find it increasingly difficult to finance their pension obligations. The growing burden on the government, which acts as the guarantor, necessitates major reform. A private, funded system, intended for all urban workers, was introduced in the mid-1990s. However, coverage is patchy, particularly in private- and foreign-owned companies, where many workers receive little or no retirement protection. Provincial governments, which are responsible for regulating most of these pensions, are making an effort to standardize a complicated array of private plans to make them easier to regulate.

Rural workers have traditionally received little or no formal pensions, relying instead on the extended family. These informal arrangements are being undermined by shrinking family size and urbanization. To address this issue, the Ministry of Civil Affairs introduced a voluntary pension system for rural workers in 1991. Participants contribute voluntarily to their retirement savings accounts, which are invested by county officials. Each year, the individual accounts are credited with an interest payment at a rate set by the Ministry. In some years, however,

---

14 Note that Figure 6 provides comparisons only to 2015.

the real interest rate has been negative. At retirement, participants receive pension payments in the form of an annuity.

While many rural workers are now participating in voluntary plans (partly through the lack of alternatives, and partly through the use of moral suasion by local officials), these plans are only contributing approximately 2 percent of a peasant's annual income.[15] This amount is insufficient to generate adequate financial support at the end of a peasant's working life. As a first step, the World Bank recommends that private insurance and investment companies be allowed to operate in rural areas to increase savings alternatives, and that a mandatory pension system be set up for rural workers to increase contributions. Of course, the administrative requirements of setting up and administering such plans among peasants and self-employed rural workers will be very challenging.

China's pension system is fragmented and inadequate according to all criteria by which it can be judged. Actuarial studies are reported to estimate that if urban China continues to rely on pay-as-you-go systems, workers will have to contribute as much as 50 percent of their salaries as pension contributions by 2050 to preserve the system's sustainability.[16] Since the pay-as-you-go pension system is limited to SOE employees, it does not play much of a redistributive role. Another problem is the lack of portability, which impedes labour mobility.

The official retirement age in China (60 for men, and 55 for women) is below the international average.[17] In recent years, due to financial distress in most SOEs, the retirement age has been reduced to 55 for men and 50 for women (or earlier) in practice in many SOEs.[18] This lower retirement age allows more young people to enter the workforce, but it increases the pension burden of the governments and

---

15 World Bank (1997).
16 Kynge (2000).
17 Certain government employees, such as officials and university professors, can retire at an older age.
18 This information is based on discussions with Chinese scholars.

the employers, because they have to fund longer, and hence more expensive, retirements.

In terms of asset allocation, the majority of pension surpluses are to be invested in government bonds and bank deposits. There are two concerns with this policy: first, these bonds are unattractive financial instruments. Bond yields have not kept up with inflation, and the treasury market in China is fairly illiquid. As a result, many workers are unwilling to allocate their savings to pension plans and the compliance rate is low. Second, when capital markets are immature and illiquid, limited opportunities for asset allocation can inhibit capital accumulation, and hence long-term economic growth. Feldstein (1998) argues that as long as alternative domestic financial assets are available to regular investors who are crowded out of the government bond market by pension funds, there will be a net increase in the capital stock (i.e., domestic savings will be intermediated into domestic investment). But when capital markets are not well developed and transparent, domestic savings may instead be hoarded (in gold, for example) or invested abroad.

Although China currently has one of the world's lowest urbanization rates, that rate is expected to increase dramatically over the next 15 years (Figure 7). As traditional farm units break up, the need for a formal system of social security, that is, a system broader than pension plans in the rural sector, will also become important. In urban centres, the continued influx of rural migrants will necessitate better enforcement of current pension arrangements, as well as reforms to improve incentives that make it attractive to workers to participate in pension plans.

Based on its findings, the World Bank (1997) has deemed the pension system in China financially unsustainable. As a remedy, it recommends a two-tier system, consisting of a social insurance scheme, and mandatory funded individual accounts. Further, it argues that for this system to be successful, China must (1) extend coverage, (2) achieve high participation rates, (3) implement financial-sector reforms, and (4) develop capital markets.

Since China's financial markets are still underdeveloped, the funded portion of the social security system requires substantial government involvement in terms of setting guidelines for asset allocation and the education of investors. In theory, it would be beneficial to allow com-

Figure 7: Urbanization rates

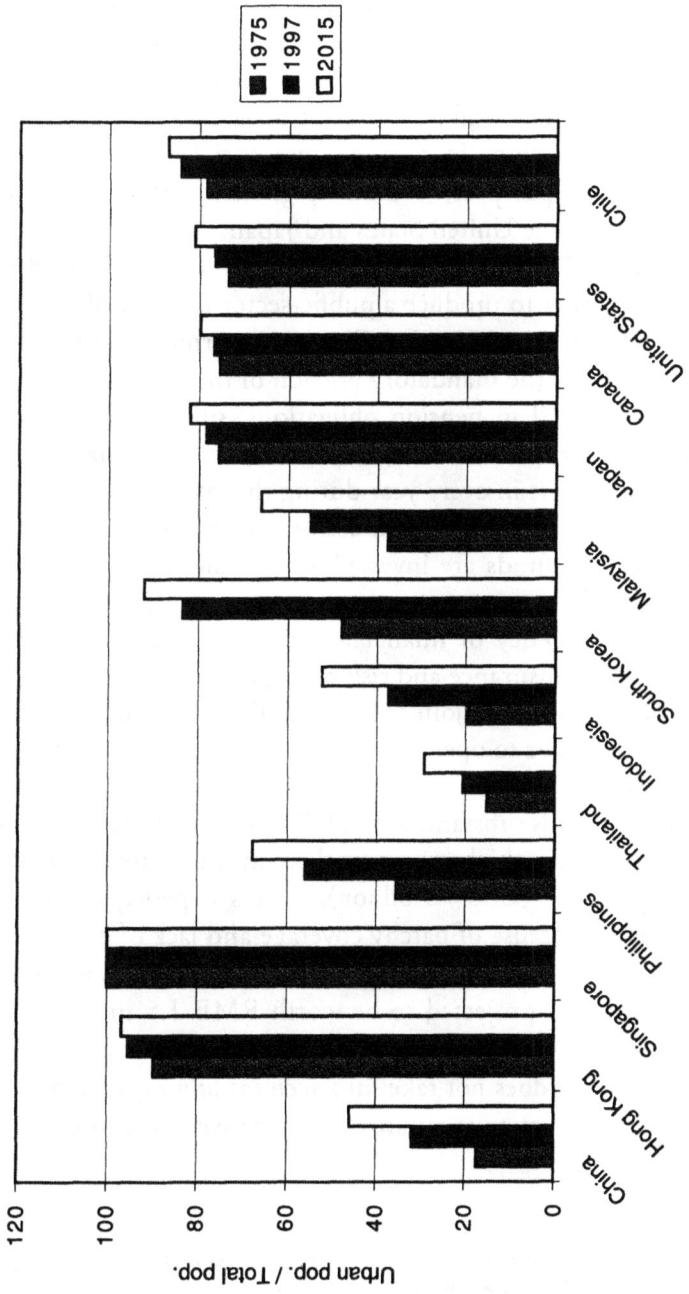

Source: UNDP (1999).

petition between public and private pension institutions, both domestic and foreign. More foreign private expertise would also accelerate modernization of the system. In practice, however, it is likely that the Chinese government will be reluctant to allow much private involvement or competition, in part because social security surpluses (at present a distant prospect) would help government fiscal balances, as is the case in both the United States and Japan.

In the late 1970s, Chile embarked on an aggressive fiscal restraint program, in order to produce a public-sector fiscal surplus to fund the pension reforms in 1981. The Chinese government currently acts as the guarantor for the mandatory portion of the pension system. When there is a shortfall in pension obligations, subsidies are drawn from government revenues. At the same time, however, China has been running a fiscal deficit in every year during the last two decades, with the single exception of 1985 (China 2000). Unless enforcement is stepped up and pension funds are invested wisely, the social security burden will put further pressure on government budgets. This concern increases the urgency of financial-market reform, particularly in the development of insurance and risk management products.

As China prepares to join the World Trade Organization, it will at least gradually have to open its doors to foreign expertise in fund management and insurance. With a large population, the potential size of the pension pool is substantial. In 2000, the size of the social insurance and welfare fund, which covers workers in urban areas, was valued at RMB 629 billion (US$ 76 billion).[19] This is perhaps a smaller sum than expected because of patchy coverage and lack of efforts to ensure workers are contributing regularly and in the correct amounts. In 10 years, the fund is projected to be worth RMB 1.5 to 2 trillion (US$ 180–240 billion).[20] This estimate is considered to be on the conservative side, since it does not take into account any expansion of the formal pension system to rural areas, or improvements in earnings (and

---

19 Telephone interview with Ms. Wei Jue, Deputy Director of the Social Welfare Division, Ministry of Finance, China.
20 Ibid.

hence higher total contributions). Since financial-market liberalization and gaining know-how in RMB-denominated products will take time, the Chinese pension market is not an immediate prospect for foreign fund-management and insurance companies. A horizon of 10 to 15 years may be more realistic.

Finally, as China relies more heavily on a funded system, it must provide its workforce with basic education in personal finance and investment. A survey conducted by Xiao, Xu, and Peng (1999) found that 90 percent of 500 workers surveyed in Southern China would welcome education programs on saving and investment. So far, any effort by foreign financial-services companies has been limited to token seminars targeted at government officials in charge of pension reform. Perhaps a more comprehensive and longer-term partnership in investment education can be established.

This description of the current arrangements in China raises the question of what should be done over the long term. The authorities have demonstrated a preference for a funded system (as indicated by Hong Kong's decision to adopt a funded system). But there is a downside in terms of social welfare and population coverage. If China were to adopt a funded pension system it would not mature for up to 50 years. Those who are currently close to retirement would not benefit. In addition, the slow pace of financial-market development implies that extensive government regulation would be required. Although the funded alternative looks preferable on the criteria of sustainability and portability, it would be costly in terms of social welfare and institutional infrastructure. On the other hand, expanding the pay-as-you-go system would provide instant pensions for the elderly, but would clearly be unsustainable over the long term. The best solution seems to be to adopt elements of an unfunded pay-as-you-go system, to help in the government's redistribution role, along with the funded alternatives.

The route forward

The analysis in this chapter implies that East Asia will see substantial pension reform in the years ahead, particularly because of the rapid ageing under way in Japan, followed some years later by rapid ageing in China. Anticipating these changes, the World Bank recommends a two-pillar pension system consisting of a public, pay-as-you-go system, and a private, funded system of individual accounts. Ideally, this set-up would be supplemented by employment-sponsored pensions. Both Japan and China are considering a move in this direction. Two separate systems (a two-pillar system) may provide a suitable mix, but they involve large costs in terms of management and enforcement. More importantly, the demographic realities will exert further pressure on the pay-as-you-go systems.

We believe other alternatives should also be explored, such as collapsing the two-pillar system into one by phasing out the pay-as-you-go system, as Chile has done. The alternative chosen depends on the role that the pay-as-you-go system is meant to play. If it is meant to provide relatively risk-free retirement protection, some alternatives are available. For example, insurance products or asset-allocation rules can achieve the same level of safety in retirement protection. If, however, the pay-as-you-go system is meant to play a redistributive role in society – for example, by requiring the young rich to finance the old poor – then there are other policies that can achieve the same effect, such as tax increases for younger taxpayers and increased expenditures on the elderly. These are questions that are worth exploring. Politically, it is perhaps difficult to remove an existing pay-as-you-go system completely. However, gradual opting out has been successfully implemented in countries such as Chile.

In conclusion, the systems that evolve in each country will depend in part on societal preferences. At the same time, the issue of sustainability and feasibility cannot be ignored. Chile, where the government has phased out the pay-as-you-go system, is essentially putting the responsibility for retirement in the hands of workers and reducing the role of the government. This is true also in Hong Kong and Singapore. Of course, there are short-run and long-run considerations that must be factored into the analysis in terms of how long it takes for such systems to mature and pay off: immediate for a pay-as-you-go system and much longer for a funded one. These are important issues for countries like China, where a large group of existing workers would need some kind of retirement income. It is because of this problem that a gradual phasing out of any pay-as-you-go system is preferred. Gradualism does not take away any benefits that are currently promised and provides a framework for a sustainable long-run pension system. At the same time, income-tested welfare benefits can be made available to those that fall below some minimum level of retirement income.

APPENDIX: COUNTRY STUDIES

China[1]

Overview
System type: two-tier (1) compulsory, unfunded pay-as-you-go, defined benefit for employees at state-owned enterprises; and (2) voluntary, funded, defined contribution for urban workers.

Before the economic reforms in the early 1980s, state-owned enterprises (SOEs) dominated the Chinese economy, and provided their (essentially urban) workers with an "iron rice bowl": workers at SOEs were taken care of for life. Pension arrangements were in the form of a pay-as-you-go system. Retirement benefits were taken from current operations, and counted as costs. If that led to a loss, it was absorbed by the government. The move to a more market-oriented economy has had a devastating impact on SOEs, as they are not able to compete in the new economic environment. With a rapidly ageing workforce, SOEs – those that manage to stay afloat – find it increasingly difficult to finance their pension obligations. The growing burden on the government, which acts as the guarantor, necessitates major reform in the social security system.

The trend thus far has been toward partial privatization. The current arrangement, revamped in the mid-1990s, can be described as a three-pillar system. It consists of (1) the old pay-as-you-go system, which is meant to provide a basic pension for subsistence; (2) a funded system in which workers make regular, mandatory contributions to their individual accounts; and (3) voluntary savings.

---

1 This analysis applies only to systems available to urban Chinese.

There are several types of funded pension schemes to which workers can contribute. Below are two examples:

- Industry scheme: This scheme is set up for workers within the same industry. Examples are the People's Bank of China pension fund, railway industry pension fund, and judiciary-sector pension fund for lawyers.
- Local scheme: This scheme is set up for workers within the same municipality. An example is the Shanghai City pension fund, which was one of the first such funds, set up in 1993. Most SOE pension funds belong in this category.

Regulatory framework
The Ministry of Finance is the official governing body. Day-to-day administration is conducted by labour departments at the municipal level, subject to approval at the provincial level.

Provincial governments are making an effort to standardize pension plans to make them easier to regulate. Currently, many workers have little or no retirement protection, so a goal of policy has been to expand participation.

Participation
The pay-as-you-go system was instituted in the 1950s for urban workers at SOEs only. The relatively new funded portion is intended for all urban workers, including those who work in public, private, and foreign-owned companies. However, coverage remains patchy in non-SOE companies.

Funding and management
The pay-as-you-go system is financed by a payroll tax that is equal to roughly 9 percent of wages, and applies only to employees of SOEs. An employee who has worked for 40 years is entitled to a pension that is equal to 20 to 25 percent of the regional average wage. Employees with a shorter work history receive a proportionately smaller pension.

The funded system introduced by the reforms in the 1990s requires a contribution rate of 10 percent of wages, with the employer and the employee each contributing half. This contribution rate is set to increase to 15 percent. (However, the actual contribution rate and the split between the employer and the employee vary significantly across funds.) Contributions are made to individual accounts, which are managed by municipal or provincial authorities. Upon retirement, the employee is entitled to an annuity roughly equal to 35 percent of his final year's wages.

The management of pension funds is gradually being shifted from the government (local finance bureaus) to the insurance industry. Domestic insurance companies are emerging as the main players today. Foreign insurance companies have had limited opportunities in China. At the end of 1998, five wholly foreign-owned and five foreign joint-venture insurance companies were allowed to sell individual policies (with restrictions placed on the location of operation). Another 40 or so have offices in China, but were only permitted to advise, not underwrite.[2]

According to official guidelines, 80 percent of pension surpluses[3] are to be invested in government bonds, and the rest in bank deposits, which have experienced negative real returns in recent years. Very recently, however, some liberalization has taken place, and up to 5 percent of pension assets can be invested in equity funds (not individual equities). Compliance with these guidelines, however, appears to be low. For example, the Ministry of Finance estimated that only 10 to 30 percent of fund surpluses were actually invested in government bonds at the end of 1996.[4]

Hong Kong

Overview
System type: compulsory, funded, defined contribution.

According to recent estimates, the percentage of individuals aged 65 and over was slightly above 10 percent. This percentage is projected to increase to 13 percent by 2016, and to 20 percent by 2036 by the government. Up to the early 1990s, less than one-third of the workforce in Hong Kong had some form of retirement protection.[5] Hence, the government has been under pressure to set up a formal system of retirement benefits.

Enacted in August 1995, the Mandatory Provident Fund (MPF) Schemes Ordinance was implemented on December 1, 2000.[6] The MPF is employment-

---

2 West and Goodkind (1999).
3 Surpluses are defined as the amount in excess of two months' worth of pension outlays.
4 West (1999).
5 "Introduction to MPF," Mandatory Provident Fund Scheme Authority website: www.mpfahk.org/.
6 Until this date, private-sector pensions were set up on a *voluntary* basis, and governed by the Occupational Retirement Schemes Ordinance (ORSO), passed in October 1993. The ORSO maintains a registration system and its main goal was to ensure that the retirement schemes are properly administered and funded. Members of the ORSO have the option to switch to an MPF scheme. Further, in January 2000, the Mandatory Provident Fund Schemes Authority (MPFA) took over the role of administering the ORSO.

related and privately managed. The amount of accrued benefits is directly related to the contributions made and the return on assets.

There are three main types of schemes:

A. Master trust scheme: This scheme is designed for small- to medium-size companies and self-employed individuals. By pooling together contributions, members enjoy a higher degree of efficiency resulting from economies of scale.
B. Employer-sponsored scheme: This scheme is suitable for large companies with enough employees to form its own scheme.
C. Industry scheme: This scheme targets workers in industries with high labour mobility, such as those who work in restaurants and construction. The advantage of the industry scheme is that a member does not need to change schemes if he changes employment within the same industry, as long as his new employer also participates in the industry scheme.

Regulatory framework
MPF schemes are privately managed by approved trustees, but regulated and supervised by the government via the Mandatory Provident Fund Authority.

Participation
Members of the workforce between the age of 18 and 64 are required to participate. This applies to self-employed individuals, as well as part-time and temporary workers. Exempted individuals include domestic workers; self-employed hawkers; civil servants and teachers who are already covered by statutory pension and provident fund schemes; recent expatriates[7] or expatriates who are already covered by overseas retirement schemes; and members of the Occupational Retirement Schemes.

Funding and management
If the scheme member is an employee, he and his employer each contribute 5 percent of his income. However, if the scheme member's monthly income is less than HK$ 4000 (US$ 513), then he is exempted from making his share of the contribution. If the scheme member's monthly income is *above* HK$ 20,000 (US$ 2571), then the scheme member and his employer are required to contribute HK$ 1000 (US$ 129) a month. Self-employed individuals contribute 5 percent of their income. Mandatory contributions are tax-deductible, subject to a maximum of HK$ 12,000 (US$ 1542) per year.

All parties can elect to make extra contributions in addition to the mandatory

---

7 Those who have been working in Hong Kong for less than one year.

amount, and they have the option to contribute on a monthly or annual basis. Contributions are made to registered MPF schemes managed by the trustees, which are typically large investment companies. Trustees are selected by employers, but employees have some flexibility in the choice of investment products.

To limit risk exposure, investment guidelines have been set as follows: (1) at least 30 percent of the scheme assets must be held in or hedged to Hong Kong dollars; (2) no short selling is allowed; (3) the holding of a security cannot exceed 10 percent of any investment fund; (4), same as (3), but applied to a class of securities issued by the same issuer.

Scheme members who have reached the age of 65 can make a lump-sum withdrawal from the MPF. Early withdrawal is permitted under specific circumstances, such as death, early retirement (age 60 or above), or permanent departure from Hong Kong.

Japan[8]

Overview
System type: compulsory, unfunded pay-as-you-go, defined benefit.

Japan's demographic changes are far more dramatic than that of any other developed country, making pension reform all the more urgent. These demographic changes, together with poor financial management of pension assets, have resulted in very large unfunded liabilities in the Japanese pension market. Reforms implemented in 1997 included the liberalization of pension markets and deregulation in financial markets, but this has not satisfied many critics who continue to argue that these reforms are not sufficient to solve the looming pension crisis in Japan. The proportion of private-sector workers in Japan and in the United States that are covered by private pension plans is about the same, whereas the pension assets in Japan are only one-seventh what they are in the U.S. What is missing from the Japanese reform are the following fundamental aspects: (1) the move toward a funded, defined contribution system; (2) privatization of government-organized pension plans; and (3) the privatization of the postal savings systems (see below).

One of the major obstacles to change in the Japanese pension system is the *keiretsu* relationship between pension plan sponsors and investment management companies. In such an economic structure, the performance of the fund manager

---

8 Much of this discussion derives from Nishi (1998) and the MHLW website (Japan, 1999).

is of secondary importance because appointments are driven by business relationships.

There are two main sources of retirement income:

A. Public pension schemes

Employee Welfare Pension Insurance: This plan covers salaried employees of private corporations. The contribution rate is 17.35 percent of gross monthly earnings to a maximum of 575,000 yen per month, plus 1 percent of the previous year's bonus. Contributions are shared by the employee and the employer, and benefits are paid out at age 60. This age is being increased gradually to 65 by 2013.

National Annuities: These cover self-employed workers and Japanese residents other than those covered by welfare pension insurance. Contributions are fixed at 12,700 yen per month, and are adjusted upwards by 500 yen annually until they reach a ceiling of 21,700 yen. Contributions are mandatory for those between the ages of 20 and 60. Contributions are only made by the annuity participant.

National Annuities Fund: This fund was established in 1991 to supplement the basic plans above. Pension premiums are freely set by the self-employed up to a ceiling of 68,000 yen per month.

Mutual Aid Pension: Provides coverage to national and local government employees, public and private sector educators and school staff, and employees of agricultural and fishing cooperatives.

B. Private pension schemes

Corporate pension plans: These are organized by corporations and professional associations. They include both tax-qualified pension and a non-tax-qualified pension plans, as well as an employee benefit plan. Both the employee and the employer make contributions.

Personal pension plans: Designed for self-employed people, these can be purchased through the post office, life insurance companies, and trust banks.

Private savings: A large part of savings are deposited in postal savings accounts (in Japan, as in Great Britain, post offices serve as quasi-banks). These funds are under the supervision of the Ministry of Posts and Telecommunications. These deposits are re-deposited with the Ministry of Finance's Trust Fund Bureau (TFB). Over the 1996–97 period, the return on assets invested by the TFB was about 5 percent, but a large part of the funds are used to fund government projects. Thus, the Ministry of Finance has resisted the privatization of the management of these funds.

Regulatory framework

In 1997, Japanese employee pension funds were freed from the 5-3-3-2 rule (50 percent in principal guaranteed investments, no more than 30 percent in Japanese equities, no more than 30 percent in foreign securities, and a maximum of 20 percent in real estate). In 1999, all rules on who can manage pension funds in Japan were abolished.

Also, there has been an accounting change: reporting market rather than book values makes the underfunding more clear – now, the falling asset values of funds will be reflected in regular performance reviews, unlike the case when one uses historical costs. This change, along with increased competition, should reward those who perform well. Beginning in 2000, Japanese corporations are required to have more open and clear disclosure of financial reports, especially in their pension assets and liabilities.

The largest obstacle to reform in the Japanese pension system is the rivalry between the Ministry of Finance and the Ministry of Health and Welfare. The former regulates trust banks, insurance companies, and investment advisory companies, whereas the latter regulates the pension plan sponsors. One of the major problems with the Japanese pension system is that there is no well-defined law or obligation for Japanese board members to manage pension assets for the benefit of the plan participants. This is in sharp contrast to the U.S. case, where there are clear rules on fiduciary responsibilities of pension fund boards. In Japan, it is unclear as to who is legally accountable for pension fund management. As a result, the Japanese government is being pressured to introduce rules that mandate the priorities of pension plan managers.

Participation
The pension system in Japan is fairly extensive, and all workers to the age of 60 (soon to be increased to 65) have access to at least some component of Japan's pension system.

Funding and management
Investment Advisory Companies (IACs) manage pension funds, but are more specialized than trust banks because the latter manage pension funds, among other things. Most Japanese IACs are subsidiaries of Japanese brokerage houses, banks, trust companies, and insurance companies, and as a result have extensive business relationships with Japanese pension-funds and members of Japanese business networks. These relationships are exploited extensively and hence serve as a major strength for Japanese IACs.

Most Japanese IACs are not as internationally known as their foreign counterparts. Japanese IAC employees tend to be less qualified, and have less global investment experience.

The liberalization of the pension market began in 1995, mainly as a result of pressure from the U.S. In that year, Japan and the U.S. signed an accord that would allow U.S. firms to compete for management of Japanese pension assets. In 1996, the Pension Service Public Welfare Corporation, which acts as pension manager for the Ministry of Health and Welfare, began appointing non-Japanese investment managers. Furthermore, US$ 180 billion were allocated to each of three investment management firms, two of which were foreign. This was a significant departure from past practice and implicitly signals the government's approval for other pension funds to also appoint non-Japanese asset managers. This trend was extended to the private sector as well when corporate leaders such as the Sony Corporation withdrew money managed by Japanese life insurers and reinvested mainly with U.S. and European fund managers. These decisions were in large part the result of the relatively poor performance on the part of Japanese fund managers.

Foreign fund managers operating in Japan, including Barclays Nikko, Schroder, Mercury, Deutsche Morgan Grenfell, Goldman Sachs Investments Advisory, and Jardine Fleming Investment Advisory recorded 200 to 600 percent increases in pension assets in the 1996 to 1998 period. Their pension assets grew twice as fast as those of their Japanese counterparts.

Specialized foreign exchange banks no longer have a monopoly, hence making it easier for individuals and companies to move large sums of money abroad. As a result, there is more competition in the market for foreign exchange, and this will stimulate foreign securities investing. In addition, the postal savings system is also set to be privatized, involving some US$ 2.5 trillion.

By 1990, the pension debt in the public pension system reached 137 percent of GDP. It is anticipated that absent significant changes to the public pension schemes, premiums would grow until 2045. The Japanese pension market is about one-third the size of the U.S. pension market. The allocation of Japanese pension assets is far more conservative than asset allocation in the U.S. In 1994, Japanese corporate pension assets were allocated as follows: 37 percent invested in fixed-return products, 26.6 percent in bonds, 17.2 percent in domestic equities. In the U.S., 62.6 percent of corporate pensions were invested in equities and 26.9 percent in bonds.

Singapore[9]

Overview

System type: compulsory, funded, defined contribution.

Singapore has an employment-related Central Provident Fund (CPF) scheme, established in 1955. The CPF is different from other pension schemes in the

---

9 Singapore (www.cpf.gov.sg) and Ng (1999).

sense that its function is not limited to providing financial support for the retired population. Contributions and accrued benefits can also be used for other purposes, such as housing, medical expenses, and education. Hence, the CPF is a multidimensional scheme. Its goal is to encourage Singaporeans to save and essentially take care of themselves in all respects at an early stage, with minimal government assistance.

The typical CPF member starts with five types of accounts:

- Ordinary account: Savings in this account can be used for housing, education, and to top up parents' Retirement accounts (see below).
- Medisave account: Savings in this account are for meeting approved medical expenses (for example, hospital bills and certain outpatient treatments), and for purchasing medical insurance.
- Special account: Savings in this account are reserved for old age and contingency purposes.
- Investment account: This account comes under the regulation of the CPF Investment Scheme. Funds here can be used for investment in financial assets such as government-approved unit trusts, stocks, bonds, gold, and insurance policies. Currently, there is a 50 percent limit on stocks and a 10 percent limit on gold.
- Retirement account: When the CPF member reaches age 55, he can start withdrawing savings from his Ordinary and Special accounts.[10] At the same time, he must open a Retirement account. Upon opening this account, the CPF member has to deposit an amount equal to the "Minimum Sum." The Minimum Sum Scheme (MSS) is the part of the CPF, which is specifically designed for retirees. It serves as a safety net and so this amount cannot be touched.[11] Starting at age 62, the legislated retirement age in Singapore, CPF members receive a monthly income from their Retirement accounts.

Regulatory framework
The CPF is regulated by the Singaporean government. Among the Fund's many

---

10 Beginning at age 55, a CPF member can apply for withdrawal once every three years, i.e., at age 58, 61, etc. A member can also apply for withdrawal on the ground that he has been unemployed for six months.
11 The "Minimum Sum" is an amount specified by the government. The MSS is a way to lock up a retiree's savings and guarantee that he will receive a stable monthly income. As of July 2000, this sum is equal to S$ 65,000 (US$ 37,790). This amount need not all be in cash. Up to S$ 40,000 can be in pledged property. The Minimum Sum will be increased by S$ 5000 a year until it reaches S$ 80,000 by the year 2003.

administrative roles, the government sets guidelines for the CPF Investment Scheme. Under this scheme, CPF members aged 21 or over may use their savings in excess of the specified Minimum Sum amount to invest in financial-market instruments (via the Investment account). The government also sets, on a quarterly basis, the interest rates, which can be earned in the Ordinary, Medisave, Special, and Retirement accounts.

Participation

The CPF covers all employees who are Singapore citizens and permanent residents. Self-employed individuals are only required to contribute to the Medisave account.[12]

Funding and management

Both the employer and the employee contribute to the CPF. Members aged 55 or below contribute 20 percent of their monthly income, while their employers contribute 12 percent, for a total of 32 percent.[13] Monthly contributions are subject to a maximum of S$ 720 for employers, and S$ 1200 for employees. Contributions are not tax-exempt.

For members aged 55 or under, three-quarters of each contribution goes to the Ordinary account, and the rest is split between the Medisave and the Special accounts. If a member wishes to participate in the CPF Investment Scheme and meets the criteria, savings from the Ordinary account can be transferred to the Investment account.

Initially, the CPF scheme had minimal impact on the Singaporean capital market, since contributions were held mostly in deposits (see Davis, 1995: 253–54). In November 1998, investment guidelines for CPF-approved unit trusts were liberalized to allow CPF members to diversify their investments. More choices are also available: as of March 2000, 25 fund managers and 65 unit trusts were approved under the scheme.

However, the government still controls the list of "approved assets" that CPF members can invest in under the CPF Investment Scheme: fixed deposits, endowment insurance policies, unit trusts, fund management accounts, bonds guaranteed by the Singaporean government, gold (up to 10 percent of savings in the Investment account), and listed shares and corporate bonds (up to 50 percent of savings in the

---

12 In July 1992, the CPF scheme was extended to include self-employed individuals. However, they only have to contribute 6 to 8 percent of their income (depending on age), and only to the Medisave account.
13 If a CPF member continues to work after age 55, the total contribution rate is reduced.

Investment account). Moreover, all investments must be in Singapore dollars. Foreign equities and corporate bonds may be held indirectly through unit trusts.

For retirees, there are three ways they can invest their Minimum Sum in their Retirement accounts: purchase a life annuity, keep it at an approved bank, or leave it with the CPF board as a deposit.

Canada

Overview[14]
System type: two tier – (1) compulsory, unfunded pay-as-you-go, defined benefit and (2) voluntary, funded, defined contribution.

Canada's retirement-income program has three pillars, and represents a balance between a basic minimum income paid to all seniors, an earnings-related public pension scheme, and a targeted supplement to low-income seniors. This program is supplemented by voluntary tax-sheltered savings schemes. As in many other countries, the future sustainability of Canada's public pension system is threatened by demographic changes: the proportion of seniors is expected to stabilize after 2030, and the Canada Pension Plan (CPP) was expected, absent any reforms, to run out of reserves by 2015. The chief actuary for the CPP projected that contributions to the unfunded pay-as-you-go CPP would be required to increase to 14.2 percent of pensionable earnings by 2030 if no changes were made. To avoid these steep increases in required contributions, the federal and provincial governments introduced changes to the CPP that have returned it to sustainability.

The three pillars of Canada's Retirement Income Program are:

A. The Old Age Security (OAS) program '
• Old Age Security is available to all citizens, but is taxable.
• Guaranteed Income Supplement: Eligibility is income-tested.
• Spouse's Allowance: Eligibility is income-tested.

These components provide a basic amount of retirement income for retired Canadians. Benefits are paid out of the general revenues of the federal government, and cost about $22 billion in 1997. The 1997 federal-provincial agreement on the CPP will see the introduction of a new Seniors Benefit, which will result in a consolidation of the OAS and the GIS into one benefit.

---

14 For further information on the Canadian pension system, see the following Government of Canada website: www.hrdc-drhc.gc.ca/.

B. The Canada Pension Plan (CPP)[15]

This plan is a compulsory, defined benefit, pay-as-you-go pension scheme. It applies to all workers between the ages of 18 and 70. Both employees and employers contribute an equal amount, equal to 4.95 percent of pensionable earnings between $3,500 and $37,400. (The current rates are 4.3 percent, but are legislated to increase to the higher rate in 2003). Self-employed workers are required to contribute at the combined rate.

C. Private Retirement Savings Plans

Registered Pension Plans (RPPs), Deferred Profit-Sharing Plans (DPSPs), and Registered Retirement Savings Plans (RRSPs) all have a tax-deferral benefit. This benefit amounts to an interest-free loan on the deferred income tax as well as the tax deferral on the earnings. Withdrawals are treated as regular taxable income. Contribution limits to these plans are a function of taxable income and are capped at $13,500 annually. This limit is scheduled to increase to $15,500 in 2005, and thereafter be indexed to the growth in the average wage rate. Withdrawals from these plans must begin by age 69. Unused RRSP deduction room can be carried forward indefinitely. There has also been some accommodation of flexible pension plans that would allow for additional contributions without reducing annual RRSP contribution limits.

Regulatory framework

The CPP is not counted as part of the government's budget, and has its own "independent" actuary who issues an annual independent report. The operation and sustainability of the CPP is therefore more visible and transparent than it would otherwise be. It was made clear in the chief actuaries' 1995 report that reforms were needed to prevent sharp increases in contributions with the retirement of the baby-boom generation. Canada's Retirement Income Programs are regulated by the Office of the Superintendent of Financial Institutions (OSFI), a federally mandated institution that also regulates banks, insurance companies, and provincial regulatory agencies.

Participation

The OAS program applies to all Canadians aged 65 and over. The CPP applies to

---

15 The province of Quebec has its own pension plan called the Quebec Pension Plan rather than the CPP. The two plans are very similar. For example, contribution rates for the QPP have been scheduled to increase to 9.9% as well. For details on the QPP, please see the QPP website: www.rrq.gouv.qc.ca/an/english.htm.

all employed and self-employed people between the ages 18 to 70 years. Private retirement savings plans are voluntary. In 1997, 95 percent of all seniors received OAS; 29 percent of all tax filers contributed to RRSPs, and the average contribution was $4000. The tax benefits of these contributions amounted to $7.36 billion. Finally, 42 percent of all paid workers belonged to an occupational pension plan.

Funding and management

In 1997, pension income was $80 billion, 56 percent from public pensions ($22 billion from the OAS/GIS [27.5 percent]; $23 billion from CPP/QPP [28.8 percent]) and 44 percent from private pensions ($35 billion).

In 1995, the chief actuary for the CPP made it clear that reforms to the pubic system were required to prevent steep increases in contribution rates. The changes, legislated in 1998, include the following:[16]

a. Accelerate the contribution increases to build up a larger reserve base to prepare for the retirement of the baby-boom generation.
b. Invest a portion of the reserves – currently, 14 percent – by an independent CPP Investment Board to take advantage of higher equity returns. (These reserves were originally invested solely in federal and provincial securities.)
c. Tighten the administration of benefits and reduce disability payments in order to moderate rising costs.

The contribution rate is legislated to increase to 9.9 percent by 2003 and remain at that level thereafter. The 9.9 percent contributions are shared equally by the employee and employer. Reform of this second pillar of Canada's public pension scheme was made easier by its smaller size relative to that in other countries. For example, in 1997, this accounted for only 28.8 percent of income for those aged 65 and over.

There is strong competition among Canadian financial institutions for RRSP savings. These savings can be invested in a wide variety of financial instruments. The deposits are protected by the Canada Deposit Insurance Corporation.

Chile

Overview

System type: mandatory, funded, defined contribution. (The old unfunded, pay-as-you-go system is being phased out.)

---

16 Government of Canada, 1999.

Chile's adoption of a system of privately managed, individually-based pension accounts has been credited as being a major impetus to the above-average performance of the Chilean economy. Furthermore, its success has served as a model for pension reform globally, despite the large fiscal impact that results from such reforms: the unfunded liabilities of the pay-as-you go system were estimated at that time to be 80 percent of GDP. The groundwork for the reforms began in 1974, when the government implemented a program of fiscal restraint necessary to implement the planned privatization of the social security system. There were two important changes implemented: first, there were uniform rules set for all pensions, and second, uniform retirement ages were instituted (65 for men and 60 for women, representing an increase of about five years for the average worker). The new system was able to set contribution rates low enough so that net take-home pay increased by about 11 percent.

Over the period 1981–97, the assets inside the privatized pension system grew to US$ 33 billion, and the annual real return over this period exceeded 11 percent per annum.

The two pension schemes currently in effect in Chile are as follows:

A. The pay-as-you-go system
In 1955, there was one pensioner for every 12.2 active workers contributing to the Chilean pension system. This changed dramatically over the subsequent 25 years: in 1980, this ratio had dropped to only 2.5. In 1979, there were 32 pay-as-you-go pension funds in Chile, each servicing different occupational groups and offering significantly different benefits across occupations. Surpluses in these funds were transferred to the government. In 1974, contributions to these pay-as-you-go pensions represented 50 percent of worker's monthly salaries. By 1980, this number dropped to between 34 percent and 42 percent of pensionable salaries.

B. Fully-funded investment accounts
In 1981, the Chilean government introduced privately invested savings accounts (PSAs). The mandatory minimum contribution to these PSAs is 10 percent of the worker's monthly salary, which reflects the amount that would be needed, assuming a 4 percent real return, for workers to achieve a pension of 70 percent of their salaries upon retirement.

The amount of pension benefits depends on the salary of the individual over the contribution period and on the performance of the investment portfolio for the individual's PSA. However, a minimum pension is guaranteed by the government. Those with 20 years of contributions but whose pension is below the legally defined minimum pension would receive the minimum pension from the government, but only after the individual's PSA runs out. Those without 20 years of contributions can apply for a welfare-type pension at a lower rate.

In 1981, at the time the funded system was introduced, workers had two choices: they could opt out of the pay-as-you-go system and into the privatized system, or remain in the public system. Over 95 percent of Chileans have now chosen to opt out. Those who opt out receive a "recognition bond" that reflects the capital they have invested in the pay-as-you-go system. These highly traded bonds carry a 4 percent real return, and must be deposited in the individual's PSA. They can be redeemed upon retirement.

The 10 percent minimum contribution into the PSA reduces taxable income, and the returns earned in the PSA are tax-free. Taxes are paid when funds are withdrawn during retirement. Neither the employee nor the employer pays a social-security tax to the government.

Individuals receive a passbook that gives the value of their retirement account. They receive updates every three months on the performance of their portfolio. All PSA assets must be invested in traded securities, and hence there is a market value for every worker's account each day. Since the PSAs are portable, it is easy for individuals to move their PSAs from one company to another. This feature improves labour mobility, and therefore enhances allocative efficiency in the economy.

Regulatory framework
The pension funds and the companies that manage them are separate legal entities. This set-up is meant to protect the funds from possible bankruptcy of the management companies. These companies are overseen by the AFP Superintendency. Strict limits are imposed to ensure that these funds are invested in highly diversified portfolios.

Participation
Participation in the previous pay-as-you-go system peaked in 1973, when 73 percent of active workers were contributing to the system, and fell gradually to 64 percent in 1989. This trend reflected two things: the evasion of paying into the system and an increase in unemployment rates. (There was little relation between worker's contributions and the benefits from participating – contributions were therefore seen as a tax on labour and hence contributed to poor labour-market performance.) Between 1977 and 1980, fiscal transfers equal to 2.6 percent of GDP were required to meet pension obligations. It was the unfairness and the increasing fiscal consequences that spurred the reforms of 1981.

The private system includes both public and private employees, but excludes the police and the armed forces. Self-employed people enter if they wish.

Funding and management
The PSAs are managed by fund management companies (AFPs), which operate in

a highly competitive industry with few barriers to entry. The fund managers are not allowed to undertake any other business. Since individuals are free to transfer their accounts from one AFP to another, there is a healthy level of competition among AFPs for new clients. Since PSA members can assess their account balance at any time, there is a high degree of transparency. This feature imposes an additional discipline on AFP management to perform well at the risk of losing clients.

REFERENCES

Baillu, Jeanine, and Helmut Reisen. 1997. "Do Funded Pensions Contribute to Higher Savings? A Cross-Country Analysis." In *Maintaining Prosperity in an Ageing Society: The OECD Study on the Policy Implications of Ageing. Ageing Working Paper* 5.1. Paris: OECD.

Campbell, John, and Martin Feldstein, eds. 1999. *Risk Aspects of Investment-based Social Security Reform*. Chicago: University of Chicago Press.

Canada, Government of. 1998. "1998 Changes to the Canada Pension Plan." Available at www.hrdc-drhc.gc.ca/isp/cpp/cpplcqa.shtml.

- 1997. "Securing Canada's Retirement Income System." Ottawa: Department of Finance. Available at www.fin.gc.ca/pam/pam-e.pdf.

Canada, Government of. Department of Finance. 1999. "Canada's Response to The Questionnaire for the 2000 Report on the follow-up to 'Maintaining Prosperity in an Ageing Society.'" Available at following OECD website: www.oecd.org/subject/ageing/country/Canada.pdf.

Canada Pension Plan Investment Board. 2001. *Annual Report*. Available at www.cppib.ca.

China, Government of. 2000. *Statistical Yearbook of China*. Beijing: State Statistical Bureau, China Statistical Publishing House.

Davis, Philip E. 1995. *Pension Funds, Retirement-Income Security and Capital Markets: An International Perspective*. Oxford: Clarendon Press.

Economist. 1995. "Is Welfare unAsian." February 11: 16–17.

Feldstein, Martin. 1998. "Social Security Pension Reform in China." *National Bureau of Economic Research Working Paper* no. 6794. Cambridge, Mass.

Feldstein, Martin, and Elana Ranguelova. 2000. "Accumulated Pension Collars: A Market Approach to Reducing the Risk of Investment-based Social Security Reform." *National Bureau of Economic Research Working Paper* no. 7861. Cambridge: Mass.

Hong Kong. Health and Welfare Bureau. 1999. "Policy Objectives: Care for the Elderly." Available at www.info.gov.hk/pa99/english/obje.htm.

Japan. Ministry of Health, Labour and Welfare Pension Bureau. 1999. "Framework for the 80-year Life Span." Available at www.mhlw.go.jp/english/org/policy/p36-37.html.

Kohl, Richard, and Paul O'Brien. 1998. "The Macroeconomics of Ageing, Pensions and Savings: A Survey." In *Maintaining Prosperity in an Ageing Society: The OECD Study on the Policy Implications of Ageing. Ageing Working Paper* 1.1. Paris: OECD.

Kynge, James. 2000. "China's Burden of Age." *Financial Times*, June 1.

Ng, Edward. 1999. "Central Provident Fund in Singapore: A Capital Market Boost or a Drag?" In *Rising to the Challenge in Asia: A Study of Financial Markets. Volume 3, Sound Practices.* Manila: Asian Development Bank.

Nishi, Norio. 1998. "The Transformation of the Japanese Pension Market." *National Bureau of Asian Research Working Paper* no. 14. Seattle.

Pesando, James E. 2001 (forthcoming). "The Canada Pension Plan: Looking Back at the Recent Reforms." In Patrick Grady and Andrew Sharpe, eds., *The State of Economics in Canada: Festschrift in Honour of David Slater.* Montreal: McGill-Queen's University Press.

Peterson, Peter G. 1999. *Gray Dawn.* New York: Three Rivers Press.

Pinera, Jose. 1997. Transcripts of congressional testimony in front of U.S. Ways and Means sub-committee on social security. See Cato Institute homepage, www.cato.org.

Ruiz-Tagle, Joaquin Vial, and Francisca Castro. 1997. "The Chilean Pension System." In *Maintaining Prosperity in an Ageing Society: The OECD Study on the Policy Implications of Ageing. Ageing Working Paper* 5.6. Paris: OECD.

Samwick, Andrew A. 2000. "Is Pension Reform Conducive to Higher Savings? *Review of Economics and Statistics*, 82/2: 264–72.

Singapore, Government of. 1999. *The CPF News Line: A Corporate Newsletter of the CPF Board*, no. 5, August (available at www.cpf.gov.sg).

Turner, Dave, Claude Giorno, Alain De Serres, Ann Vourc'h, and Pete Richardson. 1998. "The Macroeconomic Implications of Ageing in a Global Context." In *Maintaining Prosperity in an Ageing Society: The OECD Study on the Policy Implications of Ageing. Ageing Working Paper* 1.2. Paris: OECD.

United Nations Development Program (UNDP). 1999. *Human Development Report 1999.* New York: Oxford University Press.

United States Social Security Administration. 2000a. "The Future of Social Security." SSA publication #05-10055.

– 2000b. "A Brief History of Social Security." SSA publication #21-059.

Watanabe, Shunsuke. 1997. "The Social Security Crisis in Japan." Speech delivered at a meeting organized by Consulate General of Japan, Boston. Available at www.mofa.go.jp/j_info/japan/socsec/watanabe.html.

West, Loraine A. 1999. "Pension Reform in China: Preparing for the Future." *Journal of Development Studies*, 3: 153–83.

West, Loraine A., and Daniel Goodkind. 1999. "Pension Management and Reform in China." *National Bureau of Asian Research Working Paper* no. 15.

West, Loraine, and Kevin Kinsella. 1998. "Pension Management and Reform in Asia: An Overview." *National Bureau of Asian Research Working Paper* no. 11. Cambridge, Mass.

World Bank. 1999. *Human Development Report*, New York: Oxford University Press, United Nations Development Program.

– 1997. "Old Age Security: Pension Reform in China." In *China 2020*. Washington: World Bank.

Xiao, Jing J., Yinzhou Xu, and Leiqing Peng. 1999. "Worker Responses to Chinese Pension System Reform: Differences by Enterprise Type." *Proceedings of Asian Consumer and Family Economics Association*. Available at www.uri.edu/hss/hdf/xiao/pub/acf99.pdf.

National Pension Fund Websites

Canada
Canada Pension Plan: www.hrdc-drhc.gc.ca
Quebec Pension Plan website: www.rrq.gouv.qc.ca/an/english.htm
CPP Investment Board: www.cppib.ca

Singapore
Central Provident Fund, Government of Singapore: www.cpf.gov.sg

Hong Kong
Mandatory Provident Fund, Hong Kong: www.mpfahk.org

Japan
Ministry of Health, Labour, and Welfare, Japan: www.mhlw.go.jp

United States
U.S. Social Security Administration: www.ssa.gov/

The challenges of attaining security in the Asia Pacific

BRIAN L. JOB[1]

A paradox

Richard Solomon, current president of the U.S. Institute for Peace and former Assistant Secretary of State for East Asia and Pacific Affairs neatly captured the paradoxes underlying the analysis of Asia Pacific security.[2] He began by writing:

> For East Asia at large, the decades ahead hold the contradictory prospects of economic growth along with social and political disruptions that will accompany the ongoing transformations of the still-largely agricultural societies of China and Indonesia; ... the potentially destabilizing by-play throughout the region of global market forces, and perhaps ethnic and religious strife in [various] countries.

But, then in the immediately following sentence, he stated:

> In security terms, East Asia currently enjoys what, on the surface, is a relatively benign environment.

1 Thanks to Emily Munro and Jennifer Quirt of the Institute of International Relations, UBC, for their able research assistance. The author is responsible for any errors or omissions and for the views expressed in this paper, which do not represent those of any institution.
2 See Solomon and Drennan (2001).

And, in a following paragraph ...

> Despite ... positive trends in major power relations, economic growth, the expansion of democracy, and the maturing of multilateral fora in the region, the last decade of the 20th century raised serious questions about the future of East Asia.

Thus, the analyst looking to characterize the security conditions of today's Asia Pacific region is presented with sharp contradictions and conflicting signals. On the one hand, the region can be seen to have weathered the disruptive effects of the ending of the Cold War remarkably well. It has avoided the wars and state collapse that have plagued other regions. Potentially explosive security crises have been defused through major-power diplomacy; e.g., North Korea's development of nuclear weapons, India's and Pakistan's going nuclear, and the Taiwan Straits crises of the mid-1990s. Yet, from another perspective, the picture is less positive. Northeast Asia, in particular, continues to be heavily militarized, the use of force is threatened, and weapons systems that could substantially destabilize security relations are being developed and deployed. Long-standing disputes over territory and sovereignty simmer and boil up unexpectedly. Publics are inflamed by appeals to nationalism and deep-rooted cultural antimonies impede progress towards cooperation between key states.

In economic terms, prognoses are divergent as well. The need to accept principles of market economics has been embraced by all Asian states. The world's two largest polities have made remarkable progress towards fundamental reorientation of their economic life. China's admission to the WTO will represent a significant movement towards a universal, rules-based trading system. However, the downsides of economic boom and bust, of the positive and negative impacts of globalization, are also being felt throughout the region. Economic disparities, within and between countries, have triggered waves of migrating labour, tensions over borders, political unrest, and civil violence targeted against authorities or privileged minorities. Transnational security threats from terrorism, trafficking of persons, money laundering, and drug networks are advancing throughout the region and across the Pacific. The showcase regional institutions of the 1980s and 1990s appear to have run their course, stalled if not stagnating in the wake of the Asian economic crisis, widespread aversion to any functional cooperation that impinges on state sovereignty, and nervous anticipation of the consequences of a new administration in Washington itself facing an economic downturn.

Forces of democracy have made remarkable advances: South Korea, Taiwan, Thailand, Indonesia, and the Philippines have all experienced freely contested elections that produced dramatic government turnovers. Still, these new democracies are immature. Legislative traditions are weak, political parties are undisciplined, and bureaucracies are unresponsive or incompetent. Most of all, leadership is in short supply. Unable or unwilling to undertake steps to reform their economic and political systems, too many office-holders continue to rely on cronyism, corruption, or authoritarian party machines to sustain themselves. Political reform has not kept pace with economic reform; the overall combination of immature, inertial, and retrograde political systems has left the region with what some pessimistic analysts term a "governance vacuum" (*Economist*, 2001).

Comprehensive security and human security

Understanding what constitutes security in the Asia Pacific context must proceed from an appreciation of the breadth of conditions and concerns encompassed by the term "security." In past decades, Asian leaders have relied on phrases such as "national resilience" and "comprehensive security" to mobilize their populations around a singular conception of their state and to formulate grand strategies focused upon the attainment of stable and sufficient resource bases to promote prosperity. External, military threats to state security have generally been secondary considerations, both in the short and long term, to priorities of nation-building and economic development. In the post–Cold War context, external threats have largely disappeared. The preponderance of perceived threats to security arise from domestic circumstances: that is, from the absence of stable political and economic conditions, and from regimes that either do not provide for their populations or directly threaten their people through mismanagement or coercion and violence. The security at issue in these situations of "weak states" is "human security" – the provision of an adequate and safe existence for individual citizens. While Asian leaders are uncomfortable with the interventionist implications of a notion of security that gives priority to the individual over the state, at the same time they have realized that their right and capacity to govern increasingly is based upon delivery to their populations of the economic, social, and ultimately political conditions of human security.[3]

Canada's interests in the security order of the Asia Pacific have followed a similar progression over the years, i.e., expanding from a traditional state-security focus towards a human-security perspective. In generic terms, Canada has looked to the maintenance of a stable and peaceful regional environment through establishment of a sound architecture of multilateral economic and political/security institutions. From within such a context Canada can sustain its voice as a "middle power" on the geographic periphery and can protect its interests through rules-based regimes and multilateral diplomacy. Still, the Asia Pacific has proven to be a tough neighbourhood for Canada to advance this agenda. During the Cold War, the U.S.-managed security order, preoccupied with traditional notions of ideological and military threat, offered little opportunity for Canadian pursuit of multilateral security regionalism.

---

3 There are two distinctive approaches to human security in current debate. One derives from the UNDP's conception of human security as freedom from want, emphasizing food security, poverty alleviation, conditions of health, and environmental stewardship. The other follows the lead taken by Canada, under its former foreign minister Lloyd Axworthy, in defining human security as freedom from fear, i.e., emphasizing the provision of human rights, the responsibility of states for good governance, and the protection of civilians in conflict. In this paper, I opt for a practical interpretation oriented around provision of the human security conditions necessary for sustaining a peaceful and prospering domestic and regional environment – in essence a merging of elements of the two perspectives.

However, as Asian economies began to take off and Canadian trade and investment grew accordingly, Canada took the opportunity to play an active role in promoting multilateral economic institutions and principles of open economic regionalism. The immigration of large numbers of Asians into Canada's three major urban centres broadened the base of Canadian interests on social and political dimensions as well. Thus, today, Canada's primary concerns of security in Asia derive from the combination of our economic and social interests – interests that are advanced through attention to human security by Asian governments and by Asia Pacific institutions. Yes, we obviously remain attuned to the traditional crisis points in regional relations – the Taiwan Straits, the Korean Peninsula, and the South China Sea – but increasingly these too are seen as driven by policies determined by domestic circumstances of the governments involved, including the United States.

This argument is advanced below through a survey of Asia Pacific security organized along the following lines. The second section is a review of the underlying dynamics and forces of change that have swept over the region since the end of the Cold War: the ascendancy of the United States as a global power, the abandonment of ideology, the adoption of market economics, and the impact of transnational political and economic forces captured by the term globalization.

The third section focuses upon the domestic security challenges faced at home by Asian governments and societies. Particular attention is given to the conditions of social dislocation, civil conflict, and leadership crises faced in varying degrees by almost all Asian countries. The fourth section takes up the traditional security agenda: relations among the major powers, the residual Cold War crisis points (the Taiwan Straits and the Korean Peninsula), the dangers of militarization and arms build-ups, and the absence of a regional security framework. Once again contradictions are apparent. In a region of relative great power equanimity, the use of force remains a proclaimed option to settle disputes and states continue to sustain and acquire destabilizing offensive weapons systems.

The final section briefly concludes by attempting to bring all these factors into perspective by re-emphasizing the predominance of economics and domestic conditions for Asia Pacific security. It is the unavoidable necessity of participation in the world economy, coupled with the demands, met and unmet, of populations' safety and well-being that drive the security dynamics of the Asia Pacific. The advancement of Canadian interests in the human-security conditions in the region therefore requires that our economic, foreign assistance, and political/security policies be coordinated to address the human-security needs of Asian societies.

Underlying dynamics and tensions

The regional security order of the Cold War

When considering the present, it is worth recalling the parameters of the Cold War era. The Asia Pacific regional order was sustained through a framework of alliances and client-state relations based on an ideological division that defined not only security, but also political and economic, relationships. The U.S. dominated the Asia Pacific through its hub-and-spokes bilateral arrangements, reinforced by its naval preponderance, forward presence, and nuclear deterrent. While this security architecture kept the major powers from fighting each other directly (i.e., after the Korean War), it certainly did not guarantee peace, nor American victory in land wars on the Asian continent. However, with the communist states unable to sustain a united front, regional dynamics became centred on the geopolitics of the triangular relations among the U.S., China, and the Soviet Union.

In economic terms, the region was bifurcated as well. The centrally planned economies remained isolated from the regional and global economy, their systems gradually sinking under the weight of party decision-making and misallocation of resources. On the other hand, the opening and growth of the U.S. market for Asia and the building of the Japanese and then Korean economies, followed by the integration of Southeast Asia into the regional economy, proceeded according to the principles of open markets. Economic regionalism, therefore, was open and multilateral, in sharp contrast to the bilateral, closed regionalism in security matters.

On the political spectrum, Asian domestic regimes ranged from hard authoritarianism to soft authoritarianism to controlled democracies. Devoted to centralized agendas of regime solidarity and nation-building, one-party systems predominated, ranging from autocratic, Leninist party systems (as in China, Vietnam, and North Korea) to managed democratic systems. The latter, as in Japan, Taiwan, India, and Malaysia, saw a single party sustained in power by an entrenched coalition of business, political, and bureaucratic interests. These regimes, usually with strong support from the West, delivered the domestic and regional stability that facilitated economic growth. As time went on, the price (in literal and figurative terms) of this relative stability came to be the support of patronage and "crony capitalist" systems. These effectively undermined both the economic and political foundations of their countries. While they survived, indeed prospered, throughout the late 1980s and into the 1990s, their demise was inevitable, leaving in their wake weakened states unable to cope with the human security needs and demands of their populations.

The basic features of the post–Cold War security order

For Asia, the ending of the Cold War had two fundamental impacts: the demise of the Soviet Union and the repudiation of the communist social and economic order. With the removal of the geopolitical and ideological overlay of the Cold War, the Asia Pacific regional order over the past decade has been reshaped and realigned in response to the synergistic impact of five structural and ideational forces.

The establishment of the U.S. as the dominant regional and global power

Whereas multipolarity was the byword of the early 1990s, by decade's end the unipolar fact was indisputable. The Gulf War and Kosovo conflicts were benchmarks in demonstrating the superiority of the United States in military and technological terms; the economic crisis reinforced the dominant place of the U.S. economy and its role in global financial management. In the Pacific, the power of the U.S. navy is unchallenged; the U.S. alliance framework has been reoriented and reinforced as the lynchpin of regional security. What is at issue, however, is not the objective capacity of the United States, but instead the subjective questions of how it will define its role in the Asia Pacific, the strategic configuration and deployment of its forces, and the nature of its commitments vis-à-vis Taiwan and the Korean Peninsula.

The abandonment of ideology

There has been a remarkable transformation of relations among Asia Pacific states. Virtually all states have fully engaged their bilateral relations with Asia Pacific countries. Two remarkable events in the year 2000 culminated this process: President Clinton's visit to Vietnam and the North-South Korea summit of Kim Dae Jung and Kim Il Song, the latter effectively ending the Cold War of Northeast Asia. The removal of ideological definition to interstate relations has brought into synchrony the dynamics of political/security and economic dynamics on a region-wide basis. Security regionalism, involving the acceptance of principles of cooperative security and the initiation of regional multilateral security forums, has followed in the footsteps of intraregional economic interdependence and economic regionalism. This is, in my view, the primary reason that relations among the major powers of East Asia are at historically peaceful levels.

The wholescale adoption of market economic principles

At the domestic level, the abandonment of ideology was realized through the decisions of particular communist systems to become market economies. Indeed, it was China's decision in 1978, ten years before the end of the Cold War per se, that gave full impetus to the tide of economic integration of Asia into the global economy. (Twenty-two years later, the final hold-out, North Korea, has admitted the failure of centrally-planned economic life and professes to be reforming its autarkic economic and social existence.) However, having dispensed with their doctrinal creeds, regime leaders now confronted the dilemma of how to legitimize and sustain control over populations whose lives are no longer dependent upon hierarchical

party direction. As long as economic times were good, i.e., populations were satisfied with rising standards of living, the political leadership of Asia could sustain itself on the basis of "performance
legitimacy." But this was a temporary bargain. The economic crisis of
1997 brought to a crashing conclusion the processes of economic dislocation and the effects of rising economic disparities that had been
gradually exposing the weakness of Asian states, in both practical and
ideational terms.

The rise of civil society, globalization, and democratization
The synergistic effects of these various forces can not be considered
separately nor are they yet adequately understood by either decision-
makers or analysts. The rise of civil society in Asia has been the result
of the opening of economies to the vicissitudes of international trade
and investment; the penetration of Western commercial, popular, and
political culture; and the impact of the sustained effects of the western
education of Asian elites. In this context, the rise of urban middle
classes, fed up with their exclusion from patronage and influence networks, could have been expected, as in Taiwan and South Korea. Similarly, one watches the incremental creep towards greater openness and
accountability in China. What has been surprising, and of concern
from a security perspective, has been the mobilization of the popular
masses at local, national, and transnational levels. Regimes have been
brought down, as in Indonesia and the Philippines. Central governments fear the loss of local and provincial control in the face of violent
movements expressing economic, social, or religious grievances.

The domestic security context: governance and human security

Asian societies are still recovering from the shock of the economic crisis of 1997. Region-wide GDP fell over 7 percent in 1998, with key
countries like Indonesia experiencing far more severe drops (up to 40
percent).[4] The crisis brought home the realization that economic

---

4 Asia Development Bank figures.

reform cannot outpace political reform; economic progress cannot substitute for sound political management or indefinitely postpone political reform. Thus, while there have been significant shifts towards transparency, regularity, and democracy in Asian states, largely through elections bringing new regimes to power, transitions have been rocky. With these regimes lacking deep roots in civil society and facing strong opposition from vested interests, their survivability, let along their capacity to implement reforms, remains in doubt. Pessimist analysts speak of the "realistic resignation to prolonged instability and economic malaise" (Vatikiotis 2001a). While this perhaps is an overly bleak characterization, it nonetheless highlights the security implications of the contemporary domestic situation throughout much of Asia.

Two recent sets of studies reinforce these concerns. Mansfield and Snyder (1995) highlight the consequences of changes of government, particularly rapid transitions to democracy. New democratic regimes are not less likely to become engaged in external conflict. Any sudden change in government, either towards democracy or authoritarianism, brings with it the likelihood of an extended period of civil unrest and domestic violence. Second, recent research conducted by the World Bank provides evidence that economic progress is contingent upon establishment of "good governance."[5] Establishment and maintenance of a sound political order, control of corruption, maintenance of the rule of law and a sound regulatory framework, and accountability and transparency are necessary perquisites for sustained economic development.

Assuming, as did many Asian leaders and Western observers before 1997, that economic growth per se was paramount – that performance legitimacy was sufficient to cement the loyalty of the population and that rules-based systems could be established later – proved to be an expense misconception, in both economic and human terms. Moving towards more sound and responsive political orders, while at the same

---

5 See Kaufmann et al. (1999).

time mitigating the fractious tendencies associated with political transition, constitutes a primary security challenge of Asian countries.

A crisis of governance

Unfortunately, most Asian states today exhibit symptoms of being what analysts refer to as "weak states" – states lacking coherent strength on dimensions of institutional capacity, human and non-human resources, and societal cohesion.

There are two elements to the notion of institutional infrastructure: the capacity and competence of the state bureaucracy, i.e., its capability to administer and regulate; and the effectiveness and responsibility of the state's political institutions, i.e., its party system, legislative bodies, and executive councils. Most Asian states are deficient in both aspects; although it might be argued that states like Japan and India are more competent on administrative and political dimensions, respectively. As discussed above, states that have made sudden transitions to democracy or who have upset the hold of long-standing party machines, cannot be expected overnight to build or renew patterns of disciplined party politics and responsible representation of interests. Situations of civil disorder arise when mass publics, frustrated by their lack of voice in government, conclude that demonstrations and violence are the most effective routes to attain results. One sees this result not only in the riots in Jakarta, but also in the local demonstrations and disturbances by Chinese villagers seeking redress against corrupt local officials or arbitrary taxation policies.

Maintaining an efficient and even-handed bureaucracy requires substantial resources and the inculcation of a culture of public service. Neither are found in abundance in many Asian states. State budgets for administration, never generous, have been cut drastically in the aftermath of the economic crisis. Civil servants, especially at lower levels, are virtually required to "supplement" their salaries in order to sustain themselves. At higher levels, the stakes and potential pay-offs are much higher. Absent a tradition of rectitude and effective watch-dog institutions, the levels of corruption throughout Asian bureaucracies range from serious to rampant.[6] Public outrage at the excesses of their leaders has been a major element in fuelling the popular uprisings and civil disorder in Pakistan, the Philippines, and Indonesia.

If, on the one hand, the problem is that the institutions meant to provide representation, regulation, and accountability are not yet rooted in Asian states, the corresponding problem is that traditional elements resistant to reform remain firmly entrenched. These, variously, take the form of party apparatchiks who control key bureaucratic channels (as in Vietnam), powerful governmental agencies with their own agendas (as in Japan), business conglomerates that buy politicians (as in Japan, South Korea, Thailand, Indonesia, etc.), and the military (e.g., in Myanmar [Burma], Pakistan, China, and Indonesia). Political leaders can only go so far in alienating these sectors of their societies, because in the final analysis, "under ... reformist leaders compromise is an essential ingredient of stability" (Vatikiotis 2001a).

The military play an important role in the life of Asian states (as will be discussed below regarding their size and the economic burden they place upon the state). Political leaders depend upon the military to bolster their authority and to sustain order within state borders. The "line of command" can be direct, as in Pakistan or Myanmar, but is more generally indirect, as for example in Indonesia, Vietnam, Laos, and even China. In extreme instances, the military operates independently of political authority, collaborating with business interests or other national militaries for its own purposes. The Myanmarese and Thai militaries, for instance, have cooperated for many years along their borders in illegal logging, mining, and smuggling activities. Principles of civil–military relations are evolving throughout Asia. Establishment of civilian authority over the military is grudgingly being accepted in societies like Indonesia, where traditionally the military

---

6   Transparency International is one of several institutions that attempts to rate levels of corruption in cross-national comparison. On the "2000 Corruption Perceptions Index," for instance, excepting Singapore which ranked 6th, the next-ranked Asian country was Japan (23rd), with Vietnam (76th) and Indonesia (85th) at the bottom of the list. As a benchmark, Canada was ranked 5th and the U.S. 14th.

has been viewed as the guardian of the state, its protector against suspect politicians. Keeping the military out of commercial activities is also difficult, especially as governments such as China's find it hard to provide compensatory resources for foregone profit.

The lack of leadership

The history of post–Second World War Asia has been dominated by leaders who loomed almost larger than life in imparting their vision to their people and the region as a whole. Mao and Deng in China, Sukarno and Suharto in Indonesia, Marcos in the Philippines, Lee Kwan Yew in Singapore, and dynasties of LDP leaders in Japan and KMT leaders in Taiwan.

Today, such leadership is in short supply. Neither democratic nor authoritarian states in Asia have the benefit of strong helmsmen. Consider, for example, the following:

- Myanmar, ruled by a besieged but defiant military junta
- Pakistan, controlled by a military regime, popularly regarded as preferable to recent "democratic" leadership
- Vietnam and Laos, governed by geriatric, communist cadres
- Japan, in a state of inertia, shuffling from one ineffective leader to another
- Malaysia, dominated by a leader willing to sacrifice the legitimacy of state institutions to satisfy his political ends
- South Korea, headed by a visionary leader stymied by traditional power brokers of politics, economics, and the bureaucracy
- Thailand, unable to excise "business" from politics, albeit with a functioning electoral process
- The Philippines, in the hands of an inexperienced politician brought to power through a "soft coup"
- Indonesia, floundering under post-Suharto leadership

Generalization regarding this phenomena is difficult. One syndrome finds leaders whose criteria for popular support paradoxically appear to be their absolute lack of experience in their countries' national political processes, e.g., Estrada in the Philippines. Another syndrome features leaders whose suitability for office derives from their familial ties to past national figures, e.g., Megawati Sukarnoputri in Indonesia or Mrs Bhutto in Pakistan. A further syndrome is of leaders who have simply outlasted and outmanoeuvred their rivals, e.g., in Japan and in the authoritarian contexts of Vietnam, Laos, Myanmar, and to a certain extent China.

The underlying dynamic is one of changing political cultures. The personality and strength of previous leaders was rooted in the social revolutionary and nation-building ethos and circumstances of their times. Thus, until we reach a more general settling of contemporary political orders in Asian societies, a milieu in which leaders are effectively grounded, the staying power and effectiveness of political leaders will remain problematic.

The human-security consequences of weak states

Contemporary Asia presents stark examples of states that are unable and/or unwilling to provide for the well-being of their populations. The most extreme case would be North Korea, its people suffering isolation, starvation, and extraordinary authoritarian control by a regime absolutely committed to retaining power. Another would be Myanmar, whose regime sustains its autocratic control by actively supporting the manufacture and trafficking of drugs and related illegal activities. Dwelling on these examples, however, does not give an adequate overall picture of the human-security condition of Asia.

People in need

Poverty is the pervasive human security condition of Asia. While substantial progress in raising living standards has occurred over the past three decades, over 20 percent of Asia's population continues to exist below internationally defined poverty levels.[7] Indeed, economic

---

7 Asia Development Bank figures, 1999. See www.adb.org/.

growth has exacerbated, rather than alleviated, the circumstances of many. Regional and national disparities have become more pronounced, in part due to government policies that favour one area over another. Traditional agricultural regions have been hard hit through the combined effects of natural disasters, urbanization or migration to urban centres, and the removal of state-supported prices. Governments, having abandoned "iron rice bowl" systems, lack the resources to provide alternative social safety nets for their populations.

Disparities in China are particularly acute. The prosperity of the coastal regions does not extend to those inland. Recent studies indicate that 90 percent of those living in absolute poverty reside in China's western regions. Regional disparities, as measured by per capita GDP and by comparison of consumer expenditure patterns, have increased 10- to 12-fold over the last decade.

Yet these circumstances are by no means unique to China. The economic crisis saw GNP drop from 1996 to 1998 by almost 40 percent in Indonesia, 25 percent in Thailand, and 17 percent in Malaysia, while at the same time it rose 20 percent in China.[8] Recovery, especially in Indonesia, has been slow, confounded by continuing political turmoil and governmental incompetence, which stymie efforts at economic recovery and repel foreign investors. The proportion of Indonesia's 200 million people who now live in poverty has dramatically increased post-crisis, in conditions that fuel regional discontent, separatist movements, and ethnic and religious communal hostility.

Civil violence
Interstate violence is a rare phenomenon in Asia, the dispute over Kashmir being the one long-standing interstate conflict incurring regular casualties. Certainly, the primary cause of violent death is intrastate conflict. Table 1, which provides an overview of conflict in Asia in the 1990s, highlights the concentrations of severe civil violence: in South

---

8 World Bank Report 1999/2000 figures, in current U.S. dollars, as cited in Asia Pacific Foundation of Canada, 2000: 77.

Table 1: Conflict in Asia in the 1990s

Country	Inter-state conflict	Conflicts over territory or secession	Conflicts against or by government	Date(s)	Description
Bangladesh		Chittagong Hill Tract		1982–98	– claims of indigenous people; leader charges that a 1998 peace treaty is not being honoured – reports of between 3000 and 20,000 deaths – reports of up to 50,000 CHT refugees in NE India
Cambodia			Khmer Rouge	1979–98	– 1991 peace accords between the Khmer Rouge and the government; UN-supervised elections in 1993 Khmer Rouge continued attacks; in 1998 all remaining KR forces surrendered – sporadic fighting in the North continues as does government in-fighting
			Anti-regime	2000	– in 2000 violent attacks in the capital were carried out by anti-government forces
China	China-Taiwan			1940s–	– dispute over sovereignty
	Spratly Islands			1988–	– disputed claims to these islands, involves Vietnam, Indonesia, Malaysia, Taiwan, Philippines, and Brunei
				1984–	– Siachen (1000 deaths)
		Xinjian		1997	– Islamic insurgents, separatists, with continued harsh Chinese government crackdown

Table 1 (continued)

Country	Inter-state conflict	Conflicts over territory or secession	Conflicts against or by government	Date(s)	Description
India	Kashmir	Punjab		1948–	– 23,000 deaths; UN operation since 1948
				1948–	– Sikhs are demanding more autonomy, or a separate state called Khalistan
					– *Minor.* Assam, Manipur, Nagaland, Tripura, Bodo – mostly minority populations seeking more autonomy or independence
Indonesia	East Timor			1975–99	– 203,000 deaths; UN operation; independence with a referendum in 1999
		Aceh		1976–	– Free Aceh Movement controls approximately half the villages in Aceh; 3000 deaths – with domestic human-rights organizations charging over 800 killings in Aceh in 2000
		Irian Jaya		1963–	– Free Papua Organization poorly organized, trained, and equipped; 30,000 deaths
		Kalimantan		1997–	– Maduras trans-migration to Kalimantan created conflict with indigenous Dayaks; renewed violence in 1997; 4000 deaths
		Moluccas		1999–	– Christian-Muslim discord in the northern Moluccas; communal warfare with 3000 deaths
			Anti-government	1997–	– Dissatisfaction with Suharto and subsequent Habibie and Wahid administrations, coupled with continued economic crisis
					– *Minor.* Ambon and central Sulawesi; anti-Chinese riots in Jakarta in May 2000

Table 1 (*continued*)

Country	Inter-state conflict	Conflicts over territory or secession	Conflicts against or by government	Date(s)	Description
Laos			Anti-regime Anti-government insurgency	1999–2000 1975	– Series of bombings in the capital; 40 injured – no arrests – Hmong of Laos: long-standing anti-communist insurgency; re-ignited in mid-2000 with low-level hostilities
Myanmar			Democracy movement	1985–	– 9000 deaths; anti-govt. movement led by Aung San Suu Kyi
		Shan		1962–	– independence movement; recent media coverage of adolescent soldiers; God's Army Drug trade; Shan State Army under leadership of Khun Sha
		Kachin		1961–94	– located on the Chinese border, the Kachin Independence Organization signed a peace agreement with the Myanmar Government in 1994
		Karen		1945–	– armed self-determination conflict, with high-level hostilities since 1949; ongoing clashes over the Thai border – *Minor:* Mon, Arakan, Kaya
Pakistan	Kashmir			1948–	– up to 23,000 deaths; UN operation since 1948
Philippines		Mindano		1968–	– 121,000 deaths thus far; in 2000 negotiations between the governments and the Moro Islamic Liberation Front (MILF) fail; Abu Sayyaf Group (ASG) extremist group explode bombs killing 11 and kidnap 21 tourists on Malaysian resort island

Table 1 (concluded)

Country	Inter-state conflict	Conflicts over territory or secession	Conflicts against or by government	Date(s)	Description
Sri Lanka		Tamil		1983–	– Approximately 66,000 lives lost; Liberation Tigers of Tamil Eelam (LTTE)

Notes: (1) All figures of deaths as reported in IISS sources. (2) The Spratly Islands dispute is listed only for China. It could be represented as an inter-state conflict for each of the other claimant states: Vietnam, Indonesia, Malaysia, the Philippines, and Brunei. (3) There is growing evidence of a conflict between Myanmar and Thailand; see Montesano (2001). (4) The table does not include mention of incidents involving North and South Korea, which have been ongoing for over four decades. Of particular note are the naval encounters of 2000 over North Korean maritime boundary incursions. See Shinn (2001).

Sources: Wallensteen and Sollenberg (2000); International Institute of Strategic Studies (2000a); Montesano (2001); Federation of American Scientists (2001); Gurr et al. (2000).

Asia, with intrastate conflicts in Bangladesh, India, and Sri Lanka; in continental Southeast Asia in Cambodia, Laos, and Myanmar; and separately in China, the Philippines, and Indonesia. The available data on casualties are incomplete. Certainly they do not reflect the overall human tragedies of these conflicts, namely, the destruction of local economies, the terrorization and ethnic cleansing of civilian populations, and the attendant spread of disease and damage to the environment. The security and stability of Asian states, including India, Pakistan, Indonesia, Myanmar, the Philippines, and Sri Lanka, are threatened by violent movements advancing ethnic and religious causes.

Voluntary and involuntary movements of people
People fearing for their lives or experiencing desperate economic hardship have traditionally responded by relocating within their own countries or across borders. These movements may be voluntary, as people search for employment, or involuntary, as they flee danger and conflict by relocating within the borders of their own state – thus becoming IDPs, internally displaced persons – or across borders into other states – thus becoming refugees. Tables 2 and 3 give an indication of the massive numbers of people caught up in such movements across Asia. UNHCR figures place the total number of refugees, asylum seekers, IDPs and other persons of concern at over 7 million in 2000. As indicated in Table 2, the single largest concentration of refugees (over 2 million) is located in Pakistan; these persons having fled the violence and natural disasters of Afghanistan.[9] The Asian states of origin of the largest refugee populations are China, East Timor, Myanmar, Sri Lanka, and Vietnam. However, the number of refugees is dwarfed by the estimates of internally displaced persons. It is not surprising that Sri Lanka, Myanmar, East Timor, and Indonesia lead this list.

---

9 Note that Table 2 does not record the movement of persons in the year 2000, but rather the location of refugee populations at the end of 2000. Some of these refugee populations may have initially fled their home countries over a decade ago; e.g., Afghanistan and Vietnam. The East Timor refugees would have been the most recent group.

Table 2: Refugee and IDP populations, Asia 2000 (reported by country of origin and destination)

Country	Refugees in	Refugees from	Internally Displaced Persons
Australia	57,658		
Bangladesh	21,627	2,559	60,000–80,000
Cambodia		36,678	
China	294,110	107,796	
East Timor		40,000	300,000–400,000
India	170,941	6,604	
Indonesia	122,618	8,904	800,000
Japan	3,752		
Korea, North			As many as 100,000
Korea, South			
Laos		17,154	
Malaysia	50,487		
Myanmar		135,645	500,000–1,000,000
New Zealand	4,923		
Pakistan	2,001,466	3,385	30,000–110,000
Philippines	176	45,415	200,000
Sri Lanka		101,206	706,500
Thailand	104,965		
Vietnam	15,000	369,134	
Afghanistan		3,567,000	600,000–800,000
Iran	1,868,000	74,600	

Notes: (1) Chinese IDP data is unavailable. Fluctuations in data for Myanmar and other states produce somewhat unreliable data. See www.refugees.org/world/countryrpt/easia_pacific/cambodia.htm for a country report and explanation of these fluctuations for the pre-2000 period. There were no Cambodia IDPs in 2000, although it should be noted that at the end of 1998 there were 22,000, and massive repatriation is said to have taken place.   (2) UNHCR numbers of less than 100 are not reported. An IDP is defined by the UNHCR as "persons who are displaced within their country and with whom the UNHCR extends protection and/or assistance pursuant to a special request by a competent organ of the United Nations" (UNHCR 2001, "Provisional Statistics on Refugees," Table 1; online: www.unhcr.ch/statist/2000provisional/tab01.pdf. p. 4). Therefore they only record Sri Lankan IDPs (at 706,500) as the IDPs in question for the countries in the table. The bulk of the IDP data is taken from the U.S. Committee for Refugees (2001), Country reports.   (3) Afghanistan and Iran are not technically in Asia, both for Canadian government and UNHCR statistical purposes. Pakistan is, however, and the refugee population there is Afghan.

Sources: United Nations High Commission for Refugees (2001); U.S. Committee for Refugees Country Reports (2001).

Table 3: Refugee and IDP populations, regional comparisons, 2000

Regional	Refugees	Asylum seekers	Returned refugees	IDPs and others of concern	Total
Africa	3,253,250	61,110	933,890	1,732,290	6,250,540
Asia	4,781,750	24,750	617,620	1,884,740	7,308,860
Europe	2,608,380	473,060	952,060	3,252,300	7,285,800
Latin America and the Caribbean	61,200	1,510	6,620	21,200	90,170
North American	636,300	605,630			1,241,930
Oceania	64,500	15,540			80,040
Total	11,675,380	1,181,600	2,509,530	6,890,530	22,257,340

Note: Number in Asian "IDP and others of concern" column – 1,884,740 – does not correspond to number of IDPs and Others of concern on other charts UNHCR has published. These should be seen as definitional problems. See the UNCHR, "Who Is a Refugee?", available online at www.unhcr.ch/un&ref/who/whois.htm, and 1997 UNHCR Handbook on Determining Refugee Status; www.unhcr.ch/refworld/legal/handbook/handeng/hbtoc.htm.

Source: United Nations High Commission for Refugees (2000).

Refugees and IDPs present two types of security concerns. In humanitarian terms, they represent tragedies of human lives. The bulk of these populations consist of women and children, many of whom have little hope of returning to safe and productive lives in their countries of origin. In political/security terms, refugees and IDPs are of significant concern (Weiner, 1996). Not only do they bring substantial economic burdens to their destination countries, they also can become threats to their host's domestic stability and foreign relations. Refugees populations may disturb the ethnic or religious divisions within their new countries; they may unite with those of common ethnicity or religion within their host countries to resist its government. (Note, for example, the support for Islamic militancy in Pakistan, supported by Afghani refugees.) Refugees may utilize their host country as a base for activities within their country of origin. This can lead to outright conflict between the two states in question, as is threatened today, for example, between Thailand and Myanmar. Host countries, even if they wished to do so, will find it difficult to control the activities of their refugee populations. Refugee camps have become the training grounds for insurgency movements, as well as key nodes in smuggling, terrorist, and trafficking networks.

Transnational criminal activity

Weak states lack the capacity to enforce domestic laws and international obligations systematically. Their economies are usually in disarray; regular productive activities will have collapsed in conflict zones, with people desperate for alternative sources of income. In such circumstances, transnational crime flourishes. The black market of goods and services may be the only functioning market. People will be attracted or coerced into illegal activities such as logging and mining, drug production and distribution, and trafficking of goods and people.

Transnational criminal activity in the Asia Pacific has reached levels that pose significant threats to state and human security. In some instances (e.g., Myanmar) the state itself has been corrupted by the collusion of its regime in transnational crime. Continental Southeast Asia has become a major supplier of drugs, natural and synthetic, to the U.S. and Canadian markets. Criminal networks have extended their activities to include money laundering, smuggling of illegal immigrants, sex-trade activities, weapons smuggling, and technology crime.[10] National law-enforcement agencies across the Asia Pacific struggle to combat transnational crime, with varying degrees of success. Their opponents are well organized and well financed, often with the tacit or direct support of government officials. The threat posed by transnational crime, including terrorism, will continue to escalate as long as key Asian states remain weakened by internal conflict, poor economic conditions, and corrupt business and government officials.

Indonesia

Indonesia merits specific mention. A country of over 200 million, the

---

10 One source of information on transnational crime is the CSCAP Working Group on this subject. See its website, www.cscap.org/crime.htm, for reports, publications, and additional internet links.

world's largest Islamic state, Indonesia has been the linchpin of Southeast Asia. Its leadership has been crucial to the advancement of economic and security regionalism. Its economic weight is such that it either drives or retards economic advancement in the sub-region.

In its current condition, Indonesia epitomizes virtually all of the perils to security discussed above. Its economy is fragile, its overall recovery hostage to the incompetence of its political leaders.[11] Ethnic, religious, and regional tensions threaten to Balkanize the Indonesian state. Violence persists in Aceh, Irian Jaya, Malaku, and West Kalimantan. The army has been demoralized and discredited by its record in East Timor and in other provinces. While the Indonesian political landscape has been transformed since the economic crisis hit – the Suharto regime toppled and a government elected through free elections – little else has been accomplished. The obstacles to advancing the economic, military, and constitutional reforms necessary to get the country back on track are enormous. While analysts do not foresee the break-up of the country, neither can they point to signs that suggest movement in the near term in any positive direction.[12]

How Indonesia goes will have a defining impact upon the security of Southeast Asia and will significantly influence the security outlook of the region as a whole.

The regional security context

The longer-term security imperative

By 2015 it is predicted that the peoples of the Asia Pacific will account for 54 percent of the world's population, over half of the world's economy, and a substantial portion of the world demand for energy. Thus,

---

11 That being said, analysts have been surprised by the apparent growth record of the Indonesian economy, not all of which can be accounted for by rising petroleum prices. See Liddle (2001).

12 See, e.g., the excellent series of reports on Indonesia produced by the International Crisis Group (2000) and more recent, less optimistic reports on the presidential crisis.

although this paper focuses on the short- and medium-term future, i.e., a horizon of three to ten years, one must always keep in mind that the longer-term security picture for the Asia Pacific (and for the globe) will be determined by the broader dynamics of demographic transitions, urbanization and patterns of land usage, availability and consumption of natural resources (especially energy and water), and environmental management policies implemented by Asian countries, in particular by China and Indonesia.[13]

The security dilemma of moment is one of governance, juxtaposing the capacity and will of governments to bear short-term economic and political costs – in effect to delay responding to the immediate human-security demands of their publics – in order to provide for the well-being of subsequent generations. At present, unfortunately, the shadow of the future for governments on both sides of the Pacific is very short.

The appeal of the status quo

In relative terms the Asia Pacific has weathered the past two decades remarkably well. Relations among the major powers, while rhetorically charged on occasion, have remained peaceful. Provocative bilateral actions involving the major powers, such as the bombing of the Chinese embassy in Belgrade in 1999, the recent incident on Hainan Island involving a U.S. spy plane, and Chinese missile tests over the Taiwan Straits five years ago, have been resolved. Developments that have threatened regional stability, such as North Korean development of nuclear weapons in the mid-1990s, have been managed through extensive consultation. Indeed, the primary motivation of Asian states has been (and I argue will continue to be) an economic one. That is, in the final analysis, states' security policies have been defined according

---

13 There is a substantial literature on the imperatives of the environment in the Asia Pacific. See, e.g., Dupont (1998), Elliott (2000), and the forthcoming volumes from a major CIDA-sponsored project on Development and Security in Southeast Asia.

to their individual national economic interests and, in turn, the real-ization of their collective interest in sustaining a peaceful and stable regional order.[14]

Throughout the last decade, the first preference of governments in the region has been to maintain the general parameters of the existing Asia Pacific security architecture. However, for a variety of reasons, the status quo is not a viable option for the medium to long term. North Korea as currently managed cannot be sustained; the role and presence of the U.S. in the region will evolve in response to its domestic politi-cal imperatives; the announced deployment of new weapons systems and integrated military communication and surveillance systems threatens to trigger destabilizing arms build-ups; China will be under new leadership within several years; and Indonesia will no longer be as dominant a player in regional political/security affairs.

In its present configuration the current regional order cannot accom-modate changes of this magnitude, nor is it well prepared to manage the traumatic shocks that might arise unexpectedly through develop-ments on the Korean Peninsula or over the Taiwan Straits. It is this sober realization that prompts analysts to advocate the advancement of confidence-building measures and regional-security institutions with greater capacities for preventive diplomacy and crisis management.

Geopolitical competition over regional roles

For a regional environment engaging five major powers (three of the P5, four of the nuclear powers), unipolarity will never be a preferred option for any but the leading power. China and Russia, in particular, but to different degrees India and Japan, all chafe at what they perceive as U.S. hegemony. The rhetoric of the U.S. plans calling for the coun-

---

14 The phrase "It's the economy, stupid," from the Clinton electoral campaign, epito-mized the U.S.'s preoccupation in this regard, as did the direct statement by a senior Canadian official, "Our security interests in Asia are driven by our economic interests."

tering of regional rivalries[15] and, more recently, attaining strategic dominance through development and deployment of new generations of land, sea, and space weaponry has served to inflame these geopolitical tensions.[16] So too will the U.S. "war on terrorism" in Afghanistan. U.S. tendencies towards unilateralism, such as with the Kyoto Accord or arms-control treaties (the CTBT and ABM), do not sit well with Asian states.

On the other hand, virtually all Asian states are reluctant to see the U.S. withdraw its forward presence from the region. China's position on this matter is nuanced. The PRC, in principle, is opposed to the stationing of foreign troops in other countries; i.e., in the long term, China hopes to see U.S. withdrawal from the region. In the short term, however, a U.S. presence on the Korean Peninsula is regarded as a useful constraining influence on both the North and South. There is also ambivalence concerning the U.S.-Japan relationship. Beijing sees utility in this alliance, in that its existence diminishes China's abiding concern over a resurgent Japan. However, China is clearly opposed to any enhancement of U.S.-Japanese (and possibly Korean and Taiwanese) joint capabilities targeted at China.[17]

The key bilateral relationship of the region is between China and the U.S. In this regard, China's security dilemma is acute. China appreciates the U.S.'s status as a global power, but objects to what it regards as U.S. hegemonism and unilateralism. It fears that the U.S. has chosen a strategy of containment over engagement, but has limited capacity to counter such a policy. Indeed, China creates a security dilemma for itself by broadcasting bellicose rhetoric, especially concerning Taiwan, and by building up its offensive military capabilities to counter the U.S. For the foreseeable future, however, China will

---

15 See National Institute of Strategic Studies (2000).
16 See recent U.S. government official statements and U.S. strategic planning documents.
17 From a recent interview of a senior Chinese analyst, Vancouver, May 2001.

remain frustrated. It depends upon access to the U.S. market and US technology for its continued modernization. It lacks viable partners to engage in any effective regional balancing against U.S. power. Indeed, it shares U.S. interests in maintaining a peaceful Korean Peninsula and stable regional environment. The challenge of geopolitics, therefore, is to build a framework for regional security, while managing in the short term those sensitive "hot-button" sovereignty security issues over which there is a risk of irrational action.

Sustained militarization

Defence analysts have had an abiding concern over the high levels of militarization in Asia. Even after the downsizing of most major armed forces, the region is home to the world's five largest forces. (See Table 4.) Russia with just over a million men in arms, comes fifth behind North Korea, India, the United States, and China. Of greater concern is the pattern of national military expenditures and the percentage of GDP spending that they represent. Asian states embarked on a spending spree during the boom times of the 1980s and early 1990s. Concerns that this trend was evidence of dangerous escalation and arms-racing were tempered by arguments that this spending represented either (a) necessary modernization and upgrading of smaller, more professional forces, as China maintained; or (b) show-case, high-tech equipment purchased more for reasons of status than of military utility, as was likely true of many Southeast Asian countries.

The economic crisis brought the latter type of spending to an abrupt end. However, when one examines the post-crisis data, as set out in Table 4, there remain several troubling signals. First, there is little if any diminution of military effort by those states engaged in ongoing disputes, i.e., North and South Korea, Indian and Pakistan, China and Taiwan. Second, governments involved in serious intrastate violence, such as Myanmar and Sri Lanka, divert substantial, scarce national resources to war efforts. Third, levels of support for Asian militaries can be regarded as a sign of their continued role and influence in the political lives of their countries. Cambodia, Indonesia, South (and pre-

Table 4: Summary and statistics on Asia-Pacific states' defence expenditures and armed forces

Country	Defence expenditures					Growth rate (% terms)		Number in the armed forces (1000s)	
	US$ M		as % of GDP						
	1998	1999	1985	1998	1999	1998	1999	1985	1999
Australia	7,682	7,775	3.4	2.1	1.9	4.9	3.0	70.4	55.2
Bangladesh	631	667	1.4	1.9	1.9	5.6	4.4	91.3	137.0
Brunei	386	402	6.0	6.7	6.7	3.0	1.8	4.1	5.0
Cambodia	155	176	n.a.	5.1	5.1	0.0	4.0	35.0	139.0
China	38,191	39,889	7.9	5.3	5.4	7.8	7.1*	3,900.0	2,820.0
India	13,594	14,991	3.0	3.2	3.4	6.7	5.9	1,260.0	1,173.0
Indonesia	967	1,502	2.8	0.8	1.1	−13.7	1.8	278.1	299.0
Japan	38,482	40,383	1.0	1.0	0.9	−2.6	−1.4	243.0	242.6
Korea, North	2,086	2,100	23.0	14.3	14.3	5.0	n.a.	838.0	1,055.0
Korea, South	10,461	12,088	5.1	2.4	3.0	−6.7	10.7	598.0	672.0
Laos	34	22	7.8	2.6	2.3	4.0	3.8	53.7	29.1
Malaysia	1,891	3,158	5.6	2.6	4.0	−7.5	5.4	110.0	105.0
Mongolia	21	19	9.0	1.9	1.9	3.5	3.5	33.0	9.1
Myanmar	2,142	1,995	5.1	5.0	5.0	7.0	7.0	186.0	343.8
New Zealand	898	824	2.9	1.5	1.6	0.2	4.5	12.4	9.5
Pakistan	4,078	3,523	6.9	6.6	5.7	4.0	3.1	482.8	587.0
Philippines	1,521	1,627	1.4	2.3	2.1	−0.5	3.2	114.8	110.0
Singapore	4,936	4,696	6.7	5.6	5.6	0.3	5.4	55.0	73.0
Sri Lanka	995	807	3.8	6.1	5.1	5.6	4.2	21.6	115.0
Taiwan	14,447	14,964	7.0	4.8	5.2	4.7	5.5	444.0	376.0
Thailand	2,124	2,638	5.0	1.7	1.9	−10.4	4.2	235.3	306.0
Vietnam	943	890	19.4	3.5	3.1	3.5	3.5	1,027.0	484.0
United States	279,702	283,096	6.5	3.1	3.1	4.3	4.2	2,151.6	1,371.5
Canada	7,677	7,504	2.2	1.2	1.2	3.2	3.7	83.0	60.6

*The nature and extent of Chinese defence-expenditure increases is the subject of substantial debate. Note that the table reports estimates of overall defence expenditures, estimated in terms of purchasing-power parity, thus the 7+ % increase figures for 1998 and 1999. Official government figures at market rates for the PRC defence budget show an increase of 15% 1998–1999, followed by a further 13% increase 1999–2000. Recent reports are that the 2000–01 increase will be on the order of 17%.

Source: IISS (2000b).

sumably North) Korea, Myanmar, Pakistan, Sri Lanka, and Thailand all stand out in this regard.[18]

The important question, then, is, What is being bought and deployed? By whom? And why? In this regard, the most significant development of the last decade has been the nuclearization of South Asia. While both Pakistan and India were known to be nuclear-capable states, their strategic ambiguity appeared sufficient to sustain deterrence on the subcontinent, while at the same time not violating global norms of non-proliferation. For reasons more to do with domestic politics than external security, India opted to alter its course and become a nuclear power. This has largely been interpreted as a move to achieve the status and recognition that India has long felt denied. Indeed, the declared rationalization for its decision was to mitigate the threat posed to it by a major power, China, rather than the all-too-obvious threat from a lesser power, Pakistan. Pakistan, as expected, swiftly followed suit. The result is a declared nuclear stand-off, both parties claiming that this is a more stable outcome. However, analysts are much less sanguine. They point out that this is a situation of first-strike deterrence, which encourages pre-emption. These weapons are vulnerable to command-and-control system failures and to accidental launch. With a shaky political system in one of the parties (Pakistan), and the continued conflict over Kashmir – and now Afghanistan – South Asia is clearly an insecure environment.

Arms races are considered dangerous because the historical record indicates that disputes between states engaged in arms races are much more likely to turn violent. The question then becomes, "Are the parties to the three long-standing enduring rivalries in the Asia Pacific – North and South Korea, Pakistan and India, and the Republic of China (Taiwan) and the People's Republic of China – engaged in arms-racing behavior?" Empirical investigation suggests that the

---

18 In some instances it could be argued that governments should be spending more on their militaries or allocating their military funding in different ways. Large numbers of underpaid, poorly trained, and ill-equipped soldiers can represent a liability rather than an asset – a potential security problem, rather than a means of addressing them. Indonesia might be such a case.

answer is a qualified "yes."[19] Analysis of patterns of bilateral defence expenditures reveals that arms-racing has occurred, although in an asymmetric rather than balanced fashion. Not surprisingly, Pakistan and Taiwan are seen to be reacting to the arms expenditures of their larger rivals, India and China. When weapons acquisitions themselves are analysed, the Taiwan–China relationship yields further troubling results (Job et al., 2001). The PRC and ROC already appear to be arms-racing concerning combat aircraft, competition that will intensify with the delivery of weapons over the next half-decade. In addition, arms races of ballistic missiles and surface ships loom, all in all suggesting an enhancement of the potentially dangerous security consequences of disputes over the Straits.

New doctrine and new technologies: missiles and missile defence

A more immediately contentious issue concerns the United States' announced intention to develop and deploy theatre missile defence (TMD) systems in Asia and a national missile defence (NMD) system for the U.S. (and perhaps Europe).[20] The fact that these are avowedly defensive weapons systems and that both the actuality and the date of their deployment is distant and problematic has not dampened the debate. This is because the issues at stake are only peripherally about weapons and weapons systems. At present, they have much more to do with (a) defining the roles of the major powers in the Asia Pacific security environment of the future, (b) mitigating the potentially destabilizing actions that states may take in anticipation of deployment of TMD/NMD systems, and (c) sustaining the norms and institutions of the global arms-control and non-proliferation regime.

Asian states, even those favourably inclined towards accepting TMD systems, see the U.S. push for their development and deployment as a component of an overall U.S. strategy that seeks to achieve global technological and military dominance. U.S. strategic-planning documents

---

19 Wallace et al. (1996).
20 Wilkenson (2000).

such as *Joint Vision 2010* reinforce these perceptions with their plans
to technologically revamp the U.S. armed forces, equipping them for
battle-field "management," in which U.S. forces seldom enter direct
combat. For China, in particular, the prospect of U.S.-controlled or
co-ordinated missile defence systems in Japan, South Korea, and Taiwan represents a worst-case scenario (Wallace, 2001). Effectively ring-
ing China, sych systems would represent the containment that Beijing
fears from a hegemonic and unilateralist United States. Furthermore,
China is concerned that an effective NMD system would negate its
limited second-strike nuclear capability and that an effective TMD
system could facilitate a Taiwanese declaration of independence.

In response to this prospect, China is likely to undertake steps to
counteract planned missile defence systems by developing decoys and
related technologies designed to foil the striking capacity of such systems, and by simply dramatically increasing the numbers of missiles
deployed against these systems. Indeed, China has already embarked
upon this course – the overall consequences likely to be a less stable
strategic environment.

Finally, the U.S. has made clear its intention to either bypass or
renegotiate the ABM Treaty in order to proceed to deployment of its
NMD system. President Bush has portrayed the mutual-deterrence
logic of assured second strike as being obsolete. Even though the ABM
Treaty was a bilateral agreement involving only the U.S. and the then
Soviet Union, China and other states have come to regard it as a linchpin in the structure of the contemporary nuclear order. The American
willingness to discard its ABM treaty obligations, coupled with its
refusal to ratify the CTBT and its likely refusal to sign onto the Chem-
ical Weapons Convention (CWC), place in doubt the overall arms-
control and non-proliferation regime for many other states.

The traditional hot spots

The Korean Peninsula
The dramatic gesture of the summit meeting in June 2000 between
Korean leaders was of historic consequence for the Peninsula and for

the region.[21] It effectively ended the residual Cold War of Northeast Asia, setting the stage for a melding of political/security and economic dynamics on a region-wide basis. It signified the mutual recognition of the two countries of their right to exist and interact. While unification remains a rhetorical goal for both sides, the effective desired result for both sides is the normalization of interstate relations. This significant shift in turn has opened the door for bilateral engagement of North Korea by other states, including Canada, and for its joining the ASEAN Regional Forum.

By the mid-1990s, the Kim Jong Il regime had come to face the failure of its economic system and to realize the limited possibilities of utilizing military threats to gain political and economic concessions. Kim Jong Il's requests for humanitarian assistance, and its outreach to South Korea and Kim Dae Jung, were not motivated by regime security considerations. North Korea's primary goal remains the preservation of "its way of life."

Uncertainties remain regarding the prognosis for the North and for inter-Korean developments. First, it remains to be seen whether or not the North Korean regime comprehends and is willing to undertake the fundamental restructuring of its economic and social life. To date, only incremental changes have been undertaken, largely through cooperative initiatives funded by the South.

Second, how to continue and advance North Korean restraint in its weapons-development and proliferation policies poses a difficult challenge. The Clinton administration was very close to a deal regarding North Korean long-range missile development, only to have it falter over concerns regarding verification and uncertainty over committing an incoming U.S. administration. While the North apparently has met the commitments it negotiated concerning nuclear weapons and missile testing, it continues to be a major proliferator of short-range missiles and military hardware into other regions. The North shows little sign of abating its massive homeland defence commitment. Whether a

---

21 For a fuller discussion see Job (2000).

rational concern or not, the North perceives that it lives under serious threat from the United States and its allies. Thus, the chances of success for any strategy for advancing security and stability on the Peninsula will have as much to do with subjective issues of trust as with objective reductions in weaponry.

Third, sustaining continuity and coordination of efforts by the key players dealing with North Korea, namely South Korea and the United States, appears problematic. Kim Dae Jung's sunshine policy hangs by a fragile thread within the South Korean political arena. The Bush administration in its early days purposely or inadvertently sent signals undermining Kim Dae Jung's approach. Washington has clearly staked out a more rigid position concerning any future negotiation with the North. Indeed, President Bush's agenda of increasing defence expenditures and deploying NMD was served by building up North Korea as a "rogue state" that poses a clear and present danger to the U.S.

On the other hand, it is difficult to see how a reversal of the process of engaging North Korea, however frustrating it has been, is in any one's security interests. No state is prepared to deal with the consequences of a "hard landing" scenario brought about either by the sudden collapse of the North or by the outbreak of war. While others, such as the European Union and its members and regional states like Canada, can assist in the process, resolution on the Korean Peninsula ultimately remains a matter that only the two Koreas themselves and the United States can accomplish.[22]

The Taiwan Straits
The ending of the KMT's hold on power and the election of Chen

---

22 This is not to underestimate the role of China, which for reasons of its own as well as in the interests of regional stability, continues to be the major underwriter of the North Korean regime. Its interests are complex; a demilitarized Peninsula with two states likely being its preferred outcome. Japan continues to struggle in its relations with North Korea. It necessarily must be a key player in the economic rehabilitation and reform of the North.

Shui-bian proved to be less destabilizing than Beijing had feared. Of greater concern for Chinese leaders were the initial statements and decisions made by the Bush administration. The new president appeared to break with previous, finely tuned U.S. policy that stopped short of making an explicit commitment to defend Taiwan. His administration's offer to sell advanced military equipment to the Taiwanese, while not fulfilling all of Taipei's wish list, did signal Washington's intention not to allow China to gain any significant military edge over Taiwanese forces. It remains to be seen whether or not the "normal" stalemate will continue.

The status quo is everyone's preference in the short term. In part, this is because of the strength and profitability of their respective economic relationships. In part, it is because the stated goals of the two protagonists appear irreconcilable. In part, it is because of differing perspectives on the trends of the present – Beijing looking to functional, economic integration tying Taiwan to the mainland, Taipei looking to the realization of its identity as an independent, open, democratic society (Laliberté, 1997). The dilemma faced by Chinese leaders is that the latter dynamic appears to have become firmly entrenched on the island. The post-revolutionary Taiwanese generation has few affective ties to the mainland and its system.

China thus has few options. On the regional and global diplomatic scenes, it fights a vigorous holding action against the slightest gesture that could give status to Taiwan. It utilizes strong rhetoric to discourage the electorate on Taiwan and to fend off any action by the U.S., especially the U.S. Congress, that might be construed as violating U.S.-China accords concerning the Taiwanese relationship. However, Beijing has found that when it raises the decibel level too high, its rhetoric tends to backfire. So too do its attempts to intimidate Taiwan through the show of force; the U.S. response to the 1996 missile tests serve to demonstrate the profound military superiority it enjoys.

Security analysts have three worries: first, that an aging and soon-to-be-retired Chinese leadership might seek a final solution to the Taiwan problem; second, that a Taiwanese leader could make a pre-emptive attempt to claim independence, leaving Beijing's leaders no choice but to respond violently; and third, that with ever-increasing levels of weaponry deployed around the Straits an accidental action by one side or the other could trigger a full-scale conflict. None of these three (admittedly low probability) outcomes is driven by logic. The dilemma is that domestic politics determines whether or not the first two occur. The prospect of the third is tied to the competitive arms-acquisition process noted earlier.

Building a regional security architecture: bilateral and multilateral approaches

To varying degrees since the end of the Cold War, Asia Pacific states have become convinced of the need for a framework of regional institutions for the management of security matters. This has been translated into a movement towards multilateral institutions, at the official (Track 1) and unofficial (Track 2) levels. The establishment of the ASEAN Regional Forum has built upon the modalities of Southeast Asian security cooperation, as embodied in ASEAN. Track 2 institutions and processes have burgeoned, extending from tentative initiatives at confidence building to engage academics, NGOs, experts, and officials ("in their private capacities") in dialogues across the spectrum of comprehensive security. The capstone of these is the Council for Security Cooperation in the Asia Pacific (CSCAP), an inclusive, regional institution intended to function as the Track 2 analogue for the Asean Regional Forum.[23]

The achievements of regional security institutions in the Asia Pacific must be appreciated in light of the various differing national perspectives regarding their role. For major powers, especially the U.S., matters of security remain bilateral. Multilateral institutions are a helpful supplement to bilateral arrangement, useful for dialogue and confidence building, but not dispute management. Most Asian states are leery of any tendency towards creating institutions that might impinge

---

23 See Ball (2000).

upon national sovereignty. Accordingly, they are unwilling to see the CSCAP or the ARF or even ASEAN establish a formal institutional base or be given any mandate for direct action.

The dilemma, however, is that the region remains without any substantial mechanism for the management of security crises. Instead, the fallback is a reliance on ad hoc consultation among the major powers in circumstances that threaten regional stability, e.g., in response to the North Korean threat of nuclear development. Yet ad hoc processes are subject to the vagaries of bilateral relations. They do not facilitate cooperation on a broader spectrum of security concerns, such as arms control and non-proliferation; nor do they provide any standing platform for early warning, preventive diplomacy, or crisis management.

On the economic dimension, principles of open regionalism have prevailed, it being in the interests of the U.S. and Japan, as well as the smaller economies, to sustain open market access. Thus, the development of the Asia Pacific Economic Cooperation (APEC) forum advanced apace with the economic boom of the 1980s and 1990s, as did parallel, Track 2 entities that brought together private and public-sector representatives on a regular basis. The economic crisis of 1997 exposed several telling shortcomings of this institutional framework. First of all (and not surprisingly), it was incapable of coordinating a response, albeit a limited one, to this full-scale economic disaster. The pre-eminent role of global institutions, effectively under U.S., leadership had to be brought to bear, albeit belatedly. Second, the failure of this regional institutional process. to respond to the broader context and vulnerabilities of Asian societies to the impact of economic change and sudden shocks became apparent. As the leaders of the World Bank themselves acknowledged, the economic crisis was, in effect, a crisis of human security leading not only to dramatic economic loss but also to social and political disruption.

Defining and advancing Canadian security interests

Canadian observers regard the Asia Pacific security environment as being largely stable as far as major power relations are concerned. Serious concerns, however, are raised over the potential for conflict in South Asia and the collapse of Indonesia. The situations on the Korean Peninsula and over the Taiwan Straits are regarded as having a high potential for a security failure; however, in neither case is violence between the major protagonists viewed as likely in the short to medium term.

Canada's engagement in the Asia Pacific has undergone subtle changes over the past decade. While Canada now makes a conscious effort to be seen as having a relevant role in the region,[24] the traditional security concerns noted in the last paragraph do not preoccupy Canadian foreign and defence policy officials. Canada's recent military presence in the region as part of the UN Mission to East Timor – a multilateral, peacekeeping deployment of armed forces and civilian police – epitomizes the two key dimensions of Canada's security policies towards the Asia Pacific. First, we have sought to create and support multilateral approaches to regional security management. Canada actively encouraged ASEAN efforts to create the ARF; it was an innovative force in the development of Track 2 security dialogues in regional and sub-regional contexts. Second, Canada through its foreign ministry and aid agency, CIDA, has become increasingly focused upon alleviation of the human-security conditions of Asian societies. As has been argued above, this approach is in tune with the security needs and looming security dilemmas of the short and medium term in the Asia Pacific.

That being said, from Ottawa's point of view Asia Pacific regional institutions have lost momentum. The APEC forum appears to have run its course and ceded much of its role to the WTO. On the security side, the ARF appears unlikely to move beyond its current status as a meeting place, although it remains valuable. Track 2 institutions are undergoing a metamorphosis. Those that engage participants who represent governmental positions will continue to exist as confidence-

---

24 See Sens and Job (2001) as well as the chapters by Job in the annual *Asia Pacific Security Outlook* volumes of 1998, 1999, and 2000.

building mechanisms, designed to socialize and engage states less familiar with the norms and processes of multilateralism. Those that engage representatives of civil society and are more responsive to the interests of Asian citizens per se are likely to have more effective impact upon human-security problems. In the last few years Canada has focused its efforts, largely through CIDA-funded programs, on fostering the development of civil-society organizations, both nationally and regionally.

Bilateral relations on security matters have been cultivated as well. Beginning in 1996, an active Canada-Japan Agenda of Security Cooperation has supported consultation among officials, academics, and NGOs. Canada, at official and unofficial levels, now conducts security discussions with numerous others, including North Korea, Mongolia, South Korea, China, and most Southeast Asian states.

Although a new Liberal majority government and a new foreign minister came into office in 2001, observers have noted little overall change in Ottawa's approaches to Asia. Investment and trade relations remain a high priority, with China, Japan, and Indonesia sustaining their central place on the official, bilateral agenda. Notably, Canada has taken steps to re-engage its relationship with India. While the rhetoric of human security has been toned down, the reality of Asia Pacific security, as outlined above, dictates that Canadian policy may well become more rather than less oriented towards human-security considerations.

REFERENCES

Alagappa, Muthiah. 2001. *Coercion and Governance: The Declining Political Role of the Military in Asia.* Stanford, CA: Stanford University Press.
Asia Development Bank. 1999. www.adb.org/.Documents/EDRC/Briefing_ Notes/BN017.pdf.
Asia Pacific Foundation of Canada (APF). 2000. *Canada's Asia Review.* Vancouver: APF.
Bajpai, Kanti. 2000. "Human Security: Concept and Measurement." *Kroc Institute Occasional Paper* no. 19:OP:1. August.

Ball, Desmond. 2000. *The Council for Security Cooperation in the Asia Pacific: Its Record and Its Prospects.* Canberra: Strategic and Defence Studies Centre.

Calder, Kent. 2001. "Regional Security in Asia." *Foreign Affairs*, 80/1: 106–22.

CSCAP (Council for Security Cooperation in the Asia Pacific) Working Group. www.cscap.org/crime.htm.

Dupont, Alan. 1998. *The Environment and Security in Asia Pacific.* Adelphi Paper 319. London: International Institute of Strategic Studies.

Economist, The. 2001. "The Greatest Leap Forward." April 7: 17.

– 2000. "The Future That Might Have Been." December 16: 84.

Elliott, Lorraine. 2000. "Environment, Development and Security in Asia-Pacific: Issues and Responses." In Mely C. Anthony and Mohamed Jawhar Hassan, eds., *Beyond the Crisis: Challenges and Opportunities*, 2: 175–206. Kuala Lumpur: Institute for Strategic and International Studies Malaysia.

Federation of American Scientists. 2001. "The World at War." Online: www.fas.man/dod101/ops/war/index/html.

Gurr, Ted Roberts, et al. 2000. "Peace and Conflict 2001: A Global Survey of Armed Conflicts, Self-Determination Movements, and Democracy." Center for International Development and Conflict Management. Online: www.bsos.umd.edu/cidcm/peace.htm.

International Crisis Group (London). 2000. *Indonesia's Crisis: Chronic but Not Acute.* See www.intl-crisis-group.org/.

International Institute of Strategic Studies (IISS). 2000a. "The 2000 Chart of Armed Conflict." London: Oxford University Press.

– *The Military Balance: 2000–2001.* London: Oxford University Press.

Job, Brian L. 2000. "Implications of Recent Developments on the Korean Peninsula for Regional Security Cooperation." Paper presented to the Seventh Meeting of the CSCAP North Pacific Working Group. Manila, December 9–10.

Job, Brian L., and Michael D. Wallace. 1997. "The China-Taiwan Enduring Rivalry: Militarized Disputes, Rhetorical Complexity and Arms Racing?" Paper presented to the International Studies Association, 38th annual convention, Toronto, 18–22 March.

Job, Brian L., Michael Wallace, Jean Clermont, and André Laliberté. 2001. "Rethinking Arms Races: Asymmetry and Volatility in the Taiwan Case." *Asian Perspective*, 25/1.

Kaufmann, Daniel, Aart Kraay, and Pablo Zoido-Lobaton. 1999. "Governance Matters." *World Bank Policy Research Department Working Paper* no. 2196. www.worldbank.org/wbi/governance/gov_data.htm.

Laliberté, André. 1997. *Taiwan: Between Two Nationalisms.* Vancouver: UBC Institute of International Relations.

Liddle, William. 2001. "Indonesia in 2000." *Asian Survey*, 41/1: 208–30.

Manning, R.A. 2000. "The Asian Energy Predicament." *Foreign Affairs*, 42/3: 73–88.

Mansfield, Edward, and Jack Snyder. 1995. "Democratization and the Danger of War." *International Security*, 20/1: 5–38.

Montesano, Michael J. 2001. "Thailand in 2000." *Asian Survey*, 41/1 (January/February): 171–80.

National Institute of Strategic Studies. 2000. *Strategic Assessment 1999: Priorities for a Turbulent World*. Washington: National Defense University.

- 2000. *Strategic Assessment 1999: Priorities for a Turbulent World*. Washington: National Defense University. Online: www.ndu.edu/inss/sa99/sa99cont.html.

Sens, Allen, and Brian L. Job. 2001. "Canada 2001." In Richard Baker and Charles Morrison, eds., *Asia Pacific Security Outlook 2001*. Tokyo: Japan Centre for International Exchange.

Shinn, Rinn S. 2001. "North Korea: Chronology of Provocations, 1950–2000." CRS Report for Congress. Washington: Library of Congress.

Solomon, Richard H., and William M. Drennan. 2001. "The United States and Asia in 2000." *Asian Survey*, 41/1: 1-2.

Transparency International. 2000. "2000 Corruption Perceptions Index." www.gwdg.de/~uwvw.

United Nations High Commissioner for Refugees (UNHCR). 2001. "Provisional Statistics on Refugees and Others of Concern to the UNHCR for the Year 2000." www.unhcr.ch and www.refugees.org.

- 2000. "Refugees by Numbers, 2000 Edition." www.unhcr.ch.

U.S. Committee for Refugees. 2001. "Country Report: Bangladesh." Online: www.refugees.org/world/countryrpt/scasia/bangladesh.htm.

- "Country Report: Burma." Online: www.refugees.org/world/countryrpt/easia_pacific/burma.htm.

- "Country Report: East Timor." Online: www.refugees.org/world/countryrpt/easia_pacific/easttimor.htm.

- "Country Report: Indonesia." Online: www.refugees.org/world/countryrpt/easia_pacific/indonesia.htm.

- "Country Report: Pakistan." Online: www.refugees.org/world/countryrpt/scasia/pakistan.htm.

- "Country Report: Philippines." Online: www.refugees.org/world/countryrpt/easia_pacific/philippines.htm.

Vatikiotis, Michael. 2001a. "Trouble at the Top: Asia's Blundering Leaders." *Far Eastern Economic Review*, January 11: 14–19.

- 2001b. "From Chaos to Despair." *Far Eastern Economic Review*, February 15: 17.

Wallace, Michael D. 2001. "China and Missile Defence." Paper presented to annual meetings of the International Studies Association.

Wallensteen, Peter and Margareta Sollenberg. 2000. *Journal of Peace Research*, 37/5 (Stockholm: Swedish Institute of Peace Research).

Warr, Peter G. 2000. "Poverty Incidence and Economic Growth in Southeast Asia." *Journal of Asian Economics*, 11/4 (Winter): 431–42.

Weiner, Myron. 1996. "Bad Neighbors, Bad Neighborhoods: An Inquiry into the Causes of Refugee Flows." *International Security*, 21/1: 5–42.

Wilkenson, Dean A. 2000. *Ballistic Missile Defence and Strategic Stability*. Adelphi Paper 334. London: International Institute for Strategic Studies.

World Bank. 2000. "Table: Poverty Line and Number of Population Below the Poverty Line 1976–2000." Online: www.worldbank.or.id.

Canadian business in East Asia: Better than expected

KEITH HEAD AND JOHN RIES

At the time the first volume in this series was published in 1995, there was much talk in the business media that Canada was "missing the boat" by not having a larger business presence in East Asia. Our initial paper assessed these concerns by examining Canada's trade and investment position in the region and discussing the reasons why the returns to additional business there might be higher than those earned elsewhere. At the time of the Asian crisis, a period characterized by dramatic currency depreciation and contraction of economic activity, Canada was at least temporarily thankful that it had missed this boat. Countries that had not, such as Australia, saw significant markets close and suffered economically. In more recent years, growth has resumed and substantial business opportunities in East Asian economies have reappeared.

In our contribution to this final volume in the series, we re-examine the Canadian business presence in ten East Asian economies to see to what extent Canada has been successful in tapping into these markets. The first portion of the chapter will be devoted to compiling information from a variety of sources to construct a picture of Canadian business in Asia and to ascertain how it has evolved over the decade. The picture that emerges from this section is that Canadian business in East Asia seems to have remained fairly small.

A small business presence in East Asia might be not surprising or alarming, however. After all, these are distant countries with unique cultures and business practices. With the exception of Japan and China, the East Asian economies are very small relative to that of Canada's primary trading partner, the United States. To fully assess how well Canada is doing in a target market, we need to formulate a clear idea of what should be expected. The second section of the chapter benchmarks the Canadian experience in these economies against those of other developed, non-Asian countries. We utilize detailed trade statistics for ten Western countries exporting to the ten East Asian economies and construct a benchmark useful for gauging relative performance.

In the analysis, we assess the Canadian performance against that of other exporting nations disaggregated by industry. The broad picture that emerges is that Canada's export performance is on par or even better than most of the comparison group. Its strongest performance is in the food, wood, and metal industries even after we make adjustments for Canada's comparative advantages in these industries. Canada's performance, however, is outstripped by Australia. We find that Canada is particularly successful in Japan, China, and Indonesia but unsuccessful in other East Asian markets.

The third section examines trends in Canada's and other exporters' performances over time to assess Canada's prospects for the future. Our analysis reveals that exporter performance has been converging towards the constructed benchmark. However, this adjustment is slow, implying that unusual early success in reaching particular markets may be expected to continue into the future. On the other hand, it is likely to be difficult to dramatically increase exports in markets where an exporter has performed poorly.

Canadian business presence in East Asia

As with our earlier study, we consider ten economies in East Asia. At times, it will be convenient to group the five into two groups. The first group comprises Japan and the four tigers – Taiwan, Hong Kong, Singapore, and South Korea. The second group includes Indonesia, Thailand, Malaysia, Philippines, and China. Figures 1 and 2 depict each economy's growth rate of real per capita GDP from 1991 to 2001.

Figure 1: Per capita real GDP annual growth rates, 1992–2001

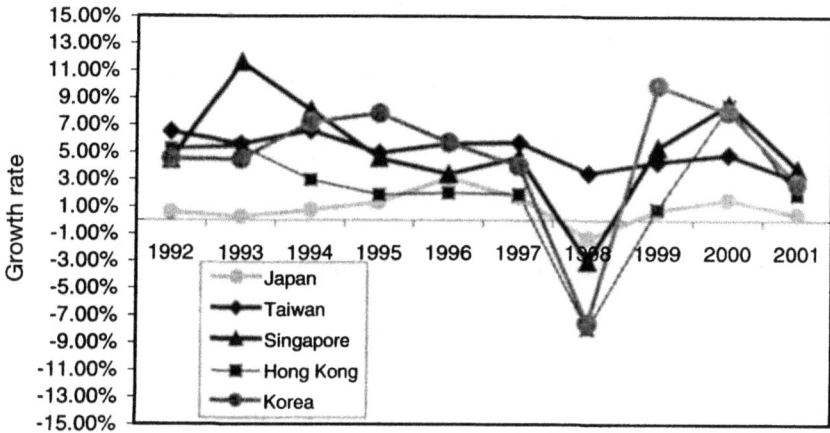

Source: World Bank.

Figure 2: Per capita real GDP annual growth rates, 1992–2001

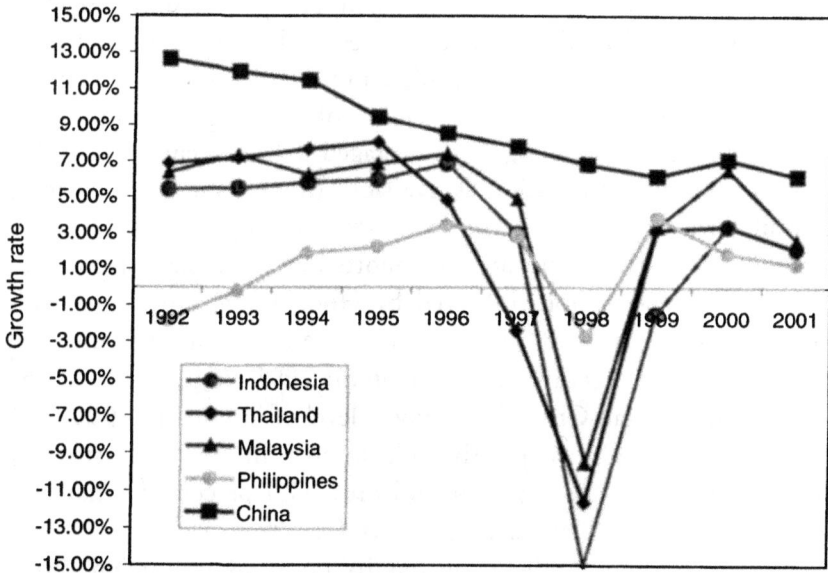

Source: World Bank.

The 1998 Asian crisis is quite evident in the figures, which reveal that all the economies experienced contraction in 1998 except for China and Taiwan. The most pronounced declines are for Malaysia, Philippines, and Indonesia, calculated as −9.54, −11.65 percent, and −15.06 percent respectively.

The negative growth of GDP was short-lived, however, as the economies rebounded and registered positive growth in 2000. In that year, with the exception of the Philippines and Korea, per capita GDP growth exceeded 3 percent. The 2001 figures are those estimated by the World Bank. They foresee a slowdown in growth, generally in the range of 2 percent. China is projected to have the fastest growth, estimated at 6.2 percent.

Table 1 provides information on the market size and market potential of these economies. The first column lists population and the second column income. Obviously, the ten economies are of varied sizes. China's 2000 population is 1.26 billion, but its income level is a modest US$ 3800 measured at purchasing power parity exchange rates. Japan has a large, wealthy population, but the previous figures showed extremely low growth of incomes in Japan. Hong Kong and Singapore are rich but small, and the other economies exhibit varying market sizes.

The second two columns of Table 1 indicate the degree of new foreign business in these economies in terms of sales of goods and foreign direct investment. Import growth averaged 8.27 percent for the nine countries where information is available (trade data for Taiwan is unavailable). China's import growth was a strong 15.95 percent. In terms of the absolute amount of imports in U.S. dollars, Japan was first with $280.4 billion, followed by Hong Kong and China with $177.9 billion and $158.5 billion. With the exception of China, the growth of imports occurred primarily in the 1991–96 period, as all the countries other than China had a lower level of imports in 1999 than they did in 1996. On the positive side, imports in 1999 grew strongly in some countries – 29.1 percent in Korea, 17.1 percent in Thailand, and 12.7 percent in Malaysia.

The last column in the table reports on flows of foreign direct investment (FDI) into Japan, Singapore, Korea, Malaysia, Thailand,

Table 1: Economic characteristics of East Asian economies

Country	Population, 2000 (millions)	GDP/Capita at PPP,* 1999 (US$)	Annual import growth average % change, 1991–99	Average annual FDI** inflows, 1991–98 (US$ millions)
Japan	126.5	23,400	4.23%	1,473.0
Hong Kong	7.1	23,100	7.98%	n/a
Singapore	4.2	27,800	7.81%	6,543.2
Taiwan	22.2	16,100	n/a	n/a
Korea	47.5	13,300	7.59%	1,958.5
Malaysia	21.8	10,700	9.39%	4,730.5
Thailand	61.2	6,400	4.82%	2,798.5
Philippines	81.2	3,600	12.72%	1,191.4
Indonesia	224.8	2,800	3.97%	2,779.4
China	1,261.8	3,800	15.95%	30,105.0
East Asia	1,858.3	13,100	8.27%	51,579.5

*Purchasing power parity
**Foreign direct investment

Sources: World Bank, except GDP/capita is from CIA World Factbook.

Philippines, Indonesia, and China (data for Hong Kong and Taiwan are not available). FDI figures reflect investments where the investor has a controlling stake. Total investment in the eight countries averaged US$ 51.6 billion in the 1991–98 period. The lion's share, $30.1 billion, went to China. Malaysia, Thailand, and Indonesia were the next biggest recipients of FDI, averaging $4.7 billion, $2.8 billion, and $2.8 billion.

Figure 3 provides a bit more detail in the evolution of FDI in Asia. In 1985, there was little investment in the region. The large explosion of investment occurred in the early 1990s, with investment levelling off in the 1996–98 period. Again, this figure shows that China has been heavily favoured by investors.

Overall, the information presented so far indicates that the attractiveness of Asia is largely confined to China. Its steadily growing economy is a source of demand for foreign goods. Investors are attracted to China's large market as well as its low-cost labour. However, there are positive developments in other countries. Taiwan, Singapore, and

Figure 3: Inflows of foreign direct-investment to East Asia, 1985–98

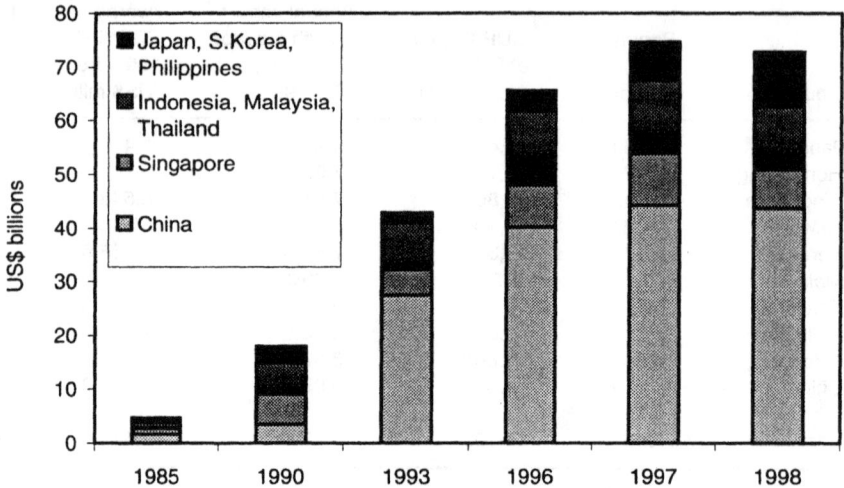

Source: World Bank, World Development Indicators.

Hong Kong boast relatively wealthy economies that are continuing to grow. Malaysia, Thailand, and Indonesia strongly increased their imports in 1999 and continue to be hosts to significant foreign investment. Now we turn to Canadian data to see how Canada has fared in the region over the past decade.

Figure 4 shows Canada's trade position with the ten economies over the 1984–2000 period. It does not present a pretty picture if one's objective is steadily increasing exports and positive trade balances. Over the entire period, Canada has run a merchandise trade deficit. This deficit bounced around in the range of 5 to 20 percent of total trade until 1997 when it began to grow, attaining a level of 41.3 percent of total trade in 2000. In absolute terms, the deficit was C$ 27.7 billion that year. Canadian exports to East Asia peaked in 1995 at C$ 24.4 billion, declined to C$ 17.7 billion in 1999, and rose slightly in 2000. In 2000, Canadian were exporting C$ 4.8 billion less to Asia than they were in 1995.

We note that there is likely to be downward bias in the export fig-

Figure 4: Canadian trade with East Asia, 1984–2000

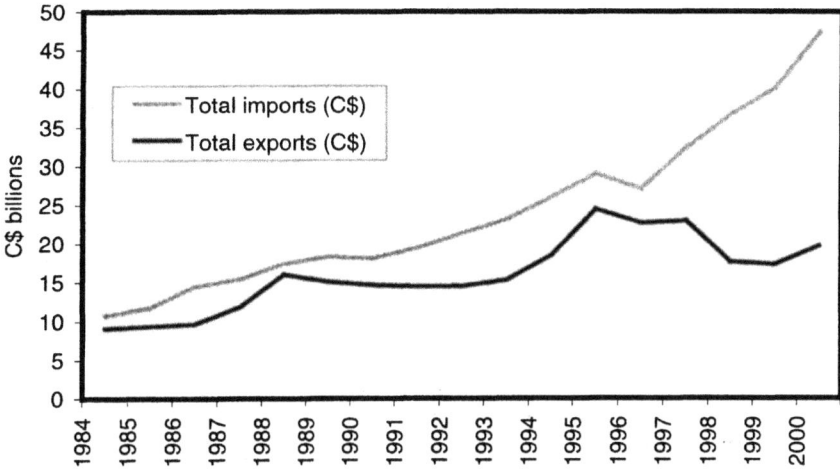

Source: http://strategis.ic.gc.ca.

ures represented in Figure 4. Statistics Canada (www.statcan.ca/english/sdds/2201.htm) reports that "Custom-based export statistics may understate and/or incorrectly portray the destination of exports." This occurs because "the country of final destination is inaccurately reported" or "Customs are typically more vigilant with respect to goods entering the country than they are for goods leaving the country." It is likely that some Canadian exports to East Asia are routed through the United States and not properly reported. Thus, the Canadian trade deficit may not be as large as Statistics Canada data indicates.[1] However, under-reporting should not underlie the increased trade deficit that has occurred over time.

Figure 5 reveals that Canada ran a merchandise trade deficit with every single one of the ten East Asian economies in 2000. The largest deficit, C$ 9.42 billion, was with China, followed by Japan with a C$ 6.3 billion deficit. The figure shows that these are the two most impor-

---

1 We thank Ed Safarian for alerting us to this issue.

Figure 5: Trade flows between Canada and ten East Asian economies, 2000

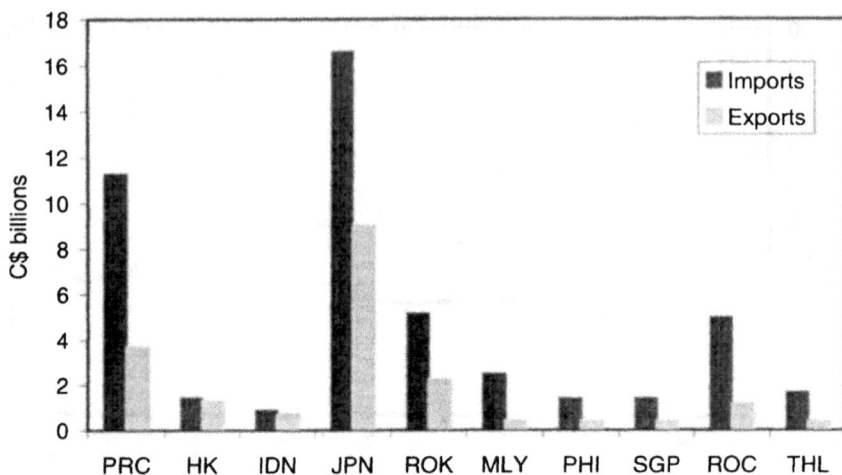

Source: http://strategis.ic.gc.ca.

tant trading partners for Canada, with Japan by far the largest destination for Canadian exports. The backdrop for these numbers is Canadian trade with the United States. In 2000, Canada exported C$ 358.9 billion to the U.S. and imported C$ 229.3 billion. Total trade with Asia, equalling C$ 67.0 billion, pales in comparison.

Figure 6 depicts the commodity composition of Canadian exports to East Asia. The majority of Canadian trade is in natural resource-intensive products. The largest items are pulp (15 percent of exports), wood (12 percent), cereals (5 percent), and coal (5 percent). The figures in parenthesis represent the export share in 1992. They reveal some volatility – pulp's share was 7.5 percent in 1992 but 15 percent in 2000 – but the overall picture is the same. Canada's export success revolves around natural resources.

Services constitute a growing share of Canadian trade with East Asia. Excluding payments to capital services, services trade comprises commercial services, travel services, and transportation services. Commercial services include financial, information, and construction services, as well as royalty and license fees. In our initial contribution to

Figure 6: The composition of Canada's exports to East Asia, 2000.

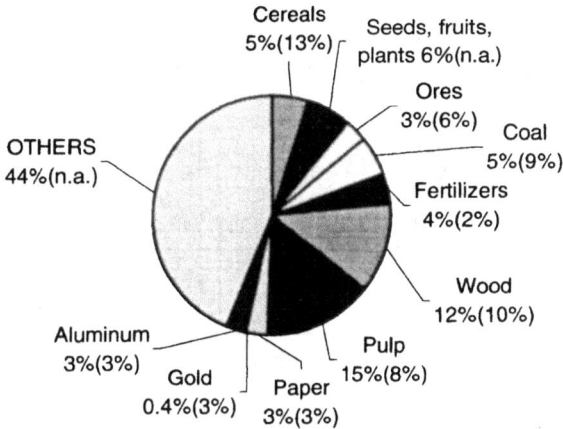

Note: Numbers in parentheses show share in 1992.

this series, we postulated that Canada might have a role in contributing to the growing service sectors of the East Asian economies.

Table 2 reveals that Canada has had modest success selling services to East Asia. In 1998, commercial services were C$ 1.58 billion against C$ 1.37 billion in imports. These exports represent a small portion of Canada's C$25 billion in commercial-service exports that year, of which sales to the U.S. accounted for three-fifths. However, commercial-service exports to East Asia have more than doubled since 1993. Sales of commercial services were fairly evenly distributed across the ten East Asian economies. The economy with the largest commercial-service trade with Canada is Japan to whom Canada exported C$ 333 million and imported C$ 808 million. Trade in travel and transportation services to East Asia was roughly the level of trade in commercial services in 1998. That year, Canada exported C$ 1.3 billion in travel services and imported C$ 491 million. Exports of transportation services were C$ 1.1 billion and imports C$ 1.4 billion. Exports of travel and transportation services to East Asia have not been growing as fast as exports of commercial services.

In 1998, Canadian exports of commercial, travel, and transporta-

Table 2: Canadian trade in commercial services, 1991–98 (in millions of dollars)

	East Asia		United States		World	
	Receipts	Payments	Receipts	Payments	Receipts	Payments
1991	461	458	6,243	9,275	9,814	13,208
1992	549	427	7,052	10,031	11,080	14,050
1993	709	572	8,332	12,046	13,113	16,859
1994	886	742	9,843	13,706	15,492	19,602
1995	1,156	892	10,412	14,520	16,805	20,260
1996	1,378	950	11,553	16,420	19,357	22,381
1997	1,499	1,084	13,264	17,615	21,936	24,792
1998	1,580	1,366	14,846	19,254	25,039	27,466

Source: Statistics Canada, catalogue #67-203.

tion services to East Asia totalled C$ 4 billion or 18.5 percent of total exports (services plus merchandise) to the region. This is up from a total of C$ 2.2 billion (13.4 percent of total trade) in 1992. While service exports to East Asia are small relative to Canadian trade worldwide, at least they are growing, a trend that contrasts with the shrinking Canadian merchandise exports to the region.

Another dimension of business activity is foreign direct investment. Recall that Table 1 shows China, Malaysia, Thailand, and Indonesia to be the largest recipients of FDI, with China hosting more than half of the recent inflows in the region. FDI is valuable because it facilitates exports of goods and serves as a vehicle for lowering production costs.

Unfortunately, data on Canadian direct investment in East Asia is extremely limited. In our initial contribution to this series, we reported that total FDI in Japan, Korea, Hong Kong, Singapore, Taiwan, Malaysia, and Indonesia was C$ 6.6 billion in 1992 (Statistics Canada, 1992). Japan accounted for C$ 2.6 billion. In 1998, the latest year for which detailed data is available (OECD, 2001), Canadian FDI in the seven East Asian economies plus China had risen to C$ 11.1 billion. This number may be compared to the C$ 17.0 billion in exports to these economies. Japan's total grew to C$ 3.2 billion, while investment to China stood at C$ 464 million.

FDI data available for Japan show a significant increase in Canadian direct investment in the last few years. The stock of Canadian direct investment there jumped by C$ 1.54 billion in 2000, bringing Canada's position in Japan to $5.5 billion. This investment was smaller than Japanese direct investment in Canada – C$ 8.4 billion in 2000.

Is the level of FDI in 1998 satisfactory? The OECD reports that U.S. and Australian FDI stocks in the eight East Asian economies were US$ 105.6 billion and US$ 5.1 billion, respectively. If we normalize FDI performance by dividing the total by GDP in 1998, we get 0.012, 0.012, and 0.014 for the U.S., Canada, and Australia. Thus, Canada's FDI in East Asia appears to be roughly on par with that of the U.S. and Australia. However, the $11.1 billion stock of FDI in East Asia in 1998 is small relative to Canada's C$ 128.5 billion in the U.S. and C$ 24.8 billion in the United Kingdom in that year.

Data limitations greatly restrict our ability to draw conclusions about Canadian performance in East Asia in terms of direct investment. Comprehensive information does not exist showing Canadian investment by country and industry, making it impossible for us to pinpoint areas of strengths and weakness. We can say, however, that 1998 data and comparisons with the United States and Australia indicate that the level of Canadian FDI in the region of $11.1 billion is what might be expected given Canada's economic size.

Benchmarking Canadian trade with the region

There is a natural tendency to measure economic success in dollars and cents. However, for trade the numbers are in the millions or billions and one requires some kind of perspective to determine whether any given dollar amount represents a "success" or a "failure." Simple comparisons to the past can be misleading, since there is general growth in the world economy and particularly large growth in East Asia for most of the last quarter-century. In this section of the paper, we will provide some perspective on Canada's trading performance in East Asia by evaluating it relative to other Western countries. Our comparison group comprises the United States, the United Kingdom, Germany, France, Italy, the Netherlands, Belgium, Sweden, and Australia. Our

Table 3: Comparative performances of 10 exporting countries, 1998–2000

Exporter	East Asia export share	GDP share	World export share	Mean great circle distance	Real exchange rate
Australia	9.2	2.2	2.1	4608	0.80
Belgium	1.9	1.0	6.3	5906	0.95
Canada	4.1	3.8	8.5	7230	0.79
Germany	11.7	11.9	19.1	5791	1.04
France	5.8	8.1	10.6	6054	1.04
United Kingdom	6.4	8.3	9.6	6015	1.04
Italy	4.5	6.7	8.3	5954	0.85
Netherlands	2.4	2.2	7.1	5823	0.94
Sweden	2.2	1.4	3.0	5159	1.16
United States	51.9	54.4	25.3	7162	1.00

intention is to see how well Canada stacks up against these other economies in terms of exports, taking into consideration size, distance to Asia, the real exchange rate, and comparative advantage. We will look across industries and time, to investigate trends in Canadian relative performance and to identify areas where Canada is especially successful or unsuccessful. We will then suggest what past performance might predict for the future.

Our primary source is the *World Trade Database* compiled by Statistics Canada, which contains detailed trade data by commodity for 1980–97. We augment this with 1998–2000 trade data from the IMF's *Direction of Trade Statistics* showing aggregate bilateral trade.[2] Table 3 provides some overall information about the Western countries we consider and their trade with the ten East Asian countries. The information reflects averages over the years 1998–2000. The first column shows each exporter's share of total exports by the group to East

---

2 Statistics Canada manages the *World Trade Database* to ensure data quality. *Direction of Trade Statistics* data is more problematic. One issue is that country A's reported exports to country B tend to be lower than country B's reported imports from country A. We average reported exports and imports, because that procedure closely matched the *World Trade Database* figures for 1997, a year when data from both sources is available.

Asia. The U.S. is the dominant exporter, with slightly over half of group exports. Germany is also a large exporter, with an 11.7 percent share, followed by Australia with 9.2 percent. The other countries have small shares, with Canada having the seventh largest share of East Asian imports. One normally expects small countries to have smaller levels of exports, other things equal. Thus, to put the East Asia market shares in perspective, column (2) reports each country's share of the comparison group's total GDP. The top share, of course, belongs to the United States. Interestingly, its share of GDP is extremely close to its share of exports to East Asia. In most cases, GDP share approximates East Asian export share with one exception: Australia only has a 2.2 percent share of GDP, whereas its East Asian export share is 9.2 percent.

The third column contains information on each country's share of the group's world exports. One may hypothesize that a country will export in proportion to its GDP. A comparison of column (2) and (3) shows this not to be the case. The GDP share of the U.S. is double its world export share. Small economies near large trading partners such as Canada and Belgium show the reverse pattern, with world export shares at least twice as large as their GDP shares.

Distance between trading partners is another influential determinant of export success. Hundreds of statistical analyses of bilateral trade volumes have shown that the greater the distance between two countries, the less on average they will trade. In fact, there seems to be a law very much analogous to Newton's law of gravity in which trade is inversely proportionate to distance. That is, a 10 percent increase in distance reduces trade flows by roughly 10 percent. We follow the successful practice of these studies in measuring distance using the "great circle" formula, which requires data on the latitudes and longitudes of a central city in each country. The fifth column shows these great-circle distances between each exporter and East Asia taken as a whole. To compute a single mean distance to Asia, we weight each exporter's distance to individual East Asian economies by the share of the East Asian economy of total East Asian imports.

The column illustrates that Australia has a geographic advantage in trade to Asia. Canada and the U.S., by contrast, are at a geographic disadvantage. The column reflects a limitation of using great-circle distances to measure the distance goods must travel to reach an export market. Sweden appears to be relatively close to Asia. This may be true for goods travelling by plane. However, the distance travelled by ships hauling Swedish-made goods to East Asia is obviously much greater than the 5179 miles shown in the table. We note, however, that more sophisticated and realistic measures of nautical distance are difficult to construct and may not perform better.

A final consideration is the real exchange rate measuring relative prices between countries.[3] The last column shows the prices in each exporting country relative to the price in the United States. The figures reveal that, while purchasing power parity did not hold closely in the 1998–2000 period, prices were not wildly out of line across the countries. The extremes are a low of 0.79 for Canada and a high of 1.16 for Sweden. Thus, the relatively low price in Canada confers an advantage to Canada in competing for East Asian goods markets. Sweden, by contrast, is at a disadvantage.

Table 3 indicates that evaluating export performance is not straightforward. Clearly, the metric used to measure performance is critical. Canada's share of East Asian imports exceeds its GDP share. Thus, by this measure, Canada's performance seems good. However, its share of exports to Asia is significantly less than its share of world exports. This may be viewed to reflect negatively on Canadian trade to East Asia. Distance and exchange rates must also be factored in. In light of the considerations discussed above, we develop measures that are useful for evaluating Canada's performance across industries, countries, and time.

We now construct an index of performance in East Asia for a set of comparable exporters. It is the ratio of "raw" performance, denoted A, over a theoretical benchmark, denoted B. We define raw performance for a given country c in industry i as its exports to East Asia as a per-

---

3 We compute real exchange rates using OECD purchasing-power-parity exchanges rates and nominal exchange rates listed in *International Financial Statistics*.

centage of U.S. exports to East Asia. Thus, using *X(from,to,what)* to denote exports, and *ea* and *us* to denote East Asia and the United States, we have

$$A(c,i) = 100*X(c,ea,i) / X(us,ea,i).$$

If a country has the same raw performance as the U.S., it will have $A = 100$. However, equal performance is highly unlikely for all the reasons we have discussed before. Hence, we wish to build the insights of our previous discussion (and, of course, the academic literature on determinants of trade patterns) into an appropriate benchmark. The benchmark we will ultimately focus on comprises four factors. We shall refer to them as "advantages" because they are defined so as to make an increase lead to greater expected performance. Then, to obtain the adjusted performance measure, we divide by the benchmark, scaling down the raw performance in East Asia for a country with advantages over the U.S. (that is $B > 1$) and scaling up for disadvantages ($B < 1$). Thus, this exercise is very much like handicapping in competitive sports.

We shall define the benchmark as

$$B(c,i) = S(c)*G(c)*P(c)*C(c,i).$$

The first factor, *S*, is the size advantage. Larger economies manufacture a greater number of varieties of products. That will normally translate into increased demand. Large countries also have more workers and capital to produce goods and thus have greater potential supply. The second factor, *G*, stands for geographic advantage. It is measured as the distance of the U.S. to East Asia relative to the distance of country *c*. Relative proximity generates higher expected exports because of lower relative transportation and communication costs. In calculating distance from an exporter to East Asia, we take a mean with weights proportional to the Asian market size. The third factor, *P*, stands for country *c*'s price advantage. It is measured as the price of the representative bundle of goods and services in the U.S. divided by the price level in country *c*, with all prices converted into U.S. dollars. This relative price is the inverse of the real exchange rates listed in Table 3.

High values of P imply that country c has a currency that is undervalued relative to purchasing power parity. Ideally we would measure the price advantage at the industry level, but industry-level prices are almost always reported as indices that are not comparable across countries. Hence, we rely on OECD data on each nation's aggregate price index, which is comparable across nations and available for the entire period of our study.

The product of these three benchmarks ($S*G*P$) forms our benchmark for total trade. However, when we examine particular industries, it is important to take into account differences in *comparative advantage*. To do so we use a measure, C, that compares the share of industry i in country c's total exports with the corresponding ratio for the United States. Thus, letting w denote the rest of world, C is given by

$$C = [X(c,w,i) / X(c,w,all)]/[X(us,w,i) / X(us,w,all)].$$

This measure is essentially the same as the index of "Revealed Comparative Advantage" developed by Bela Balassa (1965, 1979). It is appealing because it does not impose a particular view of the source of comparative advantage. Anything that causes a country to orient its exports towards particular industries, whether relative productivities or factor abundances, will lead to a higher value of C.

One possible shortcoming of C is that it ignores information on what each country imports. Thus, a country that exports a large share of some industry might be importing even larger amounts. Nevertheless our interest does not lie in understanding the net direction of trade between Canada and Asia, but rather in focusing on benchmarking Canada's performance in East Asia. Hence, since C tells us what things Canada tends to export to the world, it suggests a set of goods that we should expect Canada to export in large proportions to the economies of East Asia. A possible special case is automotive trade, where both the U.S. and Canada export large amounts to each other but not overseas. We should keep this case in mind when interpreting the results.

We use $A/(S*G*P*C)$ to gauge exporter performance in East Asia relative to what we would expect based on size, geography, overall prices, and comparative advantage. The expected score is 100 since, after making the appropriate adjustments, each country should be doing about the same as the United States. Measures greater or lower than 100 represent unusually strong or poor performance in East Asia.

Table 4 factors in the necessary adjustments to raw performance sequentially until all elements of the preferred benchmark are included. It uses *World Trade Database* data averaged over the 1995–97 period. We consider all merchandise as well as trade in particular industries. The industries are food, wood, metals, machinery, and electronics. Our "food" includes both processed and unprocessed agricultural products as well as beverages. "Wood" comprises both raw and fabricated products (from logs to wooden furniture). "Metals" includes ores, iron, steel, and aluminium, as well as fabricated metal products like wires. "Machinery" includes power-generating equipment but excludes transportation equipment. "Electronics" contains office machines, telecommunications, and electrical machinery.[4] The numbers in the top panel are exports of each exporter to East Asia relative to those of the United States. Germany tops this list, reflecting that fact that it is the largest economy among our set of comparable exporters.

As we saw in Table 3, Australia does remarkably well, with total exports 17.1 percent those of the United States in 1995–97. It actually exports 42 percent more metals than the United States. Canada stands out in specific industries – wood and metals. By contrast, Canada has very few exports of machinery and electronics relative to the United States as well as other countries. The second panel shows our performance measure after controlling for relative size. Since Canada's GDP was one-twelfth the size of the U.S. in the 1995–97 period, its measure gets multiplied by 12 in these calculations. Australia, Belgium, and Sweden realize even larger adjustments. Australia seems dominant by this measure and Canada's performance now appears good.

The third set of numbers reflects additional adjustments for relative distance and prices. This knocks both Canada and Australia down a

---

4 The industries we use are aggregates of two-digit SITCs. They are food (00–11) wood (24,25,63,64,82), metals (28, 67–69,97), machinery (71–73), and electronics (75–77).

Table 4: Exports to East Asia relative to United States

Exporter	All	Food	Wood	Metals	Machinery	Electronics
A						
Australia	17.1	35.3	7.6	142.1	5.4	2.3
Belgium	4.0	1.7	1.7	8.2	3.0	1.6
Canada	9.1	14.7	54.7	28.9	3.2	2.0
Germany	26.3	3.3	10.5	41.2	65.1	14.5
France	12.4	11.4	4.3	12.4	14.6	7.5
United Kingdom	13.6	7.9	5.3	23.0	20.8	11.6
Italy	11.5	1.9	8.2	12.7	28.9	3.7
Netherlands	4.8	5.7	2.5	7.6	6.5	3.4
Sweden	4.5	0.3	7.5	7.4	6.5	6.4
A/S						
Australia	325.0	671.5	144.7	2701.0	101.9	43.7
Belgium	113.6	49.1	49.2	233.3	85.7	44.2
Canada	114.7	184.4	686.6	363.4	40.6	25.6
Germany	85.9	10.6	34.8	136.9	211.9	47.6
France	62.2	57.5	21.9	63.0	72.5	38.0
United Kingdom	85.5	49.9	33.3	144.9	131.0	72.9
Italy	74.3	12.6	53.5	81.6	186.3	23.8
Netherlands	92.8	110.0	48.0	148.1	124.0	66.3
Sweden	140.4	8.6	236.1	234.6	202.8	202.7
A/(S*G*P)						
Australia	202.3	443.5	97.6	1694.7	61.0	25.5
Belgium	107.7	47.9	48.2	219.0	78.9	40.9
Canada	99.9	161.3	600.9	316.3	35.3	22.2
Germany	89.6	11.6	37.7	139.6	214.5	48.0
France	64.6	62.2	23.6	64.4	73.2	38.0
United Kingdom	73.7	44.9	30.1	124.0	109.6	61.2
Italy	60.0	10.7	45.9	65.6	144.8	18.5
Netherlands	87.1	107.1	46.8	136.1	113.6	60.0
Sweden	136.7	8.6	238.9	225.7	191.7	192.8
A/(S*G*P*C)						
Australia	202.3	148.9	241.2	363.7	184.2	111.1
Belgium	107.7	35.1	52.6	118.8	173.2	136.6
Canada	99.9	172.4	161	176.6	67.4	61.9
Germany	89.6	18.8	41.9	91.9	164.1	84.3
France	64.6	32.9	26.5	45.8	89.9	64.4
United Kingdom	73.7	53.6	56.9	108.9	116.5	69.6
Italy	60	12.5	33.5	44.9	101	44.6
Netherlands	87.1	48.7	60.9	121.3	263.7	78.2
Sweden	136.7	25	58.1	117.8	184.2	248.9

bit relative to the United States – Canada because it is advantaged by having prices below the purchasing power parity level and Australia because it is relatively close to East Asia. Keep in mind that great-circle distances make Europe seem closer to East Asia than they are in relationship to shipping distances. This is why the European countries tend to fall when we make relative-distance adjustments.

The last panel shows our fully adjusted relative-performance measure, which now includes the adjustment for comparative advantage. The numbers in the first column reflecting all goods do not change, since a nation cannot have a comparative advantage in all goods. In this set of numbers, Canada, with a measure of 99.9 for total trade, has almost exactly the performance of the United States. Variation, however, occurs across industries. Canada does better in food, wood, and metals than even the Canadian comparative advantage in these industries would predict. However, Canada appears to be underperforming in machinery and electronics.

Australia's performance is noteworthy in it that outperforms the U.S. and most other countries across the industries. This might reflect an aspect of economic geography that we have not controlled for: remoteness. As an island nation far from the rest of the industrialized world, Australia does not have a large nearby country to serve as its primary market. Thus, it appears to be more likely to export all sorts of goods to East Asia than other countries. Another explanation for the strong performance is the concerted effort Australia has made to integrate itself into the East Asian regional economy. An explanation we dismiss is that Australian export success arises from strong FDI performance. Our earlier analysis showed that Australian FDI in East Asia is not particularly high even relative to the size of its economy.

Figure 7 plots the performance of Canada and Australia for the years 1980–2000 for our measure incorporating all adjustments. Here we utilize data from the *Direction of Trade Statistics* to update the *World Trade Database* data. A couple of patterns emerge. First, Canadian performance relative to the U.S. drifts down over time. The decline is particularly large over the 1988–2000 period, where the measure falls from 164.2 to 90.7. Canada's performance stabilized at about 90 from

Figure 7: Canadian and Australian export performance, 1980–2000

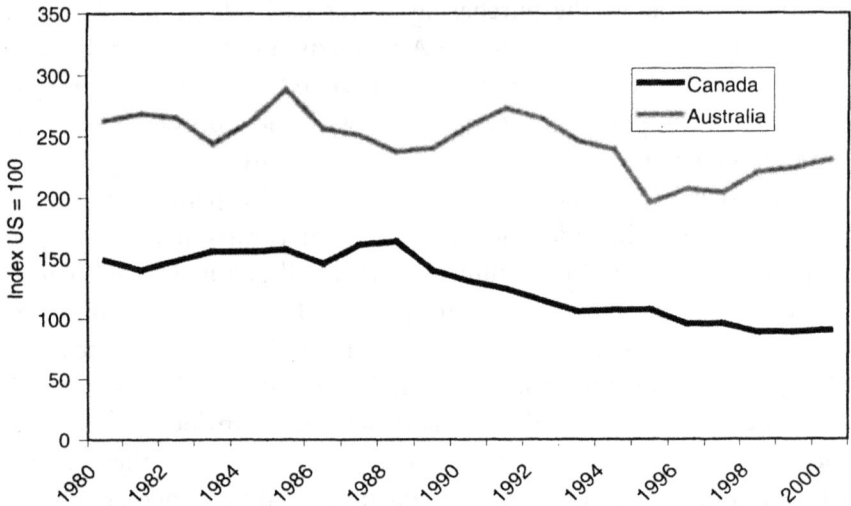

Table 5: Canadian export performance

Importer	All	Food	Wood	Metals	Machinery	Electronics
China	172.0	989.7	177.7	130.3	131.4	367.7
Hong Kong	88.4	98.2	78.2	165.7	84.5	110.9
Indonesia	153.7	712.1	162.7	92.0	115.9	96.4
Japan	138.4	155.0	196.7	276.3	43.9	25.1
Korea	87.4	93.8	112.3	160.0	68.3	56.3
Malaysia	40.8	144.0	106.0	32.2	47.1	35.6
Philippines	52.0	82.6	31.9	311.4	58.7	63.3
Singapore	25.9	53.6	88.0	68.9	61.6	34.0
Thailand	57.7	220.0	115.9	46.2	65.0	51.8
Taiwan	65.0	39.7	123.6	157.6	33.8	87.4

1998 to 2000. Australia's performance also tails off a bit throughout the mid-1990s, but then recovers to a robust 231 in 2000.

Table 5 portrays Canada's performance in specific countries averaged over the 1995–97 period. The measure includes adjustments for size, distance, prices, and comparative advantage. Relative to the United States, Canada does well in China, Indonesia, and Japan but more poorly in most other economies. Canada's success in China is noteworthy, with a measure of 172 for all goods and 989.7 for food. Canada exhibits superiority to the U.S. in electronics and machinery exports to China and machinery exports to Indonesia.

The exercise of benchmarking Canadian performance has yielded a number of interesting insights. First, Canadian success in East Asian export markets declines sharply over the 1988–2000 period. By 2000, Canada's trade with East Asia was slightly below what we might expect based on size, geography, and prices. Australia is clearly the most successful exporter to East Asia once our adjustments are included. However, Canada has some success stories. It sells large amounts of food, wood, and metal products to East Asia, even after adjusting for Canadian comparative advantage in these industries. It is particularly successful in China, Japan, and Indonesia. Canada even succeeds relative to the U.S. in selling machinery and electronics to China and machinery to Indonesia.

Canadian prospects in East Asia

We have seen that Canada's trade performance in East Asia, when properly benchmarked, is equal to or better than most comparable exporters. The question this raises is whether Canada's early relative success can be sustained in the long run or not. We formalize this question as one of the *speed of adjustment* of actual trade to the benchmark. If adjustment is quick, Canada's current successes will be fleeting and it will tend to catch up when it is behind. If adjustment is slow or even non-existent, then Canada's current bright spots will remain that way for the foreseeable future.

Macroeconomists typically measure the speed of adjustment using something called a "partial-adjustment model." In our case we are interested in how quickly (if at all) each country's relative market penetration in Asia (denoted A in the previous section) adjusts towards our theoretical benchmark (denoted B). We stipulate the following standard process:

$$\ln A(t) - \ln A(t-1) = \alpha \left[\ln B(t) - \ln A(t-1)\right] + e(t).$$

The parameter α measures the speed of adjustment. At its lowest rea-

Table 6: Adjustment rate estimates

	All	Food	Wood	Metals	Machinery	Electronics
Adjustment rate (α)	0.049	0.05	0.074	0.152	0.126	0.093
Std. error of α	(0.014)	(0.016)	(0.018)	(0.038)	(0.033)	(0.031)
Half-life (in years)	13.8	13.5	9.0	4.2	5.1	7.1

sonable value of zero, there is no tendency for Asian performance to move towards its benchmark. Instead, it follows a "random walk," with each year expected to be, on average, no better or worse than the preceding one. The maximum value of α is one. In that case we have instantaneous full adjustment. Were it not for the random shocks denoted $e(t)$, we would have $A(t) = B(t)$ in each period. For intermediate values, we have partial adjustment. Namely, each year A tries to close its deviation from B by a percent amount equal to roughly 100α. We estimate the model using nine exporters over the period 1980–97 for total trade and trade in each of our industries (the full range for which the data is available). The results are reported in Table 6. The "half-life"s we report indicate how many years it would take for an early deviation from the benchmark to disappear (in the unlikely event of no subsequent shocks). It is obtained using the formula half-life $= \ln(1/2)/\ln(1-\alpha)$.

The rather slow adjustment rates we estimate show that any particular deviation from the benchmark will be persistent but it will tend to disappear gradually, that is, it would disappear if the benchmark did not change and there were no new shocks. This does not tell us whether our benchmark-adjusted performance measures, A/B, are converging towards 100 or not. That is, it is quite possible for a series of shocks to arrive moving A away from B and then the country gradually adjusts, but, as a set, the exporters never get very close to the benchmark.

To understand this, it is useful to recall Galton's fallacy. Francis Galton, the statistician who invented regression analysis, examined the difference between the height of a son and his father. He found that sons tended to be less different from the average height than their fathers and interpreted this as evidence that all people were converging towards a common height (due to the mixing of commoners and the

Figure 8: Is performance in East Asia converging?

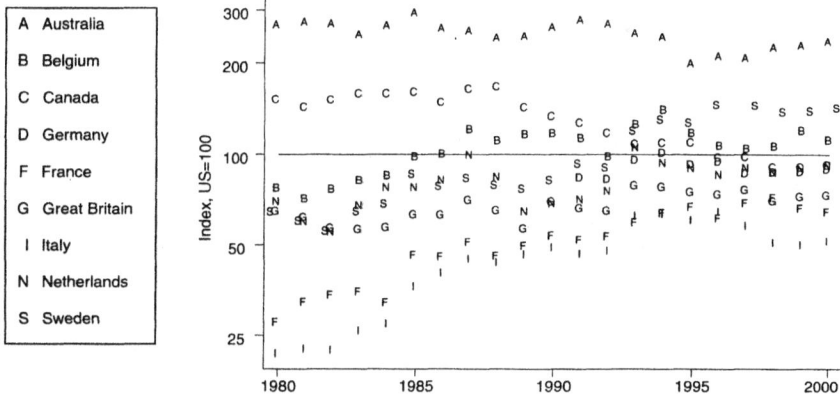

A	Australia
B	Belgium
C	Canada
D	Germany
F	France
G	Great Britain
I	Italy
N	Netherlands
S	Sweden

Index, US=100

300
200
100
50
25

1980   1985   1990   1995   2000

noble-born). In fact, the distribution of heights is not collapsing around a single value. It is just that particularly short or tall fathers are unlikely to have sons who are quite so "deviant" as themselves. Nevertheless, some average-height fathers will have tall or short sons.

In Figure 8 we show what is happening to the adjusted performance of nine exporters into East Asia for all merchandise goods when we use the *Direction of Trade Statistics* to extend the data through 2000. As before, a value of 100 indicates that the country is performing at its benchmark; that is, it is equal to the U.S. after appropriate adjustment for size (GDP), geography (distance), and prices (the real exchange rate). The diagram is shown with the index expressed in a log scale. This means that a given distance away from 100 represents the same *percentage* deviation. Thus, 100 is as far from 50 as is it is from 200. The figure seems to point towards convergence, although certain exporters continue to over- or underperform. Canada starts as an overperformer, but loses ground over time, ending up slightly underperforming relative to the United States. Australia loses some of its excess penetration as well; however, in 2000 it remains the top exporter. (Figure 7 contains the same Canadian and Australian data, but it is not portrayed on a log scale.) At the other extreme, Italy is a clear laggard in 1980, exhibits improving performance until 1997, and then its trade performance falls off in 1998–2000. Overall, Figure 8 exhibits convergence up to the 1998 Asian crisis, at which time Australia's performance outstrips that of other exporters.

From the combined information provided by the partial adjustment estimates and the figure, we conclude that there is a significant tendency for market penetration to move towards the theoretical benchmark. In the terminology used by Barro and Sala-í-Martin (1995), there is both Beta and Sigma convergence. In more colloquial terms, "high flyers" eventually fall to earth. Deviations are persistent but they gradually erode and are not simply replaced by new shocks of equal magnitude. However, this process appears to have been somewhat disrupted by the Asian crisis.

Concluding remarks

This paper shows that East Asia continues to occupy a minor role in Canada's overall international trade and investment activities. Canadian total exports to the ten East Asia economies were lower in 2000 than they were in 1995. On the surface, these facts suggest poor Canadian performance. However, we show that, when properly benchmarked, Canadian export performance is along the lines of what one might expect. The observed decline in Canada's export performance relative to other Western countries appears to represent a fall to the benchmark level. What might be of some concern is the fact that Canada's trade performance in the last three years has fallen slightly below the theoretical benchmark.

From a broader perspective, Canada's relative decline in export performance is part of a larger tendency of countries towards convergence to the benchmark. Our chapter in the first volume of this series discussed ways through which a "first-mover" into East Asia may sustain a long-run advantage. In our analysis of export performance, we find some evidence supportive of this contention. While exceptional performance will be eroded over time, the adjustment to the benchmark is quite slow. This can result in a head start delivering many years of sustained advantage.

Australia seems to be a case in point. Its trade performance in East Asia remains clearly superior to that of other Western countries. Moreover, it was able to recover from the Asian crisis quickly. While its relatively high trade with East Asia might be partly due to its remoteness from other trading partners, its ability to sustain exports levels subsequent to the 1998 collapse of the East Asian economies may indicate superior government and business policies. This suggests Canada might enhance its trade to East Asia by studying Australian strategies.

There are reasons for Canada to be optimistic about future business in East Asia. The economies have emerged from the 1997 Asian crisis and *have all begun to grow again*. We show that Canada is particularly successful at exporting to Japan, China, and Indonesia, countries with large or potentially large markets. Our analysis suggests that this success should persist for many years, resulting in a large volume of exports to China and Indonesia as these economies continue to grow and open their markets to exports.

REFERENCES

Balassa, Bela. 1965. "Trade Liberalization and Revealed Comparative Advantage." *Manchester School*, 33: 99–123.
– 1979. "The Changing Pattern of Comparative Advantage in Manufactured Goods." *Review of Economics and Statistics*, 61/2 (May): 259–66.
Barro, Robert J., and Xavier Sala-í-Martin. 1995. *Economic Growth*. New York: McGraw-Hill.
Organization for Economic Co-operation and Development. 2001. *OECD Statistical Compendium*. Rheinberg, Germany: DSI Data Source & Information.
Statistics Canada. 1992. *Canada's International Investment Position*. Catalogue no. 67-202-XIB. Ottawa: Statistics Canada.

About the authors

Loren Brandt (PhD, University of Illinois) is Professor of Economics, University of Toronto. Specializing in the Chinese economy, he has extensive experience working in China and has been involved in major collaborative projects focusing on privatization, banking reform, and property rights formation. His articles have been published in the *Journal of Political Economy*, *Journal of Monetary Economics*, *Journal of Development Economics*, and the *Journal of Economic History*. He is also one of the area editors for Oxford University Press's forthcoming three-volume *Encyclopedia of Economic History*.

Wendy Dobson (PhD, Princeton University) is Professor and Director, Institute for International Business, University of Toronto. She has served as Associate Deputy Minister of Finance in the Canadian government and President of the C.D. Howe Institute. Her most recent publications include *World Capital Markets: Challenges to the G-10* (co-authored with Gary C. Hufbauer, 2001), *Financial Services Liberalization in the WTO* (co-authored with Pierre Jacquet, 1998), and *Multinationals and East Asian Integration* (edited with Chia Siow Yue, 1997), which was awarded the 1998 Ohira Prize for the best English-language book on the Asian economies.

Keith Head (PhD, MIT) is Associate Professor of Strategy and Business Economics, Faculty of Commerce and Business Administration, University of British Columbia. He holds the HSBC Professorship in Asian Commerce and teaches courses on international business management. In 2000, he received the Killam Undergraduate Teaching Award. His research interests include multinational enterprises, international trade policy, and economic geography. His recent work includes "Increasing Returns versus National Product Differentiation as an Explanation for the Pattern of US–Canada Trade" (with John Ries, in *American Economic Review*) and *Elements of Multinational Strategy* (in progress).

Walid Hejazi (PhD, University of Toronto) is Assistant Professor of International Business Economics, University of Toronto. His research interests include the analysis of expectations in financial markets, the relationships between U.S. and Canadian financial markets, and the impact of globalization on Canada's patterns of trade and foreign direct investment. He has served as a consultant to Industry Canada and the Canadian International Development Agency.

Brian Job (PhD, Indiana University) is Professor of Political Science and Director of the Institute of International Relations at the University of British Columbia, a comonent unit of the Liu Centre for the Study of Global Issues. His research focuses on the evolving security order of the Asia Pacific region, on the promises and problems for multilateral approaches to security at the regional level, on the settlement of regional conflict, and on Canadian security and defence policy. Professor Job is a founder and Co-Director of the Canadian Consortium on Asia Pacific Security, Co-Chair of the Canadian member committee of CSCAP (Council on Security Cooperation in Asia Pacific), and Co-Chair of the CSCAP North Pacific Working Group. His recent publications include "Assessing the Risks of Conflict in the PRC-ROC Rivalry," co-authored with Andre Laliberte and Michael Wallace, in *Pacific Affairs, 2000* and "Canada: The Security Environment," in Charles Morrison, ed., *Asia Pacific Security Outlook 1999* (Japan Centre of International Exchange: Tokyo, 1998).

John Ries (PhD, University of Michigan) is Associate Professor, Faculty of Commerce and Business Administration, University of British Columbia. He holds the HSBC Professorship in Asian Business and teaches courses on international business, international trade policy, government-business relations, and the Asian business environment. His primary research interests are international trade and business and the Japanese economy (he speaks Japanese). He has published articles in numerous academic journals including the *American Economic Review*, *Journal of International Economics*, the *Journal of Industrial Economics*, the *Canadian Journal of Economics*, and the *Journal of Urban Economics*. His current research includes analysis of the effects of the Canada–U.S. FTA on North American manufacturing and of the role of vertical networks on the U.S. auto parts trade.

A.E. Safarian (PhD, Berkeley) is Professor of Business Economics at the Rotman School of Management, University of Toronto. He has also served as Dean of the University's School of Graduate Studies. His research and teaching interests include foreign direct investment, foreign trade, and public policy. He is author or co-author of a number of books and articles on these topics, including *Multinational Enterprise and Public Policy* (Edward Elgar, 1993) and *Canada and Foreign Direct Investment: A Study of Determinants* (Centre for Public Management, University of Toronto, 2001).

Pauline M. Shum (PhD, University of Toronto) is Associate Professor of Finance, Schulich School of Business, and Associate Professor of Economics, Faculty of Graduate Studies, York University. She is also the Director of the PhD Program in Administration at York University, and a Research Associate at the Institute for Policy Analysis at the University of Toronto. Her research interests include portfolio theory, corporate investment and pension reform. Her work has appeared in the *Journal of Monetary Economics* and the *Journal of Finance*, among other international journals.

Xiaodong Zhu (PhD, University of Chicago) is Associate Professor,

Department of Economics, University of Toronto. His research interests include economic development, macroeconomics, public debt
management, and financial economics. His articles have been published in *Journal of Political Economy*, *Journal of Monetary Economics*,
Journal of Economic Theory, and *Journal of Development Economics*. He
has also published articles on China and on public debt management
in newspapers such as the *Asian Wall Street Journal* and the *Globe and
Mail*.

Institute for International Business

The Institute for International Business was formed in 1998 by the merger of three entities at the Rotman School of Management: the Centre for International Business, the International Centre for Tax Studies, and Project LINK. Globalization has reshaped research and teaching in all areas of management and economic sciences. The Institute's mission is to take faculty expertise in research, and its dissemination, teaching, and international exchange, and focus it on *sustaining Canadian competitiveness* in this new global environment.

Institute research is organized around three themes:

International business research: Rapidly changing technology and the emergence of new competitors in emerging markets and the transition economies have significantly changed business strategy and management approaches. To help Canadian managers understand the strategies and business practices of their international competitors, the Institute publishes the HSBC Bank Canada Papers on Asia in cooperation with the scholarly publishing program of the University of Toronto Press.

Quantitative economic analysis: Economic intelligence and the interpretation of macroeconomic trends in major economies and potential markets require analytic strength and broad international expertise.

Through its association with Project LINK, an international research consortium headquartered at the University of Toronto that brings together economists from 80 countries, the Institute creates its own economic outlook, studies policy, and evaluates markets.

The policy environment for business: Government policy has an effect on the cost of doing business and the ability of Canadian businesses to invest in knowledge, capital, and people. Institute programs examine the effects of Canadian government policy, relative to the United States, on production and employment costs in key Canadian industries.

The Institute's research strategy is formulated in consultation with advisory committees from academe and the private sector. The program is directed by Wendy Dobson in consultation with a Steering Committee consisting of Professors Peter Pauly (business economics and econometric analysis) and Jack Mintz (tax policy and public finance).

Programs and services

Working Papers
Designed for technical audiences, *Working Papers* present the Institute's latest work in progress.

The Institute Roundtable
Monthly roundtables provide a forum for private sector decision makers to discuss developments in international business and the global economic environment. Sessions led by Associates and invited speakers focus on anticipating, interpreting, and responding to these developments.

Symposia and Seminars
Special symposia like the "Great Minds for Great Business Symposium" and special seminars are held from time to time featuring Rotman faculty and speakers from the international community, who

address issues that relate to sustaining Canadian growth and competitiveness.

The Institute for International Business
Joseph L. Rotman School of Management
University of Toronto
105 St. George St.
Toronto, Ontario, Canada M5S 3E6
Tel: 416 978 2451
Fax: 416 978 0002
email: iib@rotman.utoronto.ca